THE SWEET SPOT
ASIAN-INSPIRED DESSERTS

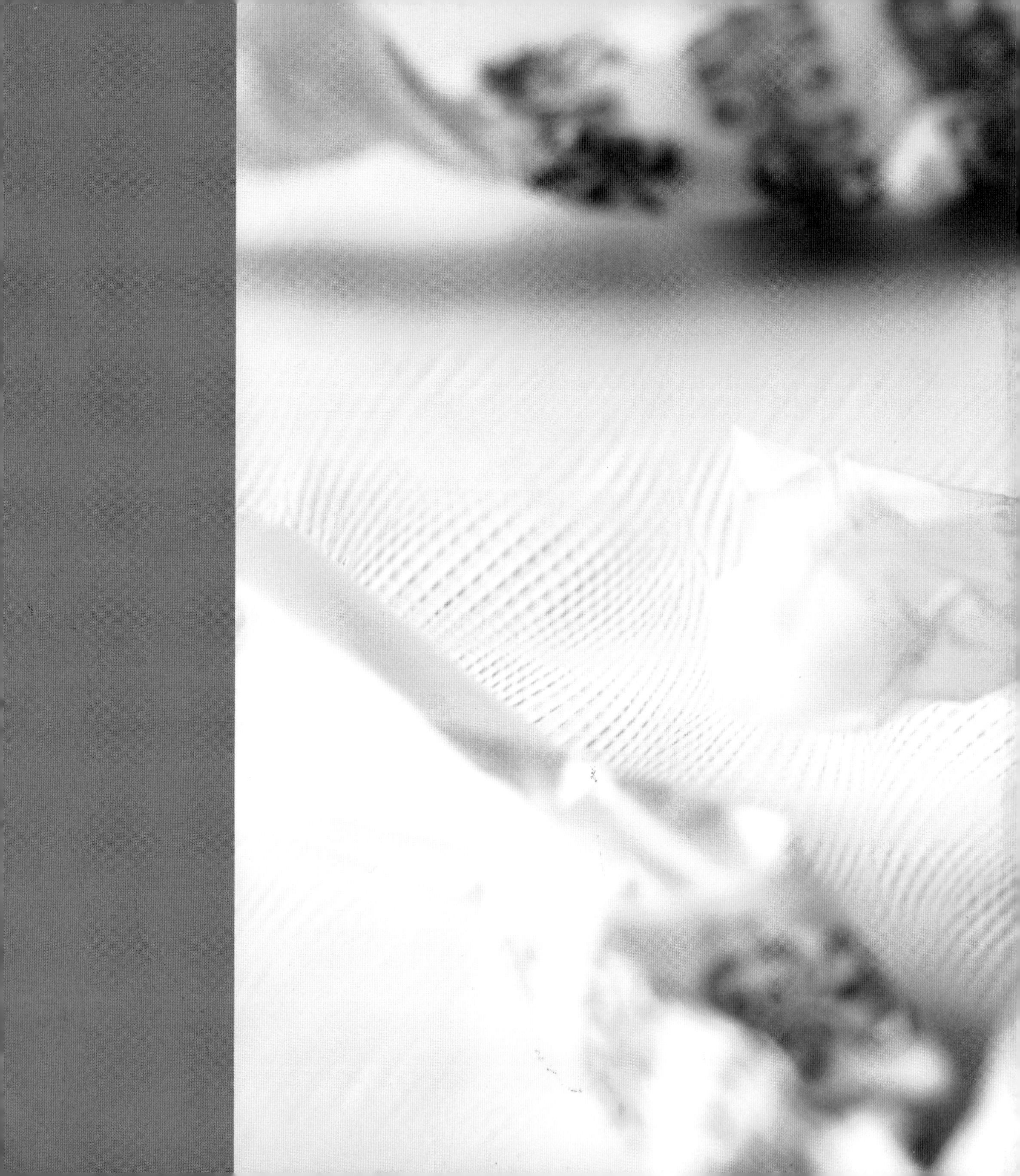

THE SWEET SPOT

ASIAN-INSPIRED DESSERTS

PICHET ONG AND GENEVIEVE KO

Foreword by Jean-Georges Vongerichten
Photographs by Pate Eng

WILLIAM MORROW
An Imprint of HarperCollinsPublishers

HarperCollins books may be purchased for educational, business, or sales promotional use. For information please write: Special Markets Department, HarperCollins Publishers, 10 East 53rd Street, New York, NY 10022.

FIRST EDITION

Designed by Lorie Pagnozzi
Photographs by Pate Eng

Printed on acid-free paper

Library of Congress Cataloging-in-Publication Data has been applied for.

ISBN: 978-0-06-085767-7
ISBN-10: 0-06-085767-6

07   08   09   10   11   WBC/TP   10   9   8   7   6   5   4   3   2   1

To Ruby, my mother, and Vibul, my father—P.O.

To David—G.K.

CONTENTS

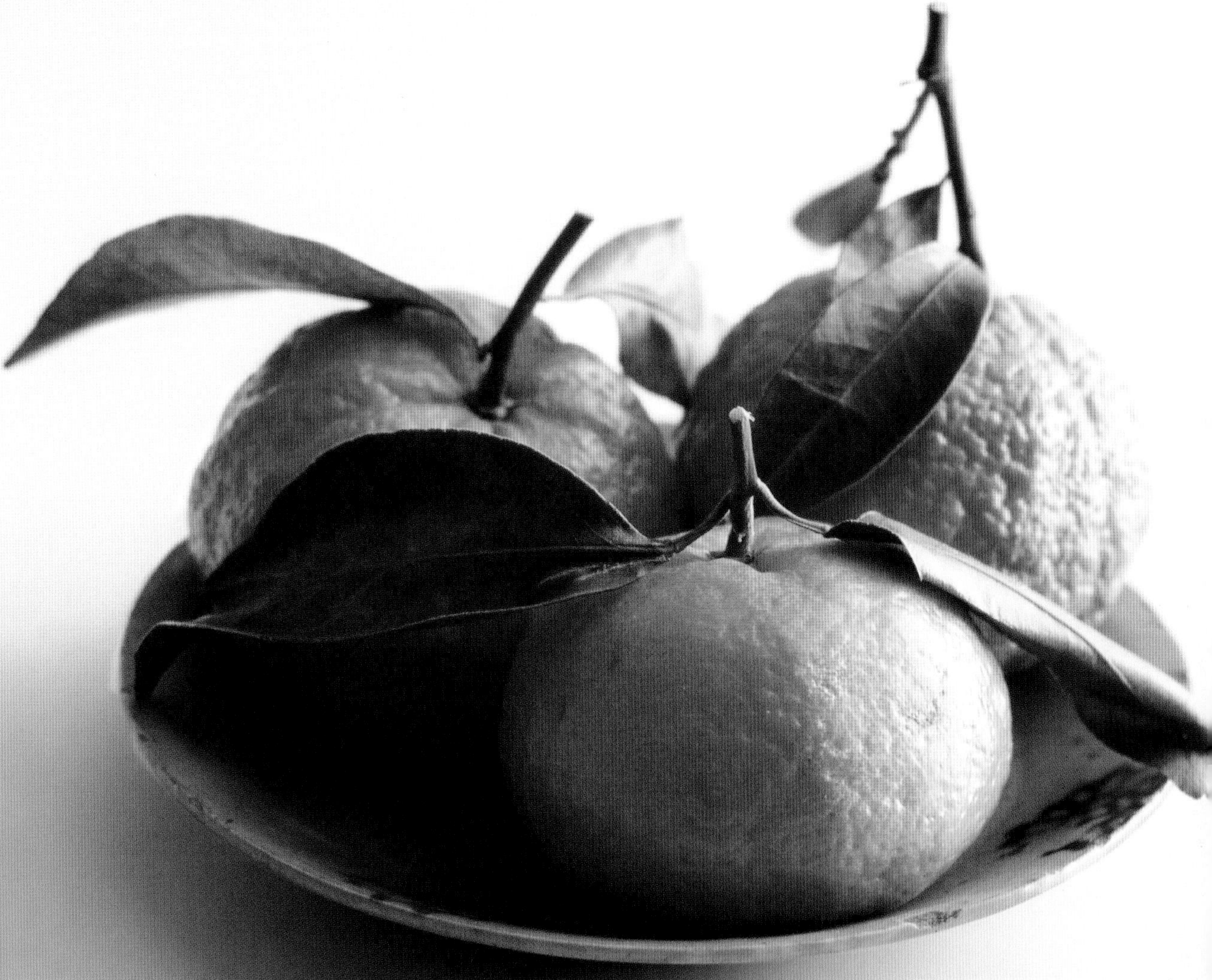

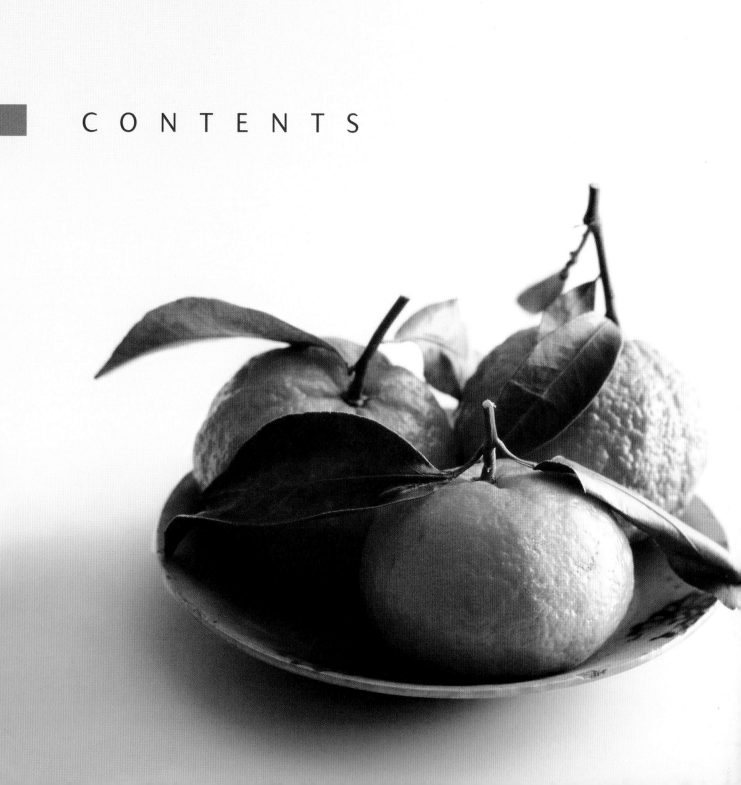

ACKNOWLEDGMENTS

This book simply would not have happened without the generous contributions of people from every corner of my life. My love and thanks go first and foremost to my mother, Ruby, who taught me many secrets, not only about cooking, but also about life. My father, Vibul, who told me that it's okay to start the day by eating dessert, has been a constant source of support and unconditional love. Stuart has been by my side through thick and thin, and I'm grateful for his unfailing love, which keeps me sane through all the stress of restaurant openings.

I owe an enormous debt of gratitude to Jean-Georges Vongerichten, who has been my mentor both in and out of the kitchen. He provided the perfect showcase for my ambitions and always believed in my work. I am also thankful for all the amazing colleagues in the Jean Georges family with whom I have had the privilege of working over the years, especially Daniel Del Vecchio and Josh Eden.

I can hardly begin to count all the pastry chefs who have provided me with friendship, support, camaraderie, and many, many delicious desserts along the way. They are too numerous to name and they know who they are. This book is also for them.

I am grateful to Simpson Wong, who provided the setting for our photography sessions at his beautiful restaurant. Equally meaningful and important are the friends who contributed props for Pate Eng's beautiful photography: Judy "JB" Prince, George Mendes, Izabel Lam, and Sylvia Weinstock. Several gifted chefs have worked incredibly hard at maintaining the deliciousness of my desserts: Melissa Sacco, Christine Ko, Helen Yoo, Marissa Martinez, Kenneth McGoey, Kiyomi Toda-Burke, Jennifer Jupiter, Alfredo Garcia, Emilio Castillo, Chieh De Jong, Roshel Yusupov, Alara Nelson, Dana Lipkin, Hayden Ramsay, Tim Roberts, and Tara DeLanghe. Most of all, I thank my successor at Spice Market and 66, the talented Frederick Aquino.

Pate Eng provided the elegant, understated photography that was a perfect match for the recipes and text. "Bar Chef" Yvan Lemoine helped out with additional photo styling. I'm very grateful to both of them for the beautiful finished product you're holding now.

I am grateful to Steven Hall and Sam Firer for getting my work out to the public even before this book.

This book is a direct result of the efforts and commitment of my agent, Janis Donnaud, who deserves my sincere gratitude.

Likewise, Harriet Bell, Lucy Baker, and Stephanie Fraser at William Morrow invested countless hours in editing this book and giving it its final form. I thank them for their patience and good sense. And a special thank-you to the design department for the lovely design and the colors, which are perfect for the recipes in this book.

And last but not least, I thank my coauthor, Genevieve Ko, for her beautiful writing and for her friendship. She has made the entire process a pleasure.

—*Pichet Ong*

It has been an immense pleasure working with Pichet from the day we met. Not only has he inspired me with his creativity and taught me an immeasurable amount about pastries, he has also been a great friend.

Thank you to Mark Bittman for introducing me to the world of food writing and for being a wonderful mentor, friend, and supporter. I am very grateful for Jean-Georges Vongerichten, Daniel Del Vecchio, and Pierre Schutz for welcoming me into their kitchens with Pichet. Without all of you, this book would not have happened. Likewise, Janis Donnaud, Harriet Bell, Lucy Baker, Stephanie Fraser, copy editor Judith Sutton, and designer Lorie Pagnozzi deserve my deep gratitude for their efforts in shepherding this project through to completion. It was a joy working with Pate Eng, a truly gifted photographer.

I appreciate those who have taught me how to cook, love food, and be a writer, namely, Roy Ip, Mark Oppenheimer, Steve Courtney, Ruth Lively, Jean Bonk, and Jennifer McTiernan-H.

I could not have done this without the support of my parents, Winston and Dorothy, and the rest of my family: Emily, Kenneth, Mike, Jim, Joyce, Drew, and Kat. A special thanks to Astrid Alvarenga for her help in our home testing sessions. My daughters, Vivien and Natalie, were eager taste-testers and "Uncle" Pichet's greatest admirers. Thank you, David, for your love, support, and unfailing generosity in all things.

—*Genevieve Ko*

FOREWORD

I first met Pichet Ong when he worked as a fish cook at my restaurant, Jean Georges, in 1997. After falling out of touch with him briefly, I was thrilled to see him again four years later. I have been recreating and reinventing savory Asian dishes for the modern palate for years, and I wanted to interpret Asian sweets in the same way. When I tasted Pichet's almond tofu at the three-star restaurant where he was pastry chef in 2001, I knew we had to work together again.

Pichet explained that he was interested in introducing New Yorkers to new Asian-inspired desserts, which was exactly what I was looking for. Pichet's enthusiasm for using Asian ingredients and techniques matched my vision for my Chinese restaurant, 66, and later, my Asian street food restaurant, Spice Market. He came on board to create Chinese desserts for 66, and his innovative style of cooking without boundaries fell easily in line with the way I see food.

At a tasting of dessert selections before the opening of Spice Market, other chefs declined his durian ice cream, made from the notoriously pungent spiky tropical fruit, but I excitedly dug in. From that moment on, I knew that Pichet and I shared a love for truly authentic Asian cuisine. And as we cooked sweet and savory dishes together over the years, I saw that Pichet also shared my zeal for flavor combinations that are fresh yet familiar—complex yet simply spectacular.

We also share the same approach to building flavors. Starting with one ingredient, tastes, textures, and temperatures are assembled layer upon layer. With that, we embrace the same Asian cooking principles, such as adding bitterness to reduce sweetness, saltiness to enhance sourness. And, with our use of exotic and truly authentic Asian ingredients, we dare to tread where other chefs have not.

More than that, I consider Pichet a fantastic friend who loves to have fun. He is a true gourmand and always in pursuit of better living through better eating. I have long envisioned the future of restaurant dining to be one that is engaging and entertaining. In Pichet, I have found someone who is more than willing to dazzle and surprise with yummy desserts that deliver as much amusement as flavor. When we opened 66, we had a lot of fun playing with iconic Chinese restaurant themes and transforming them into refined desserts with whimsical presentations. Customers loved slurping sophisticated dessert drinks through the fat straws normally found at Chinatown tapioca drink shops. The Frozen Orange Wedges, Almond and Chocolate Fortune Cookies, and Sesame Balls were also a huge hit.

At Spice Market, Pichet wowed diners once again with updated traditional street sweets from Asia. Most who ordered dishes like Thai Jewels and Fruits on Crushed Coconut Ice and Ovaltine and Milk Chocolate Kulfi with Caramelized Banana had never tasted nor even heard of anything like these desserts. But they always cleaned their plates, and they quickly made these desserts the talk of the town. Pichet is one of the few pastry chefs I know who can fashion desserts from completely new and esoteric flavors and still please everyone—unadventurous eaters and restaurant critics alike.

Even when dealing with classic ingredients, Pichet takes an original approach to technique. For example, he creams his butter with spices for cookie dough and uses fresh citrus fruit zest as an aromatic garnish. Both techniques are evidence of his training in savory cooking and his daring spirit in applying them to sweets. These finer details are groundbreaking in the world of pastry and fine cuisine.

Pichet's gift for re-creating Asian desserts for a universal palate is as evident in this book as it is on the restaurant table. He takes classic continental desserts and makes them with Asian ingredients and techniques. He takes traditional Asian desserts and adds Western flavors and textures. And, of course, he invents his own techniques and flavor combinations for truly inspired, and inspiring, desserts. With practical hints and substitution suggestions for hard-to-find ingredients, he ensures that anyone can try his desserts without compromising the integrity of his creations. No matter how bizarre and unfamiliar a dish may sound, the end product is always universally appealing.

This book is a tremendous contribution to the world of cooking literature. *The Sweet Spot* presents Asian flavors from an insider's perspective as Pichet educates and entertains, walking the line between Western and Eastern cuisine. While he has organized his recipes according to traditional Western sweet classifications, you will be tempted by scrumptious desserts you've never heard of and astounded by how the classics can be so appetizingly new. The extensive pantry, equipment section, and informative chef's tips will answer any questions you have about novel ingredients and techniques. Most of all, on every page, from the stories to the photography, you will have a taste of Pichet's passion for fabulous desserts. Be warned—that passion is contagious.

—*Jean-Georges Vongerichten*

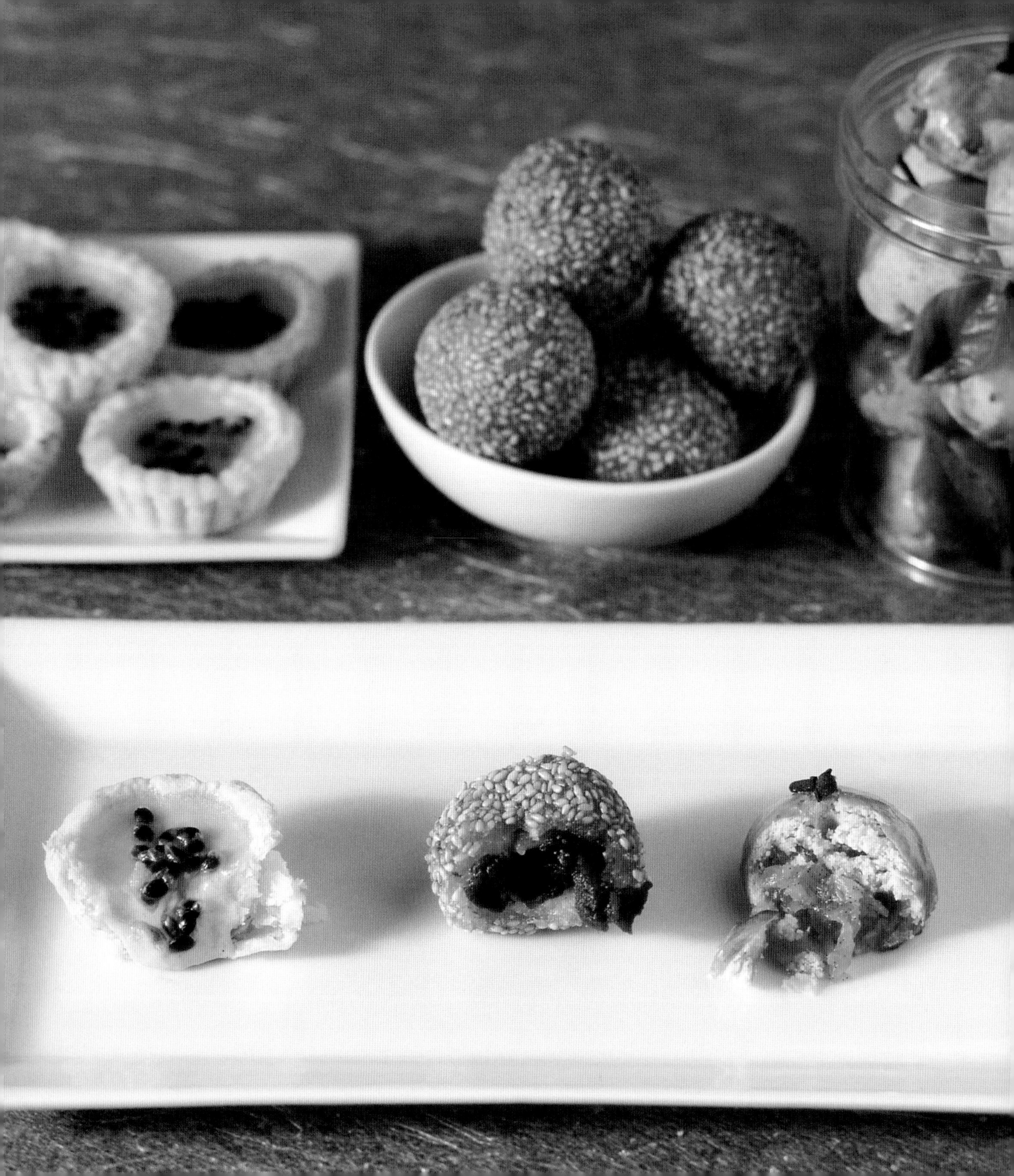

INTRODUCTION

Asian food is now as popular in American cuisine as hot dogs and hamburgers. You can order Chinese takeout in almost every town. Supermarkets across the country stock ready-to-go sushi dinners. And Asian chicken salad is as common as nachos or lasagna on the menus of many restaurants. These everyday establishments have figured out what trendier "fusion" restaurants have known for years—diners are eager for the sweet, salty, sour, and spicy tastes of Asian cuisine.

But what about dessert? Fortune cookies aside, Asian desserts remain a mystery even to many connoisseurs of Asian savory dishes. The common assumption is that desserts are simply not an important part of Asian cuisine, and that those desserts that are popular in Asia are so foreign as to be unappetizing to the Western palate. Nothing could be further from the truth. Sweets are enjoyed throughout Asia just as they are in culinary cultures everywhere—as desserts, snacks, and the occasional guilty pleasure. Although many Asian desserts take different forms than their Western counterparts, many others are deeply inspired by classic Western desserts introduced to Asia. In any case, Asian desserts share the same culinary role as sweets everywhere—to comfort, excite, and indulge.

We had our first conversation about this book over dim sum. Between bites of barbecued pork in Chinese puff pastry, we excitedly shared our passion for the Asian desserts we had enjoyed growing up on both sides of the Pacific. As we rattled off some of our favorite sweets—lemon roll cake, chocolate Pocky sticks, mango pudding—we realized that these treats, far from being foreign, were only slight adaptations of Western classics that Americans have been enjoying for decades. But not surprisingly, we also discovered a shared love of distinctively Asian desserts, like chewy sesame balls and fried baby bananas. And many of the following recipes had already demonstrated, in restaurant kitchens, how authentic Asian flavors and textures could be transformed into desserts that anyone would love. We knew the same could be true for this book.

The Sweet Spot manages to walk the fine line between the novel and the comfortable by always maintaining great flavor as the highest priority. Rather than relying on butter and sugar, these recipes highlight the vibrant fruit and floral flavors of Asia amid a range of indulgent textures. They will satisfy your sweet tooth without sacrificing the clean sophistication that is their hallmark.

You may rightly wonder whether these creations, many of which employ seemingly unfamiliar ingredients and techniques, translate to the home kitchen. The truth is, most of these recipes were created in a home kitchen. The majority of the recipe testing for this book took place not in a fancy four-star arena, but rather in a humble home kitchen, where we cooked shoulder-to-shoulder, using groceries from the local supermarket. With an electric stovetop and a convection oven, we whipped up authentic Asian desserts, such as Rasmalai with Pistachios and Rose Water, that require neither special techniques nor hard-to-find pastry tools. If a recipe did require a special tool, we would more often than not fashion one from the materials at hand. Without a cookie stencil for the fortune cookies, for example, we quickly made one out of a yogurt container lid.

Like good Asian cooks, we tried not to waste any ingredients. In the process, we ended up with some surprise desserts. After preparing the traditional Kabocha and Banana in Gingered Coconut Milk, we were left with a bunch of very ripe baby bananas. Within the hour, we were devouring the best banana bread we had ever tasted. Although neither of these desserts may ever make it onto a restaurant menu, they are perfect for home cooks. More important, although most of the recipes here are adapted from restaurant creations, none of them requires a restaurant staff to create.

While this book came together naturally and quickly, the recipes themselves are the culmination of many years of hard work and a deep familiarity with the ingredients, techniques, and flavors of Asian desserts. We set out to create vibrant desserts that would thrill and entertain while remaining accessible to the home cook and familiar to those who try them. Most of all, we set out to make these desserts fun. We certainly had fun making them, and we think you will too.

EQUIPMENT

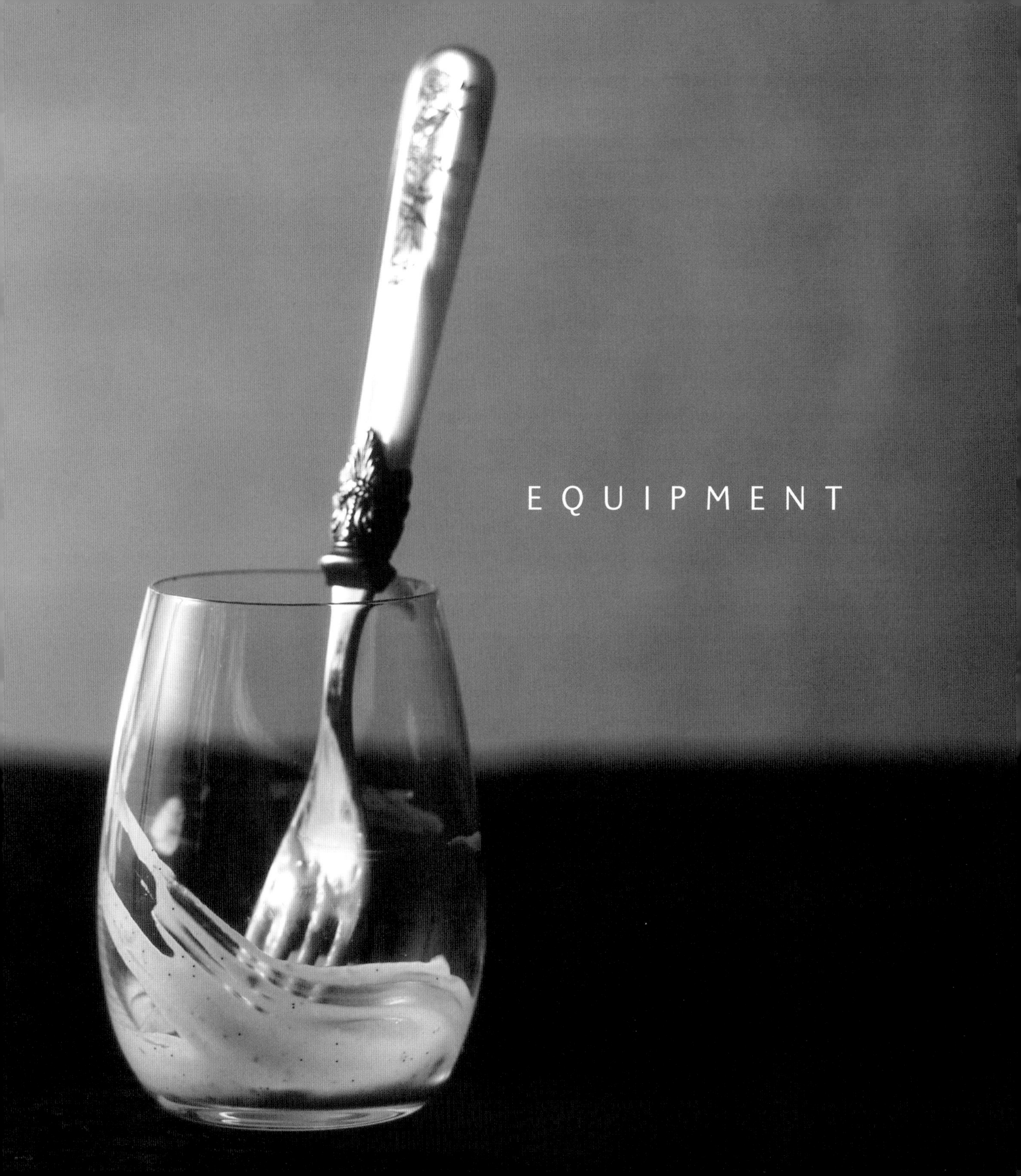

It's not true that a chef is only as good as his tools. Some of the best food I've ever eaten has been made with some pretty rudimentary equipment. But, especially in the pastry world, the right tools make any cook's tasks a whole lot easier. The following is a list of the appliances and tools that I depend upon in the kitchen. You probably have many of these items already; some of them, although essential, are also quite basic. And you certainly don't need to run out and purchase everything that you don't have—where possible, I've given alternatives to the more obscure, pricey, or otherwise difficult-to-acquire items.

YOUR HANDS

I love using machines and gadgets, but in the kitchen, my hands are my most important tool. In fact, every dessert in this book can be made entirely by hand. Learning to whisk or mix by hand will make you a better cook. For example, whipping egg whites by hand gives you a feel for the difference between soft and firm peaks, while cutting butter into flour with your fingers will help you understand what makes a piecrust tender and flaky. I almost always prefer to whip cream by hand, especially when dealing with small amounts. Not only does this save the hassle of pulling out the mixer, but I've found that hand-whipped cream tends to stay whipped longer.

APPLIANCES

Some of the following machines are essential if you intend to make some of the frozen or drinkable desserts in this book. And all of them will make your life easier, especially if you plan on making a lot of pastry. Of these, the most indispensable is a **standing mixer,** such as the Kitchen-Aid model I use at home. A standing mixer frees your hands to prepare other ingredients and allows you to add ingredients without disrupting the mixing process. Most machines come with a paddle attachment for creaming and mixing, a whisk for whipping egg whites and cream, and a dough hook for kneading stiff bread doughs. Be sure to adjust the speed as directed in individual recipe instructions. If you don't want to invest in a standing mixer, a hand mixer will also work for mixing, creaming, and whisking.

I consider a **food processor** one of the most useful kitchen machines for dessert making. I don't use it for chopping, since it does so unevenly and tends to ruin the texture of most ingredients and release too much liquid. It is, however, fantastic for making pastry crusts and doughs. It can cut cold butter into flour very quickly without warming the ingredients too much, effectively making a perfect pie or tart dough in less than a minute. A food processor also makes great cake and cookie batters, particularly those that include chopped nuts. Food processor blades differ in sharpness and speed, so keep a close eye on ingredients as you mix them. When in doubt, pulse, stop, and feel the ingredients with your fingers. **Blenders** are essential for making frozen drinks and pureeing fruits. Choose a heavy-duty, sturdy blender such as one manufactured by Vita-Mix that can easily handle ice and has a variety of speeds.

Grinding your own spices is a sure way of adding an extra boost of freshness that makes the flavor and aroma of any dessert come alive. The best tool for doing this is an electric **coffee grinder,** which is like a miniature food processor on steroids. The small blade is incredibly sharp and fast and can pulverize hard spices into fine powders. As an added bonus, if you use your coffee grinder for pastry spices, such as cinnamon and cardamom, you can grind your coffee beans in the same grinder for an exotic cup of joe. (To clean your grinder between uses, pulverize a piece of soft bread and brush out the crumbs.)

When it comes to making ice cream (my favorite type of dessert), you have two mechanical choices: an old-fashioned hand-cranked model, which looks a lot better than it works, or a modern electric **ice cream maker.** In the latter category, my favorite is the PacoJet. This beautiful, compact machine essentially pulverizes frozen blocks of ice at extremely high speed, whipping air into the mixture to yield incredibly smooth and luscious concoctions in less than four minutes. Did I mention it costs almost three thousand dollars? Cuisinart makes a perfectly acceptable machine at a fraction of the cost. Or, if you already have a KitchenAid standing mixer, you can buy the ice cream bowl and churning attachments. Whatever machine you buy, follow the manufacturer's instructions carefully.

BAKEWARE

The one piece of bakeware I can't live without is a **half-sheet pan,** or **rimmed baking pan.** Also known as a jelly-roll pan, a half-sheet pan is 12 inches wide, 17 inches long, and 1 inch deep. It's great for cakes, cookies, and brownies, as well as for savory cooking. Look for heavy-duty steel pans coated with aluminum and avoid nonstick or Teflon pans. (You can always grease or line the pan with foil or parchment paper or use a silicone baking mat to prevent items from sticking.) A quarter-sheet pan (12 × 9 inches) is also helpful when making smaller recipes.

As with sheet pans, other bakeware items should also be heavy-duty steel coated with aluminum so as to conduct heat evenly. For the cakes in this book, you'll need an **8- or 10-inch round pan,** an **8- or 9-inch square pan,** and a **13 × 9-inch pan** if you do not have a quarter-sheet pan. Breads and pound cakes require a **loaf pan,** preferably 8½ × 4½ inches. For tarts, my first choice would be the plain and simple **8-inch-diameter, ¾-inch-high straight-edged tart rings.** They can be set right on a flat baking sheet and are easy to remove. However, more traditional fluted tart pans with removable bottoms also work well. This type of pan generally results in a thicker crust, but as long as the pastry is delicious, that shouldn't be a problem. Ultimately, it comes down to a matter of personal preference. Another option is to use an 8- or 10-inch springform pan, but these make it difficult to trim the pastry. That said, the extra crust that rises up the sides can make for a beautiful rustic-style tart with an appealing handmade look. For individual tarts, of course, you'll need smaller tart rings or pans. The most common size is 4 inches in diameter.

A **9-inch ceramic or glass pie plate** is essential for pies. I also like square glass baking pans, such as the ones made by Pyrex. These are great for soft-textured desserts that don't have to be removed from the pan, such as Grand Marnier Tofu Cheesecake (page 78). They're also great for steam-baked desserts, such as Coconut Palm Sugar Flan (page 170). A **springform pan** with removable sides is ideal for cheesecakes but isn't absolutely necessary. You can wrangle a cheesecake out of a cake pan, but doing so may compromise its presentation.

Also very useful are individual **ceramic ramekins**. Ramekins come in a wide variety of shapes and sizes, but the one I use the most is the 4-ounce version, which is 3½ inches across and 1½ inches high. It is the perfect serving size and can be used for both baking and presentation. I recommend using heavier ramekins for soufflés and steam-baked custards. The Swiss company Bodum has developed oven-proof glass ramekins that can withstand high heat. These make for a great presentation. An attractive alternative to ramekins is Chinese ceramic teacups, which I like to use for desserts like Steamed Yuzu Soufflés (page 45). The thick ceramic is ideal for steaming and baking, and the smooth, rounded shape has a lovely Eastern aesthetic. They are inexpensive, durable, and can be found in most Asian cookware stores.

Before you use the sheet and cake pans, you should usually line them to prevent sticking. **Parchment paper** is ideal for the job, as it's essentially nonstick and greaseproof on both sides. Generally, you'll grease the pan, line with parchment, and then grease the parchment. Parchment paper is readily available in supermarkets and cookware stores and comes in both sheets and rolls. I prefer the sheets, as they are easier to cut to fit the shapes of the pans.

A **nonstick baking mat**, often referred to as a Silpat, after its largest manufacturer, is a reusable mat lined with silicone. Nothing sticks to it, so it's ideal for caramels and other candies. It also conducts heat evenly, which makes it a good foundation for chocolates. A Silpat also works well for thin delicate cookies, like tuiles or the fortune cookies in this book. I don't recommend using Silpats for thicker cookies or tart shells, as they don't make the bottoms crisp enough.

Once your dessert is baked or cooked, you'll want to put it on a **cooling rack**. A good sturdy cooling rack both protects your kitchen surfaces and allows for even cooling. It can also be used to support a cake or other confection on which you need to pour a liquid ganache or other topping—the excess drips right off and allows you to coat your creations evenly. One large rack, 16 × 20 inches, is sufficient.

COOKWARE

Most traditional Asian desserts are not baked, as ovens were, until recently, not a common household appliance through much of Asia. Instead, many of these desserts are cooked on stovetops. Even in Western cooking, stovetop desserts are quite common—think caramels and puddings.

Good saucepans are key to stovetop desserts. Copper-core pans conduct heat the most evenly and with the most precision, but they are also the most expensive option. Aluminum-core pans are cheaper and work nearly as well. With both types, look for nonreactive stainless steel exteriors. As with bakeware, avoid nonstick surfaces. A set of three saucepans—large (4-quart), medium (3-quart), and small (1½-quart)—is convenient.

Steaming is one of the most common techniques for cooking Asian desserts. If you already have a wok, get a steamer rack on which you can set a bamboo steamer. If you don't have a wok, you can put a steamer rack or insert into a large saucepan or casserole with a lid. If you're on a tight budget, you can always improvise by crumpling a large sheet of heavy-duty aluminum foil and setting it evenly on the bottom of a saucepan or casserole. Whatever you use, be sure to keep the steamer level and to replenish the water as needed. If you're not using a bamboo steamer, wrap the saucepan or casserole lid in a thin kitchen or tea towel to absorb any condensation—you don't want little water droplets compromising the flavor and texture of your dessert.

TOOLS

Mixing bowls come in all sizes and materials, but I rely on my restaurant kitchen–quality stainless steel mixing bowls. They are lightweight yet sturdy, nonreactive, and easy to maneuver. (If I'm mixing or whisking vigorously, I set the bowl on a damp kitchen towel formed into a ring to prevent it from slipping.) A set of three—large, medium, and small—is essential, but extra mixing bowls never hurt. You can, of course, use plastic, ceramic, or glass bowls, but they tend not to keep their contents sufficiently cold and I think they often feel clumsy.

If you have a standing mixer, you might consider buying a second mixer bowl. Many recipes in this book require two separate batches of ingredients to be mixed, and having a second bowl will save you the trouble of washing the bowl between batches.

Spatulas are essential for folding one ingredient into another. Not to be confused with the spatulas used for flipping fried eggs, rubber or silicone spatulas are also great for scraping bowls, mixing, and stirring by hand. The silicone spatulas can withstand high heats, so these also come in handy when making milk and fruit reductions or caramels. Have at least two—one large, one small—so you don't have to keep washing them.

The classic wooden spoon is stronger than a rubber spatula, although it lacks some of the spatula's versatility. Aside from stirring and mixing, a wooden spoon is the ideal tool for preparing custard, which often requires scraping the bottom of the pot. I recommend having one with a rounded edge for mixing and one with a flat edge for scraping. To test whether a custard is done, lift the spoon out of the mixture: the custard should cling to the spoon and leave a clean line when you run your finger through it. A wooden spoon is the most accurate tool for this purpose. It is also an excellent tool for creaming by hand.

Whisks are essential for the important job of whisking. A large balloon whisk is good for incorporating air into ingredients like egg whites or heavy cream. It also works well for gently but thoroughly folding in ingredients. A French-style, or oblong, whisk is great for just about everything else—beating, smoothing, mixing, and stirring. There are a number of new styles of whisks on the market, but they are more appropriate for non-pastry uses, such as sauce making. Whatever type of whisk you get, make sure it's sturdy with a flexible wire head.

Chopsticks are an essential tool in the Asian kitchen. Long wooden chopsticks are ideal for mixing liquids and deep-frying desserts such as Sesame Balls (page 196). If you're adept at maneuvering them, they give you a great deal of control when turning items in hot oil. Metal chopsticks with sharp skewer-like tips can be used to determine the doneness of cakes.

To measure ingredients most accurately, use a kitchen scale (see page 9). We include measurements by weight in this book, but, as in most cookbooks, our primary measurements are in cups and spoons. In any case, you should have a sturdy set of dry measuring cups and measuring spoons. Most professionals would argue that you must use liquid measuring cups for liquids, but I stray from the pack here. I find dry measuring cups more convenient and accurate for measuring smaller quantities of liquids: I've tested the weight measurements of liquids in dry and liquid measuring cups and the results are always the same. However, do not try to use a liquid measure for dry ingredients. For dry ingredients that are subject to settling, like flour and confectioners' sugar, I fluff the ingredient in its container with a whisk, and then scoop directly with the measuring cup. To remove any excess, I sweep the flat edge of a butter knife across the top.

For larger quantities of liquid, I prefer the plastic or glass pitcher-style liquid measuring cups. These obviously make pouring easier, and being able to monitor the level of the liquid as you pour allows you to anticipate how many portions the remaining liquid will yield.

On a number of occasions, I've had to improvise a rolling pin. But wine bottles, tall glasses, and tin cans are no substitute—the only way to achieve perfectly even and flat dough is with a good rolling pin. When you do roll out dough, turn the dough a quarter turn after each roll to ensure an even surface and prevent the dough from sticking. Lightly flour the work surface as necessary, adjusting for the stickiness of the dough. I prefer French-style rolling pins, which do not have handles on the ends. Not only do I find them easier to handle, they can also double as a tool to crush or pound ingredients like ice into tiny crystals or cookies into crumbs. Avoid washing your rolling pin with soap and water; instead, keep it clean by rubbing it with some flour to remove any oil, scraping off any stuck dough with a knife, and then rubbing it with a damp cloth.

Rather than buying a special flour sifter, you can just use a fine-mesh sieve to sift dry ingredients together. First, be sure that the sieve is completely dry. Then, simply put a small amount of the dry ingredients in the sieve and—being careful to not spill the contents over the sides—tap and shake vigorously to sift the ingredients into a large bowl or onto a sheet of parchment paper. The sieve is also an essential tool for straining liquid mixtures. Pour the mixture through the sieve and firmly press on any remaining solids to extract as much flavor as possible. If you bake often, I advise having two, one for dry ingredients and the other for liquids.

The Microplane has soared in popularity since its introduction into kitchens in the early 1990s (it began its career as a woodworking tool). It grates citrus peel and chocolate into fine little tendrils—little bursts of flavor that are pretty enough to garnish any dish. To zest citrus, firmly run the fruit against the grain of the tiny blades, turning the fruit constantly along the plane. Don't zest beyond the colored outer layer—the white pith beneath can be bitter. To zest chocolate, run room-temperature chocolate gently against the blade in long, even strokes. The Microplane can also be used to grate large hard spices such as cinnamon sticks or nutmeg.

It goes without saying that you should always keep an eye on what you're cooking. Your own senses of sight, smell, and touch are the best way to determine whether your dessert is done. The cooking times in this book are always estimates and will vary according to kitchen conditions. So look for golden brown cookies, smell for smoky caramel, and insert testers into cakes until they come out clean. That said, a good digital timer with a clear alarm will help you stay on track. Or you can just use the timer on your microwave or oven.

NONESSENTIAL TOOLS

A kitchen scale, preferably digital, is the best measuring tool for a serious pastry cook. It's the only way to achieve precise measurements of ingredients that can vary in weight when measured by volume. Flour and confectioners' sugar can be packed too firmly, brown sugar and coconut flakes too loosely. A kitchen scale will also minimize your dishwashing. Just combine the ingredients into the same mixing bowl, resetting the scale to zero between each ingredient.

A pastry bag is not just for cake decorators—it really is a nice tool to have around the kitchen if you cook often. I use one to pipe out rounds or lines of batter or to quickly fill molds. You can prepare mousses or creams ahead of time, store them efficiently in pastry bags, and pipe them out when they are ready to be served. Because pastry bags are difficult to clean and can pick up smells from mixed usage, I prefer the disposable plastic variety, simply snipping the tip to the diameter I need. In a pinch, you can substitute a large Ziploc-style bag for piping and filling and use a spoon to make rounds.

An offset spatula is another important tool that has many uses beyond cake decorating. It is basically a spatula with a metal blade that meets the handle at an angle. The "offset" blade allows for easy maneuvering. In general, it's useful whenever you need to smooth or sculpt a dessert surface. The key is to hold the flat bottom of the spatula parallel to the surface and to keep it flat as you run it across the icing or ganache to achieve a smooth, even layer. Be sure to choose a flexible spatula that will allow for freedom of movement across the surface. If the room is cold, warm the spatula by dipping it in warm water and then drying it—this will soften the icing and make it easier to work with. A 4-inch-long rounded-tip offset spatula is the most versatile and is best for details. However, longer varieties are best for handling larger tasks, such as smoothing out the top and sides of a frosted cake or spreading cake batters on sheet pans. An offset spatula can also be used to pick up cookies or tarts, and even to cut dough.

An ice cream scoop with a snap lever, while useful for scooping ice cream, is even better for scooping and portioning cookies. It's also great for portioning cake batter that will be baked in molds, such as for individual cheesecakes or cupcakes. The smallest available scoop—2 ounces—is a great tool for making chocolate truffles.

A pastry brush controls the amount of liquid you spread on a cake, along the edges of pastry, or on any other surface. A shallow spoon can do the job, but not as delicately. I also use a pastry brush to grease my bakeware, especially individual ramekins. Simply load the brush with some softened butter and brush the entire surface to ensure an even and thorough greasing. A pastry brush is also useful to brush off excess flour when rolling out dough. I like to keep a separate one for this purpose, as well as for cleaning my spice grinder.

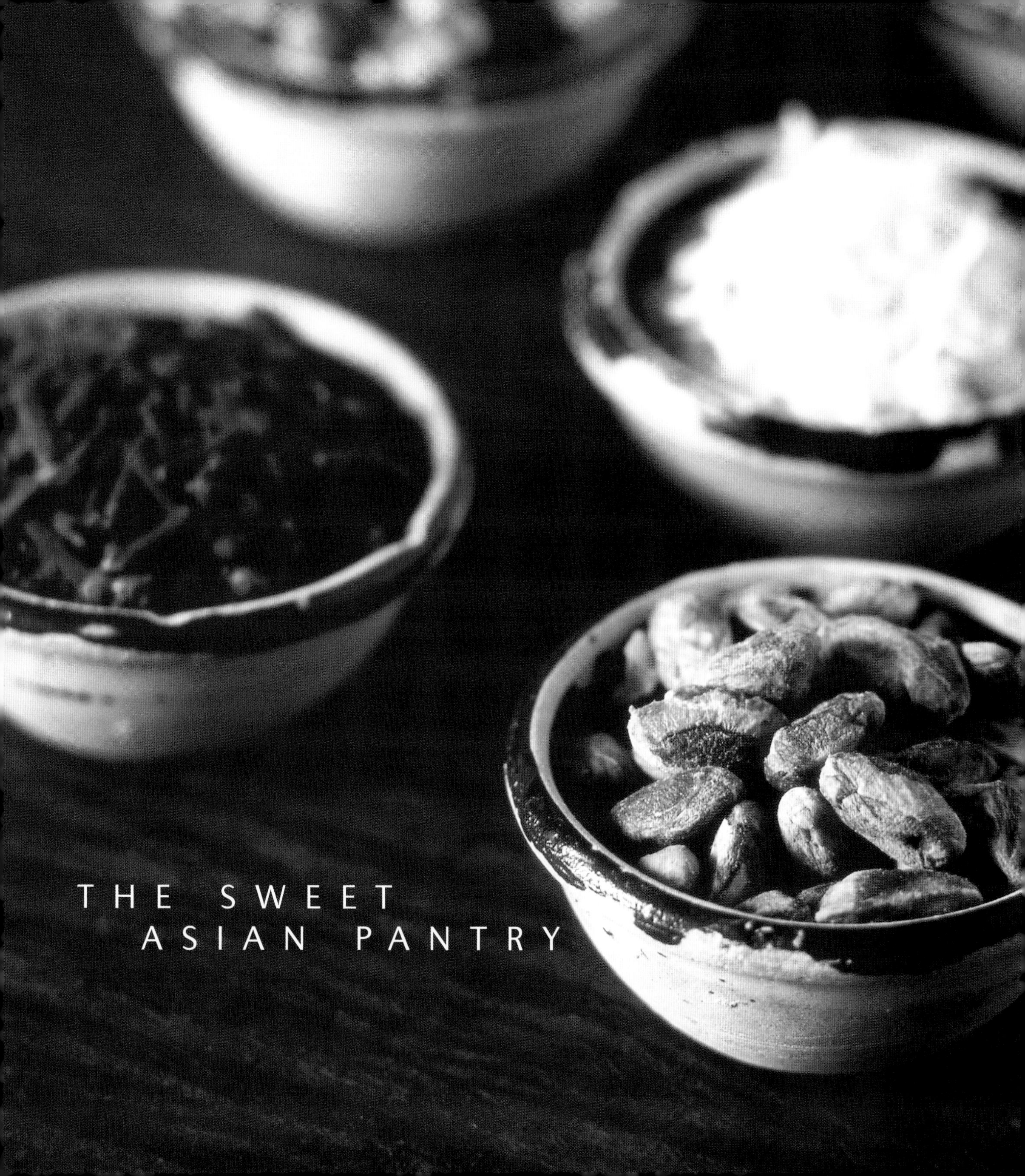

THE SWEET ASIAN PANTRY

The ingredients for the desserts in this book fall into a few different categories. For Asian desserts inspired by the West, you'll need basic Western pantry items, like flour and sugar. Most of these you probably already have, but I recommend my favorite brands below. For traditional Asian sweets, you'll have to find more unusual items, like glutinous rice flour and palm sugar. These are available in Asian and specialty food markets or through mail-order companies (see Sources). The descriptions given below will introduce you to these ingredients and how they are best used. Finally, many of the desserts based on popular Asian treats use ingredients that seem more mid-1950s American than new Asian. Sweetened condensed milk and tapioca pearls, for example, are old-fashioned staples that I make taste refreshingly new.

Although many of the ingredients below may sound unfamiliar, they are combined with items you know and love to create desserts that will please everyone. The resulting flavors are at once innovative and familiar and make for the perfect ending to any meal. Finding, choosing, and using these new ingredients will also introduce you to a world of flavors and textures that will greatly expand your culinary repertoire. Experiment and enjoy!

BEANS, either whole or mashed into a paste, are commonly used in Asian desserts. They add a distinct texture and subtle nutty sweetness while supplying protein and no added fat. SWEET RED BEANS are perhaps the most common dessert filling throughout East and Southeast Asia. Chinese dried red beans are larger and have a fuller flavor, while the Japanese adzuki variety is smaller and more delicately sweet. Dried beans are best; soak them in cold water overnight and then cook in boiling water. Canned adzuki beans can be used in a pinch. (Do not substitute red kidney beans; they differ vastly in taste and texture.)

BUTTER should be fresh. I always use sweet unsalted butter, which allows me to control the amount of salt, if any, in a dessert. Moreover, salt is a natural preservative that is added to butter to give it a longer shelf life. Although this has certain advantages, salt also inhibits the growth of the good microbes and bacteria that give butter its flavor. Plugrá, the brand I've used at every restaurant at which I've worked, is now available in many supermarkets. It is labeled "European-style butter," indicating that its fat content is higher than that of most other commercial butters, making it perfect for piecrusts and tart shells. Breakstone's butter, made in New York State, and the popular Land O' Lakes brand from Wisconsin are other excellent butters.

My recipes often call for butter that has been brought to room temperature. If you need to do this quickly, you can microwave refrigerated or frozen butter on the defrost setting in 10-second increments (do not let it melt). You can also cut the butter into small cubes and let it sit for a few minutes or beat it between sheets of plastic wrap with a rolling pin.

CANDIED GINGER adds a sugary, spicy heat to dishes. Make your own according to the recipe below, or buy it. Look for candied ginger in round coins, or slices, rather than those cut into thin strips or a tiny dice; the coins have a better proportion of sugar to ginger. I prefer candied ginger from Hawaii.

CANDIED GINGER

Makes 2 cups

Two 5-inch pieces (5⅛ ounces/145 grams) fresh ginger, peeled and cut into ¼-inch thick slices
⅔ cup (4½ ounces/126 grams) sugar

1. Bring a small saucepan of water to a boil and add the ginger slices. When the water returns to a boil, drain the ginger, rinse under cold water, and drain again. Repeat this process two more times.
2. Put the drained ginger back in the saucepan and add the sugar and ⅓ cup water. Bring to a boil over medium heat, then turn the heat down to low and simmer for 35 minutes, stirring occasionally.
3. Drain the ginger and dry completely in a single layer on a cooling rack. The ginger can be stored in an airtight container for up to 3 weeks.

CARDAMOM comes in several varieties, but these recipes call for the most common form, white cardamom, the pods of which contain tiny brown-black seeds. To ensure freshness, buy only in small quantities; the pods should be fragrant and unshriveled. Ground cardamom is used in baked goods like cookies, but use whole cardamom pods to steep or infuse liquids. To make your own ground cardamom, simply grind the seeds in a spice grinder.

CHOCOLATE is categorized according to the cacao content, which is determined by the amount of cocoa bean in the chocolate. The contents of cocoa beans are chocolate liquor, cocoa butter, and cocoa powder. The basic categories are as follows: unsweetened (99 to 100 percent cacao), bittersweet (60 to 98 percent), semisweet (50 to 60 percent), and milk (35 to 50 percent). White chocolate is not technically chocolate, as it doesn't contain any cacao but is made from cocoa butter, milk, and sugar. American brands usually include less cacao than their European counterparts, and I generally recommend that you avoid a supermarket chocolate, with the exception of Ghirardelli. That said, I don't believe there is "bad" chocolate, but with so many excellent imported brands now readily available, you don't have to settle for second best. I recommend all varieties of Michel Cuizel, Valrhona, E. Guittard, and Scharffen Berger. For milk chocolate, Fechlin has an especially milky sweet chocolate bar that works well in many Asian-style desserts. Whatever brand you buy, look for the more versatile thick bars, which you can cut into desired sizes and textures with a chef's knife.

Pistoles, which are flat rounds of chocolate, are a convenient proxy for chopped chocolate, and I often use them in brownies and chocolate chip cookies. Chocolate chips can be used in cookies but are not good for melting.

Whatever its form, all chocolate keeps well in a dark, cool place at room temperature for up to 6 months. Keep it away from spices and other strong aromatics in your pantry, as chocolate readily absorbs different scents. If you are buying in bulk, wrap the chocolate tightly and store in the freezer for up to one year. Finally, if your chocolate develops pale creamy-white spots, what is called "bloom," don't worry: it's not spoiled, and the spots will disappear when the chocolate is melted.

COCOA POWDER should contain only unsweetened cocoa powder. Avoid cocoa mixes, which contain added sugar or milk powder. I prefer Valrhona, but, failing that, choose another Dutch-processed cocoa, which is richer and darker from being treated with acid-neutralizing alkali. Cocoa powder keeps in an airtight container in a cool, dark place for up to 1 year.

COCONUTS are native to Southeast Asia. As much as I love fresh coconut, I prefer the convenience of finely shredded unsweetened dried coconut, also known as desiccated coconut. It imparts a fresh coconut flavor to my desserts

without the hassle (to put it mildly) of cracking open a rock-hard shell. If you can find only coconut chunks or wider shreds, process in a food processor until finely grated. Many ethnic grocery stores carry frozen unsweetened coconut, which is also good for steeping in milk or soaking in hot water and squeezing to make coconut milk; see the recipe below. In general, unsweetened coconut, with its natural nuttiness, is far preferable to the sweetened kind found in most supermarkets. However, you can substitute sweetened shredded coconut in these desserts if you reduce the sugar called for in the recipe by about 10 percent. For example, cut 2 scant tablespoons sugar from 1 cup. Dried coconut keeps in an airtight container for up to 3 months at room temperature or up to 1 year in the freezer.

COCONUT JUICE is the milky, floral-scented liquid found inside young green coconuts. Fresh coconut juice spoils very easily, so frozen packs are the next best thing. Look for the Bangkok Market brand, or try any unsweetened variety made without preservatives, preferably imported from Thailand or the Philippines.

COCONUT MILK is made by steeping the shredded meat of mature coconuts in hot water and then straining it. As the strained liquid sits, a thick, rich cream naturally rises to the top. The thin, milky liquid beneath is coconut milk. While it is easy to make, I often use canned coconut milk for convenience. I prefer Chaokoh or Mae Ploy brands; avoid any that contain sweeteners, additives, or emulsifiers. Coconut milk will separate while sitting in the can, so shake the can well before opening. Soaking the can in a bowl of warm water before opening makes it easier to remove all the contents.

FRESH COCONUT MILK

Makes 1 quart

1 cup (3⅛ ounces/88 grams) shredded fresh coconut or finely shredded unsweetened dried coconut

1. Put the coconut and 4 cups very hot water in a blender and puree for 30 seconds. Let the mixture sit for 30 minutes.
2. Strain the coconut milk through a fine-mesh sieve lined with cheesecloth, pressing on the coconut meat to extract as much liquid as possible. The coconut milk can be stored in an airtight container in the refrigerator for up to 3 days. Shake well before using.

COCONUT POWDER, also known as coconut milk powder, is made from very finely ground desiccated coconut. A relatively new product, this is commonly mixed with water to make coconut milk, but I use it as I would cocoa powder. It adds an earthy flavor to desserts, such as Spiced Chocolate Kringles (page 97). It can also be added to coconut milk to make it even more rich and flavorful. The Chaokoh brand is the best.

COFFEE, particularly VIETNAMESE COFFEE, is one of my favorite dessert flavors. Ground from the dark roasted *robusta* beans grown in Vietnam's highlands, the coffee is brewed through a traditional Vietnamese coffee canister. The grounds are packed into a little metal canister, which is set on top of a coffee cup containing sweetened condensed milk, and hot water is added. The coffee passes through the interior strainer and press and slowly drips directly onto the sweetened condensed milk. I use Vietnamese coffee to flavor some of my desserts and I've found that the closest substitute is New Orleans Café du Monde chicory coffee. Coarsely ground French Roast coffee beans work too.

CORNSTARCH, also known as corn flour, is a dense powder made from endosperms of corn kernels. Generally used as a thickener, it is ideal for many soft cakes and Asian pastries with fine crumbs.

CRÈME FRAÎCHE is a fermented, thickened cream with a velvety richness and a nutty tang. In France, the only ingredient is unpasteurized cream, which thickens and matures naturally. In America, buttermilk or sour cream is added to help the pasteurized cream along. Although you could use sour cream as a substitute, it really doesn't compare. Crème fraîche is available in most gourmet markets. You can make your own by mixing 1 cup heavy whipping cream with 1 tablespoon buttermilk, then letting the mixture sit at room temperature for 12 to 18 hours until thickened.

EVAPORATED MILK is more popular than fresh milk in many parts of Asia because it is canned and keeps well at room temperature. It is made by boiling half the water out of milk. With a hint of caramel, it's ideal for desserts. Brands like Carnation and Nestlé are good, but check the expiration date. Older cans may have an unpleasant metallic taste.

FLOUR is best fresh. I prefer the King Arthur and Arrowhead Mills brands, which are widely available. I also like Giusto's and Hecker's, which may be harder to find. The more common Pillsbury flour is also good. I measure flour by stirring it, scooping it with a measuring cup, and leveling the top with the back of a knife. For most recipes, I sift the measured flour once through a fine-mesh sieve.

All-purpose flour is a blend of high-gluten hard-wheat and low-gluten soft-wheat flour. It can be bleached or unbleached; I prefer unbleached.

Almond flour, also known as almond meal, is ground from whole raw almonds. You can make your own by grinding whole almonds in a food processor. Be sure to freeze the almonds first, since warm or room-temperature almonds can become almond butter when ground.

Cake flour is a soft-wheat flour with a high starch content and a fine texture. It makes exceptionally tender cakes and doughs. Slightly different is pastry flour that has a higher gluten content and is used for puff pastry and pie doughs.

Glutinous rice flour, also known as sweet or sticky rice flour, is finely ground glutinous rice. Used in many traditional Asian pastries, it is used to make sticky, chewy treats with a subtle sweetness. I usually use the Erawan brand.

Mochi flour is a form of glutinous rice flour specifically designed to make mochi, or Japanese sticky rice cakes. I prefer Mochiko brand.

Tapioca flour, also known as cassava flour, comes from the starchy root of the cassava plant and is often used as a thickener. In desserts, it creates a chewiness similar to glutinous rice flour, but the end product is less sticky. The flour becomes translucent as it cooks. I prefer Erawan brand.

FRUIT is best when fresh, local, and organic, so use whatever is in season at your farmers' market when making fruit desserts.

Asian pears are a highly prized fruit often given as gifts throughout Asia. The skin color can range from dusty brown to pale yellow, but the flesh is always refreshingly sweet, crisp, and juicy. These bruise easily, so store them carefully, preferably in the foam wrap they generally come with.

Avocados are a surprisingly versatile and delicious dessert component. Use the Hass variety, preferably from California. Avocados ripen easily at room temperature, yielding to pressure when fully ripe.

Baby bananas, also known as lady's finger or finger bananas or Manzanos, are short and stubby, about 5 inches long, with yellow skin and creamy pale yellow flesh. They are the sweetest of the banana family and develop a custard-like texture when cooked. Use them only when they are fully ripe, with a dark yellow and brown sugar–spotted skin. To keep a stash on hand, especially if you like Banana Cake (page 31), peel ripe bananas, wrap them tightly in plastic wrap, and freeze until needed.

Berries are best in the summer and should be used as soon as possible. Wash them gently and let drain slowly to avoid bruising. Check your local farmers' market for unusual varieties.

Citrus fruits, like oranges, lemons, and limes, should yield to pressure when you squeeze them. That means they're juicy. If they are hard, let them sit at room temperature for a few days.

Jackfruit, a relative of the breadfruit and the fig, is a spiny oblong fruit that is very popular in Thailand. When ripe, it tastes like a floral banana with a firm bite. You can only find it canned here, but it tastes fine once rinsed well.

Kiwis, also known as kiwifruits or Chinese gooseberries, are furry brown ovals with a juicy, tender, sweet-tart grass-green flesh spotted with tiny black edible seeds. Ripe kiwis yield to gentle pressure. The easiest way to peel a kiwi is to slice off the ends and then peel with a vegetable peeler or paring knife.

Kumquats, tiny oval citrus fruits, have a sweet edible skin and juicy tart flesh with lots of seeds. They are available fresh for a brief period in the late winter and should be firm, shiny, and bright orange. The best way to seed them is to slice them crosswise and pick out all the seeds.

Longans, a fruit whose name translates to "dragon's eyes," are somewhat similar to the lychee, with a floral translucent white flesh and a hard round seed. Usually smaller than lychees, longans have a smooth mustard-brown shell. Available fresh in late summer, longans are often dried and then reconstituted to flavor syrups used in beverages and desserts.

Lychees, also spelled litchis, are a cherished Chinese fruit. Fresh lychees, available in early summer, look like bumpy red golf balls and have a translucent white juicy flesh with a smooth brick-red seed. Canned lychees are more readily available. They taste better if you rinse them under cold water to refresh the fruity flavor and wash away the sugary syrup.

Mangoes are a luscious tropical fruit with a silky golden-orange flesh. In India, the mango tree is considered sacred—perhaps this is why the most delicious variety, Alphonso, which is incredibly aromatic with a bright orange flesh, grows there: You can find frozen or canned Alphonso mangoes here in Indian markets. I use the Ratna brand of Alphonso mango puree. Champagne, a trade name for a mango variety, is the next best mango, and is imported from the Philippines and Mexico. Flattened and oblong, it has pale yellow flesh and is best used when very ripe, with sugar spots and wrinkled skin. If you can only find the standard oval variety with green or red skin, toss the fruit in a little sugar before proceeding with the recipe.

Mangosteens (no relation to mangoes) look something like an Asian animation character. Flat and round, about the size of a tennis ball, the hard, dark purple fruit has cute round leaves fanned out like petals against the top. The milky-white fruit segments inside, which separate like a tangerine, are juicy and creamy all at the same time. Fresh ones can sometimes be found in your city's Chinatown or in specialty markets. Canned mangosteens are a relatively close approximation to the succulent real thing.

Melons range from musky cantaloupes to syrupy honeydews to crunchy watermelon, with myriad tasty heirloom varieties in between. The Asian way to choose a watermelon is to tap it and listen for a hollow sound indicating juicy sweet flesh. For other types of melons, smell the top of the melon where it was connected to the vine—it should be sweetly fragrant, like the melon itself.

Palm seeds are a crisp, translucent fruit popular in Southeast Asia. Fresh palm seeds taste like a bite out of the tropics and add crunch to refreshing desserts, but they are not available here. Canned whole palm seeds are fine, albeit a bit slimy from the sugar syrup in which they are stored. A good rinse under cold water fixes that.

Passion fruits are brownish purple on the outside and a brilliant fuchsia inside. This little tropical fruit has crunchy, edible seeds that complement the juicy pink flesh. Passion fruits—best used when soft and very wrinkled—will ripen at room temperature in a few days. Passion fruit puree is concentrated, blended passion fruit and has an aromatic sweet tartness. It is thicker and much more potent than passion fruit juice. Perfect Puree of Napa Valley makes a good version.

Persimmons are a fall-winter fruit. The Fuyu and Hachiya types are most commonly available fresh. Both have a bright red-orange thin skin and fluted olive-green leaves at the top. The Fuyu is round and somewhat flattened and best eaten alone, like an apple. It is crunchy, sweet, and still firm when ripe. The Hachiya is astringent and very bitter when hard; it should be allowed to ripen until it is so soft it feels as if the juicy flesh were going to burst through the skin. At that point, it can be halved and the flesh scooped like pudding out of its skin, to be enjoyed on its own or made into compotes or other confections.

Pineapples, gloriously sweet and tart, are available fresh year-round. The reliable variety sold in most supermarkets is pleasantly low-acid. A ripe pineapple is most identifiable by its sweet tropical perfume, most potent at its base, which should yield when pressure is applied. Avoid precut and canned pineapple, which is mushy and saccharine.

Pomegranates are a sacred fruit. They are brilliantly red inside and out, and are easier to enjoy than you may think. While the hundreds of juicy capsules inside can look intimidating, you can actually pop them out quickly. Score the pomegranate around its equator and twist it open. Hold one half cut side down in your palm over a wide bowl and tap the skin briskly with a wooden spoon—the seeds will fall right out. Pomegranate juice is easily made by pureeing the seed capsules in a blender, then straining the juice; bottled pomegranate juice, such as POM, is also now available everywhere. Pomegranate molasses is concentrated pomegranate juice with a fruity, honeyed flavor. You can find it in Middle Eastern stores. Or you can make your own: cook down pomegranate juice over low heat until it is syrupy.

GELATIN, made from animal proteins, sets desserts without adding any flavor, odor, or color. It comes in sheets, or leaves, which must be soaked in cold water until softened, and in powdered, or granulated, form, which must be sprinkled over cold water to bloom. The softened gelatin is dissolved in a warm liquid, then sets when chilled.

GINGER, also known as gingerroot, can be used either young or mature. The young, less fibrous roots have a subtle flavor that can be enjoyed raw, candied, or pickled. For the recipes here, I use mature ginger, which has a dark tan skin and distinct spiced heat. Buy fat round roots with smooth skin and peel with the edge of a spoon or a vegetable peeler. Or, if you want to keep the skin, scrub it well.

Ground dried ginger adds a nice kick to baked goods. Look for mustard-yellow powder that still has fine strands of dried ginger fibers. Be sure to use it fresh, when it still tingles your nose.

HEAVY WHIPPING CREAM, also known as heavy cream, contains 36 to 40 percent fat. Traditionally the rich layer that naturally rises to the top of a container of raw milk, heavy cream today is commercially produced with a centrifuge and then pasteurized. When whisked into whipped cream, the cream doubles in volume. In its liquid form, it adds a silky, luxuriant feel to desserts.

HONEY varies widely in flavor and texture, depending on what flower the bees fed on. Any recipe with honey will taste only as good as the honey you use, although this is often a matter of personal preference. I like fireweed or wildflower honey for general recipes, chrysanthemum for Asian-inspired desserts, buckwheat or chestnut for hearty winter sweets, and lavender for aromatic floral flavors.

HORLICKS is a powdered malted barley, wheat, and dairy drink mix popular in the United Kingdom and much of South and Southeast Asia. The description may not sound very appetizing, and it is advertised as "the great family nourisher," but it tastes wonderful when used in desserts. It adds a fuller, earthier flavor than regular malt powder.

KABOCHA SQUASH, a winter squash popular in Asia and increasingly here, looks like a green pumpkin with celadon zebra stripes. The thin skin is edible (and tasty). When cooked, the sweet, nutty flesh becomes golden yellow. Kabocha squash is available year-round in Asian and many farmers' markets. Choose a small one that has firm, dark green skin and is heavy for its size (2 pounds is ideal).

KAFFIR LIME LEAVES are double-lobed oblong leaves from the kaffir lime tree. Their unique potent floral citrus aroma adds a tart, herby aroma to desserts. They are available fresh and dried in Asian markets; the glossy fresh green leaves are far more preferable.

LARD, rendered and clarified pork fat, makes flavorful, flaky, and tender pastries. It is often used in Chinese doughs and pastries. I recommend keeping it frozen until use.

LEMONGRASS is a key herb in Southeast Asian sweet and savory cooking. It contains the same oil found in lemon peel, which gives it a distinct herbaceous citrus flavor. Lemongrass stalks are about 2 feet long, with a pale green top and creamy white bulb and violet rings between the layers. Choose firm, unblemished stalks with a strong lemon aroma. To fully release its fragrance, smash it with a skillet or the side of a heavy knife before using.

MALI SYRUP is a fragrant liquid sweetener used in Thailand. It captures the distinct light tropical perfume of jasmine flowers in a clear syrup. Hale's Blue Boy is the most widely distributed brand.

MALTOSE, also known as malt sugar, is a thick amber-colored liquid sweetener. Similar to honey but far less sweet, it becomes very soft when cooked and makes great candies that are neither too sweet nor too sticky. It is quite solid and hard at room temperature and must be softened in a warm water bath or in the microwave before use.

MATCHA, also known as *hiki-cha,* is a Japanese green tea powder made from high-quality tea leaves that have been steamed, dried, and finely ground. Whisked with hot water, it is pleasantly bitter when drunk alone. In desserts, it adds a complex smoky flavor complementary to creamy sweets. Splurge on good matcha, since the dessert will only taste as good as the tea.

MILK is available in full-fat, low-fat, and nonfat varieties. Use whole milk when making any of these recipes, fresh cheese, or other milk-based desserts. I sometimes enjoy using "non-dairy" milks in my desserts too.

Almond milk is made by pulverizing boiled almonds with hot water and straining (see below). This creamy nutty liquid has been consumed in Asia for centuries and continues to be a part of desserts there.

Soy milk, the "milk" of Asia, is made by boiling dried soybeans and straining the resulting mixture. Fresh soy milk is drunk, warm or cold, night and day throughout Asia, where it is savored for its creamy, nutty flavor. Commercial American brands tend to have a bland metallic flavor; it's best to make your own.

FRESH SOY MILK

Makes 6 cups

½ cup (3¼ ounces/90 grams) dried yellow soy
   beans, rinsed well, drained, soaked in cold
   water overnight, and drained again
⅛ teaspoon salt
¼ cup (1⅞ ounces/53 grams) sugar, plus more
   to taste

1. Put the soybeans and 3 cups water in a blender and puree until the mixture is smooth and milky. Transfer the puree to a large saucepan, add 3 cups water, and bring to a boil over high heat, stirring constantly. Turn the heat to low and simmer, stirring occasionally, for 25 minutes.
2. Strain the milk through a fine-mesh sieve lined with cheesecloth into a bowl, pressing on the soybeans to squeeze out as much liquid as possible. Stir in the salt and sugar, adding more sugar to taste. The milk can be stored, covered, in the refrigerator for up to 3 days.

Fresh Almond Milk: Substitute whole almonds for the soybeans. Omit the rinsing and soaking, and simmer the almonds until they are tender, about 1 hour. Then proceed as above.

MUKWA are candied fennel seeds from India offered throughout and after Indian meals, as fennel is said to aid digestion. The crunchy multicolor candy coatings make them a fun treat.

NUTS are always best fresh. Store them in an airtight container at room temperature and use within 3 months. If you plan to keep them any longer or are buying in bulk, wrap them tightly in an airtight container and freeze for up to 1 year. The nuts used in these recipes are almonds, walnuts, cashews, peanuts, macadamias, and pistachios. To toast nuts, simply put them on a baking sheet in a 300°F oven and toast until golden brown and fragrant, stirring every 5 minutes. Due to their high oil content, they can burn easily.

OILS from fruits and vegetables, like canola, vegetable, and grapeseed, can go rancid if kept too long or exposed to excessive heat or light. When using olive oil in desserts, buy a high-quality fruity extra virgin oil. Oils used in other desserts should be neutral in flavor unless meant to flavor the dessert, as almond oil sometimes does.

I also use a nonstick vegetable oil spray, like Pam, to grease ridged and other baking pans quickly and easily.

ORANGE BLOSSOM WATER, also known as orange flower water, is distilled from orange blossoms. The fruity perfume is heavenly and adds a sweet citrus fragrance to desserts. The water should be clear, with no added flavorings or sweeteners. I prefer Mymouné brand from Lebanon. Avoid orange extract, which is too potent to add flavor judiciously.

OVALTINE is a malted chocolate beverage mix, fondly remembered by those of a certain age. Even as an adult, I still love the flavor, and I use it in desserts for its creamy malted chocolate goodness.

PALM SUGAR, which comes from the sap of sugar palm trees, has a complex smoky sweetness. Ranging from pale tan to dark brown, this sugar comes wet in jars or dried in hard little disks. I prefer the fresh, milder flavor of the wet sugar from Thailand, which is also easier to caramelize, but it is much harder to measure than the uniformly shaped dry 1-ounce disks. You can crush the disks with a rolling pin and measure the sugar in cups. Store palm sugar in an airtight container at room temperature. Substitute light brown sugar in a pinch.

PANDAN LEAVES, also known as pandanus screwpine or bai touy leaves, are used in Southeast Asian desserts in much the way vanilla is used in Western desserts. The long forest green leaves add a sweet floral aroma and brilliant green color to many desserts. They are steeped whole in liquids, used to wrap steamed sweets, or blended with water to make an extract. The frozen leaves are available here; they impart much the same flavor, but not the same vibrant green color. To achieve the same coloring, you can use pandan paste or extract. One drop is sufficient.

RED SALA SYRUP is a red floral syrup common in Thai desserts. Hale Blue Boy is the most common brand and can be found in Thai and some other ethnic markets. You can substitute grenadine for a similar color and effect.

RICE comes in innumerable varieties, but no matter what kind you are using, always rinse it in a colander or sieve under cold water before you use it in one of these recipes. Not only does this clean the rice, it also removes excess starch that would otherwise compromise its flavor and texture.

Jasmine rice, also known as Thai hom mali rice, was originally a local specialty of villages in central Thailand, but it became a national favorite and international export in the middle of the twentieth century. Its heady floral aroma makes it popular for both savory and sweet cooking in Southeast Asia. A long-grain rice, it has a soft chewiness, so the cooked grains cling to one another while still holding their shape. When buying, look for the Thai Hom Mali Rice label and splurge on "Prime" grade. Also choose bags with the most recent date of milling and packaging for the freshest and most fragrant rice.

Sweet glutinous rice, also known as sticky rice, is related to jasmine rice and has a similar aroma and sweetness. The grains hold their shape well but are stickier and chewier when cooked. To cook the rice, soak it in cold water for at least 1 hour, or as long as overnight. Drain well, then wrap in banana leaves or cheesecloth and steam over simmering water. Do not boil the rice in water, as you do with most rice varieties. My favorite brand is Erawan from

Thailand; substitute Japanese sticky rice if that is not available.

ROSES are sometimes grown specifically for cooking, particularly in Persian and Indian cuisine. Purchase organic unsprayed dried buds and petals meant for cooking; do not attempt to dry your own petals. **ROSE WATER** is distilled from rose petals. Its floral aroma enhances many desserts, but too much will overpower other flavors. I prefer the Mymouné brand; they also make an incredible **ROSE JAM**.

SALT is now available in many varieties; kosher salt or the fine crystals of ordinary table salt are best for dissolving into desserts. **FLEUR DE SEL**, which means "flower of salt" in French, is the hand-harvested top layer of salt collected from large salt pans. The little flakes have a distinct yet delicate sea-saltiness. This gourmet treat adds a wonderful crunch and savory note when sprinkled on top of a finished dessert. For any recipes that call for fleur de sel, you may substitute Maldon sea salt from England, which has thin delicate crystals.

SESAME SEEDS have a sweet nuttiness and crunch. Both white and black ones are frequently used in Asian desserts, either whole or blended into a paste. Buy untoasted seeds and toast them yourself so you can control the degree to which they are browned. To toast the seeds, put them in a skillet over medium heat and cook, shaking the pan, until they are fragrant and, if using the white seeds, golden brown.

SILKEN TOFU is not only an ingredient in certain Asian desserts, it is sometimes dessert itself. Flavored with a little ginger syrup, it is often served like sweet custard. Made from soy milk that is coagulated but not hardened and strained, silken tofu has a unique and captivating softness. If you live near a large Asian neighborhood, look for fresh homemade silken tofu in markets.

SPRING ROLL WRAPPERS are nearly translucent paper-thin wrappers made from wheat flour, tapioca flour, and water. I prefer the TYJ brand, and I will keep a package refrigerated for only a few days before using. When fried, these wrappers take on a fantastic crispness. Do not confuse them with egg roll wrappers, which are much thicker and tougher when fried.

STAR ANISE is not related to aniseed, but it has a similar licorice scent and taste. The brick-red star-shaped spice comes from a small evergreen tree that grows in China and Vietnam. Buy small quantities at a time to ensure freshness—they should be fragrant and not too brittle.

SUGAR comes in many different forms. Keep any sugar well sealed in a cool, dry place.

Granulated (white) sugar, which is refined cane or beet sugar, is the most versatile for baking.

Brown sugar is white sugar with added molasses, which gives it a softer texture and more complex flavor. I generally prefer light brown sugar to dark, as it has a more delicate flavor. To measure, pack the sugar into the measuring cup and then level off. Be sure to store brown sugar in an airtight container to prevent it from hardening.

Confectioners' sugar is powdered white sugar. To most accurately measure confectioners' sugar, use a scale. To measure confectioners' sugar with a measuring cup, scoop up the sugar, filling the cup generously, and level the top with the back of a knife. Always sift through a fine-mesh sieve before using.

Demerara sugar is a raw sugar, like muscovado, turbinado, or sugar in the raw. After sugarcane has been processed to extract the molasses and refine the sugar crystals, the remaining sugar is called raw sugar. Use raw sugar as a finishing sprinkle on dishes to add a nice crunch without too much sweetness.

Superfine sugar, known in Britain as castor sugar, is fine-grained white sugar. It dissolves readily, which makes it ideal for cakes, meringues, and drinks.

SWEETENED CONDENSED MILK is made by adding sugar to milk and then evaporating much of the water from it until the sugar content is about 55 percent. The high sugar concentration gives it the resulting thick, syrupy consistency. The cans keep for a long time at room temperature so it is used in tropical climates without refrigeration. Sweetened condensed milk is an integral part of desserts throughout East, Southeast, and South Asia. It is used as is, cooked into a sauce, or mixed with other ingredients. I prefer the Vietnamese Longevity brand, but Nestlé, Eagle, and Carnation are also good.

SWEETENED CONDENSED MILK CHANTILLY

Makes 2 cups

1 cup (8 ounces/227 grams) heavy
   whipping cream
2 tablespoons sweetened condensed milk
⅛ teaspoon salt

Whisk the cream until soft peaks form. Add the sweetened condensed milk and salt and whisk until medium-soft peaks form. (When you lift the whisk from the cream, a peak should form and the very tip should fall back down.)

TAPIOCA is made from the root of the starchy cassava plant. It comes in various forms, but it's the little balls that are a key ingredient in Asian desserts. From 1/16 to ¼ inch in diameter, these pearls are most often mixed into warm soups and cold drinks. Flavorless and colorless when cooked, tapioca pearls primarily add a slick, chewy texture to sweets; they should be tender but retain a nice firmness. I prefer Bascom brand.

TARO is a root that has an ivory-and-lavender-swirled flesh beneath a dark, hairy, brown exterior. This starchy plant has a faint carrot-like sweetness and a creamy quality when cooked. For desserts, taro is served in slices in soups or mashed and formed into dumplings. Buy roots that feel firm and use them within a week.

TEA comes in many forms, but the loose leaves are best both for drinking and for flavoring desserts. Although there are many varieties of green and black Asian tea leaves, the one that I use the most, and the one that you can substitute in any tea dessert, is jasmine. With a faint floral aroma, it is neither too bitter nor too subtle. Store loose tea leaves in an airtight container in a cool, dark place.

THAI CHILES, also known as bird's eye chiles or Thai bird chiles, are among the hottest varieties, but I use these fresh chiles for their flavor, not their heat, in my desserts. I prefer the small red or orange riper chiles. To prepare the chiles for use in these recipes, remove the stems, cut the chiles in half lengthwise, and scrape out the seeds and the thin white membranes with a sharp knife. Rinse and pat dry, then mince. Don't use your pastry cutting board for preparing chiles, and do not touch your eyes after working with chiles. I also recommend wearing gloves when working with them.

VANILLA BEANS are a luxury, but they are worth it, especially those from Madagascar and Tahiti. The former has a more rounded flavor; the latter is plumper and full of seeds, with a hint of cherry. I also like the exotic flavor of Planifolia vanilla beans from India, but they are difficult to find. I buy vanilla beans from Mr. Recipe, which also makes other excellent vanilla products, such as ground vanilla, vanilla oil, and vanilla paste. Whichever variety you use, purchase only a few beans at a time so they stay moist and fresh. Wrap them tightly in plastic wrap and store in a cool, dry place. Do not refrigerate them. If they do dry out, put the brittle beans in the bowl of a food processor with some sugar and process to make vanilla sugar, which will keep indefinitely. To prepare fresh vanilla beans, split them lengthwise in half with a sharp knife and scrape out the seeds with the blunt edge of the knife.

Vanilla extract is readily available in supermarkets. It is much more reasonably priced, but still adds great flavor to desserts. Look for pure vanilla extract, in which the only ingredients are vanilla beans, alcohol, and water; there should be no sweeteners or flavorings added. I like the vanilla extract made by Nielsen-Massey. Vanilla paste matches vanilla extract in flavor and strength, but it also has infinitesimal vanilla seeds suspended in the syrupy mixture. These give it a more pronounced aroma.

WATER CHESTNUTS are actually tubers from a Southeast Asian water plant. When mature, they are almost golf ball–sized and have a thin brown skin surrounding crisp white flesh, which is crunchy, juicy, and faintly sweet. Fresh water chestnuts have an incomparably crisp texture and are easy to prepare. Peel off the skin with a vegetable peeler and soak in cold water until ready to use, to avoid browning. If you can't find fresh water chestnuts, you can use canned whole ones, but rinse them well under cold water to refresh them.

YOGURT is milk that is fermented and coagulated. Good yogurt contains nothing more than milk and the bacteria needed to make it; avoid yogurt with added flavorings, preservatives, and stabilizers. For the desserts here, use whole-milk yogurt for its creaminess. Stonyfield Farm is one of my favorite brands, but I also like the richness of Greek yogurt—look for labne or the Total brand.

YUZU JUICE is a potent citrus juice used in Japanese cuisine. Fresh yuzu fruits, which look like green tangerines with yellow spots, are hard to find here. Frozen and bottled juice is available in Asian or specialty markets. As the juice is often used in savory dishes as well, be sure to buy unsalted juice for these dessert recipes.

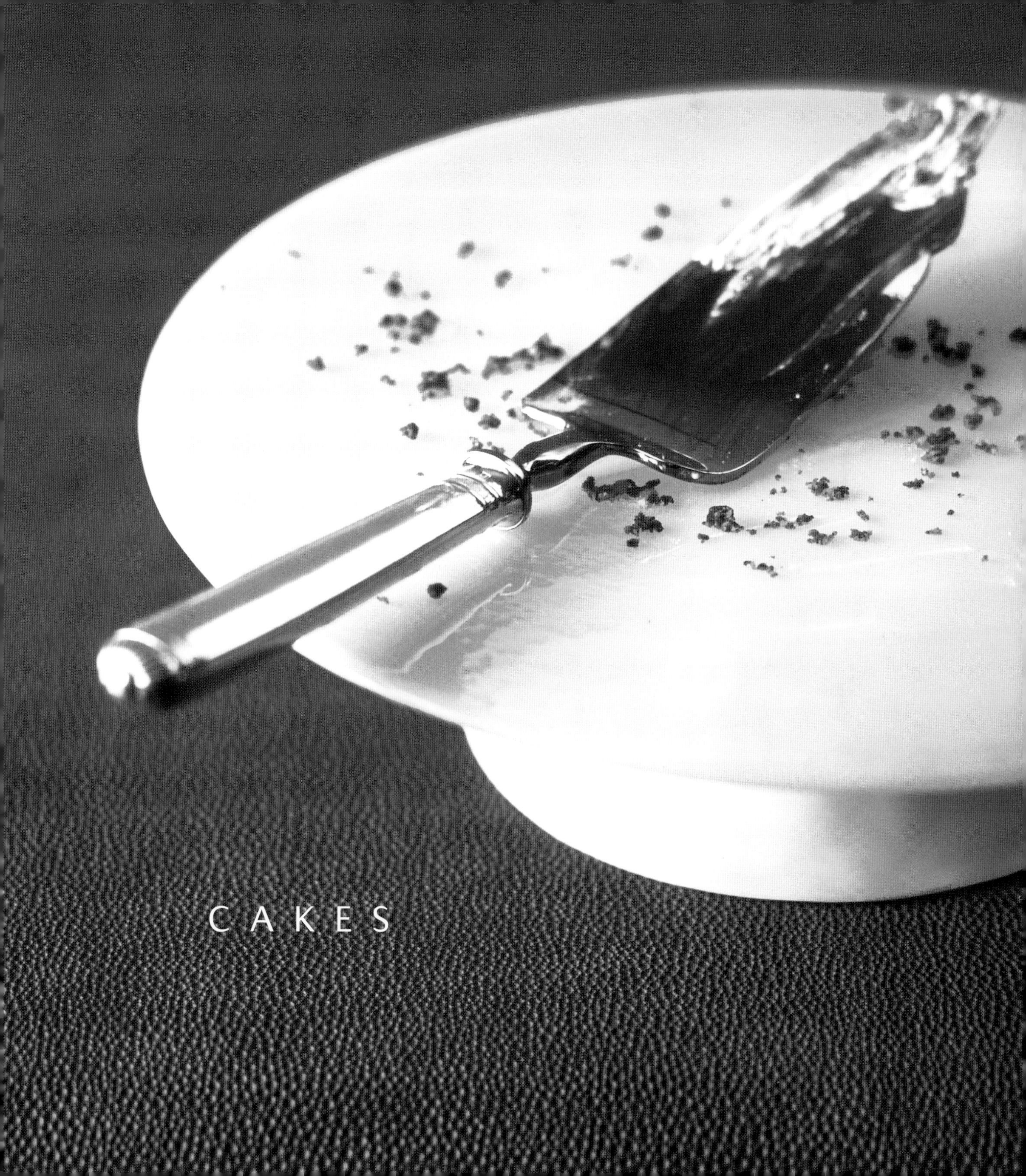

CAKES

Cakes are universally loved. They feel celebratory but not pretentious, ambitious but not absurd. No one is ever sorry to see a cake on the table. I offer a range of cake recipes here, from home-style pound and sheet cakes to special-occasion layer cakes to modern individual cakes. Besides my own takes on Western standards, I've also included a sampling of authentic Asian steamed cakes. Sometimes chewy, sometimes spongy, sometimes silken, these traditional treats are sure to surprise and please.

For all the joy they bring, cakes are surprisingly easy desserts to master. The key to doing so is to carefully watch every step. Although I offer detailed instructions for each cake in this book, I encourage you to trust your eyes, nose, mouth, and fingers even more than usual here. Don't let your kitchen appliances lull you into a false sense of security—you still have to control the speed and time of your standing mixer.

There's good news too—any "mistakes" you make can usually be fixed. If your cupcakes didn't rise quite as you wanted, just frost them more liberally. If the frosting looks grainy and isn't coming together, you probably added butter that was too cold—just keep beating, and it will soon become a smooth, luscious topping.

Some of the recipes here may look intimidating, but almost every one can be made in stages, and many of these cakes keep exceptionally well, so they can be made ahead. Besides, I've always found that the time you invest in a cake pays off in the end. Your friends may grab a cookie on their way out the door, but they'll sit down and stay for cake.

LOAF AND SHEET CAKES

The basic loaf or sheet cake is a staple at American picnics, potlucks, teatimes, and whenever else people crave a simple yet satisfying sweet. There are endless one-bowl variations on the simple butter-flour-sugar mix, but they all share a lack of pretense and a warm, inviting charm.

The appeal of these classic flavors has not been lost on Asian bakers. Rows of sweet loaf and sheet cakes line the shelves of Asian bakeries. The biggest difference between these and their American counterparts is that the Asian versions are lighter and less sweet. Also, Asian bakers naturally tend to add traditional Asian dessert flavors—such as coconut, red bean, and green tea.

Raised in Asia and America, I grew up eating both versions of these cakes and I draw on both traditions for inspiration. So, while my cakes are usually lighter and less sweet than classic American ones, I tweak those classic flavors just enough to make them especially delicious, but not too esoteric.

These cakes reflect the Asian philosophy that sweets should be good for you. I don't pretend that my desserts are low in fat or cholesterol, but in many cases I substitute an ingredient that is not only intriguing in flavor but also more healthful than what it replaces. For instance, I sometimes add yogurt to a cake to give it a creamy tartness and a rich, moist crumb that doesn't taste at all oily. That doing so lessens the amount of butter needed is an added benefit. In fact, many of these cakes use much less butter than you might expect. Instead, I use ingredients like olive oil and Kabocha squash.

The next time you want to inspire nostalgia without seeming passé, serve one of these cakes.

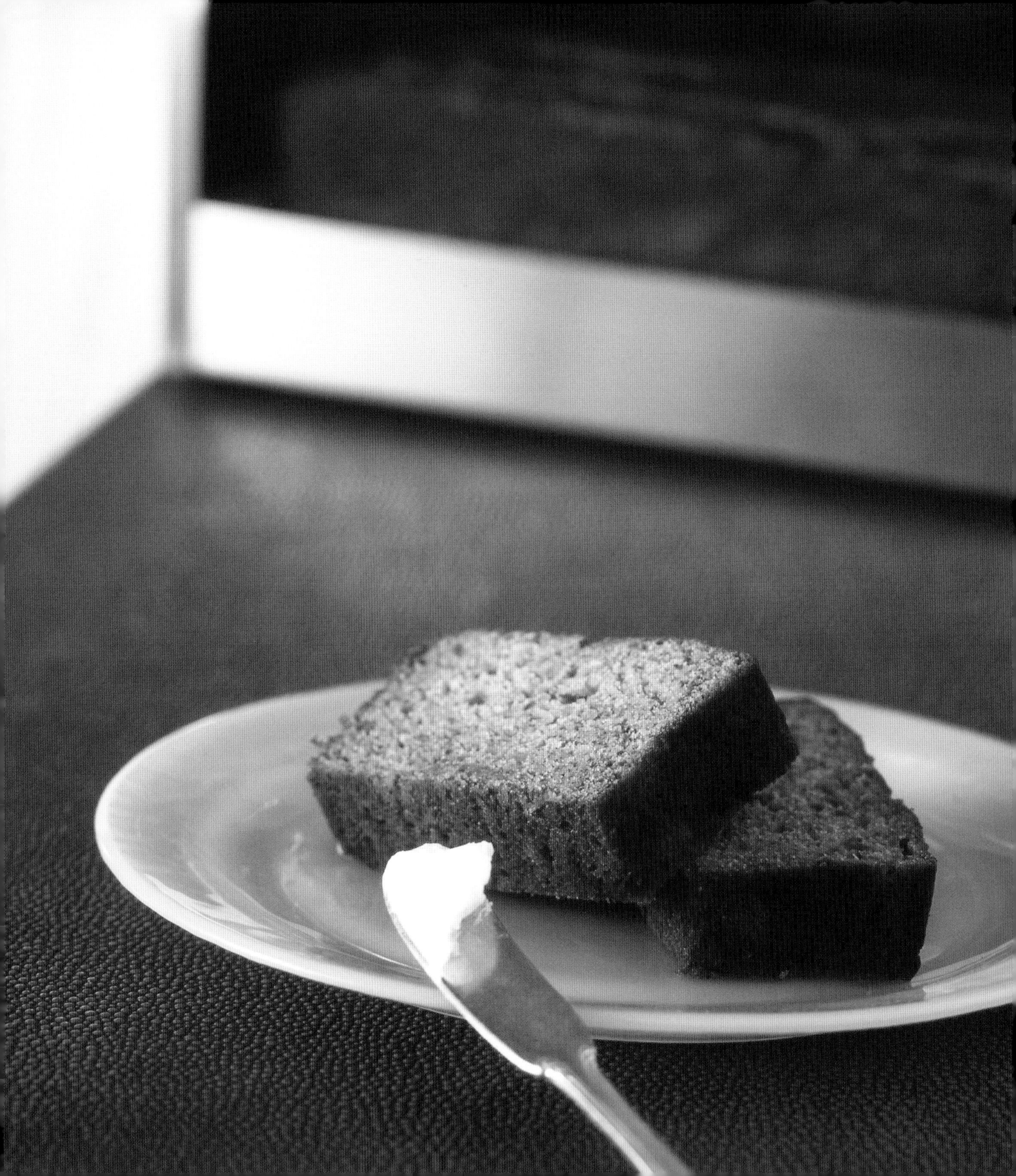

BANANA CAKE

In my humble opinion, this is the best banana cake. Ever. Baby bananas, enjoyed throughout Southeast Asia, have a distinct flavor and texture that set this cake apart. Yogurt keeps the bread-like texture light and moist, while honey adds a musky sweetness.

CHEF'S TIPS: The key to keeping this banana cake light in texture is to avoid overmixing. I make this cake a lot, so I keep containers of mashed banana—measured for this recipe—in my freezer.

⅓ cup (2¾ ounces/78 grams) unsalted butter, at room temperature, plus more for greasing the pan

1 cup (5½ ounces/155 grams) all-purpose flour

1 teaspoon baking powder

1 teaspoon baking soda

¼ cup (3 ounces/85 grams) honey

½ cup (2½ ounces/72 grams) packed light brown sugar

½ teaspoon ground cinnamon

½ teaspoon salt

1 cup (8 ounces/228 grams) roughly mashed baby bananas (about 5 baby bananas)

½ teaspoon vanilla extract

1 large egg

½ cup (4⅝ ounces/130 grams) plain whole-milk yogurt or sour cream

1 cup (5½ ounces/155 grams) semisweet chocolate chips, optional

1. Preheat the oven to 350°F. Lightly butter an 8½ × 4½-inch loaf pan and set aside.

2. Sift together the flour, baking powder, and baking soda and set aside.

3. Put the butter, honey, sugar, cinnamon, and salt in the bowl of an electric mixer fitted with the paddle attachment. Beat the mixture on medium-high speed until light and fluffy, about 5 minutes. Scrape down the sides and bottom of the bowl, add the bananas and vanilla, and beat on medium speed until the mixture looks "broken," or lumpy, about 1 minute. The bananas should be smashed, with a few small chunks remaining.

4. Turn the speed to medium-low and beat in the egg until incorporated. Turn the speed to low and gradually add the sifted flour mixture, mixing just until no traces of flour remain, about 10 seconds. Add the yogurt and mix until the batter has only a few remaining white streaks, about 5 seconds. Be sure to avoid overmixing. Gently fold in the chocolate chips, if desired.

5. Transfer the batter to the greased pan. Bake in the center of the oven until a tester inserted in the center comes out clean, about 45 minutes. Cool the cake in the pan on a rack for 5 minutes, then unmold and cool completely on the rack.

■

CONDENSED MILK POUND CAKE

Makes one 8½ × 4½-inch cake, about 12 servings

In Southeast Asia, sweetened condensed milk is often drizzled on toast as a snack. This pound cake is a luxurious homage to that treat. Using condensed milk as the primary sweetener results in a buttery cake rich in texture without being too dense. It's great on its own or as an accompaniment to tea. Slices can also be served as a more elegant dessert with some macerated berries and a dollop of Sweetened Condensed Milk Chantilly (page 25).

CHEF'S TIP: This pound cake keeps well, tightly wrapped, for up to 1 week at room temperature or up to 2 months in the freezer.

1 cup (8 ounces/226 grams) unsalted butter, at room temperature, plus more for greasing the pan

1⅓ cups (7 ounces/200 grams) all-purpose flour

¾ teaspoon baking powder

½ cup (3¾ ounces/106 grams) sugar

1 vanilla bean, chopped, or 2 teaspoons vanilla extract

½ teaspoon salt

¾ cup (8½ ounces/239 grams) sweetened condensed milk

3 large eggs

1. Preheat the oven to 325°F. Generously butter an 8½ × 4½-inch loaf pan and set aside.

2. Sift together the flour and baking powder and set aside.

3. Put the sugar and the chopped vanilla bean, if using, in the bowl of a food processor fitted with the metal blade and pulse until the vanilla bean is finely ground. Sift through a fine-mesh sieve and return the sugar mixture to the food processor. If not using the vanilla bean, just put the sugar in the processor.

4. Add the butter and salt and process until light and fluffy, about 2 minutes, scraping down the sides and bottom of the bowl occasionally. Add the condensed milk and pulse until well incorporated, about 15 times, scraping down the sides of the bowl once. Add the

sifted dry ingredients and pulse until no traces of flour remain, about 10 times. Add the eggs and pulse just until combined, about 5 times. Scrape down the sides and bottom of the bowl, add the vanilla extract, if using, and finish mixing by hand to fully incorporate the eggs.

5. Transfer the batter to the prepared loaf pan. Bake until the top is dark golden brown and a tester inserted in the center comes out clean, about 1 hour. Cool completely in the loaf pan on a rack, then unmold.

■

OLIVE OIL AND YOGURT CAKE

Makes one 9 × 13-inch cake, about 24 servings

I'll confess that this dessert is inspired more by the Mediterranean than by Asia. Although it looks like a traditional yellow cake, the olive oil adds a distinctive fruitiness and nuttiness while the yogurt adds a sweet tang and keeps the cake unbelievably moist. Although fleur de sel may seem an unusual form of "sprinkles," its mild saltiness brings out the best in this cake.

CHEF'S TIPS: Use an extra virgin olive oil that is delicious on its own, such as a fruity Spanish olive oil, like Arbequiña or Piqual.

This cake is even better the next day if you cover it tightly and set aside at room temperature overnight.

1 tablespoon unsalted butter, at room temperature, for greasing the pan

4 cups (21⅞ ounces/620 grams) all-purpose flour

2 tablespoons baking powder

3 cups (28¼ ounces/800 grams) plain whole-milk yogurt

3¼ cups (21⅔ ounces/614 grams) sugar

9 large eggs

2 tablespoons grated orange zest

1 teaspoon vanilla extract

1 teaspoon salt

1 cup (8 ounces/228 grams) extra virgin olive oil

½ cup (5¾ ounces/163 grams) orange marmalade

1 tablespoon fleur de sel or other mild sea salt, such as Maldon

1. Preheat the oven to 350°F. Generously butter a 9 × 13-inch cake pan and set aside.

2. Sift together the flour and baking powder and set aside.

3. Put the yogurt, sugar, eggs, orange zest, vanilla, and salt into the bowl of an electric mixer fitted with the whisk attachment. Whisk on medium speed until well combined, about 2 minutes. Turn the speed to low and whisk in the flour mixture until well blended, about 1 minute. Scrape down the sides and bottom of the bowl and stir the batter a few times.

4. In a small bowl, whisk together 1 cup of the batter with the oil until smooth and homogeneous. Add the oil mixture into the remaining batter in a slow, steady stream, folding continuously.

5. Transfer the batter to the cake pan. Bake until a tester inserted in the center comes out clean, about 50 minutes.

6. While the cake is baking, stir the orange marmalade together with 1 tablespoon water.

7. As soon as the cake is done, brush the top with the orange marmalade glaze and sprinkle with the fleur de sel. Cool completely in the pan on a rack.

■

HONEY CASTELLA

Makes one 9 × 13-inch cake, about 24 servings

Castella, also known as *kasutera,* is a delicate sponge cake that's popular in Japan, particularly in the city of Nagasaki, where it's served at festivals and street markets. Although the exact origins of castella are unknown, it's thought to have originated in the Castile region of Spain and to have been brought to Japan by Portuguese merchants in the sixteenth century. The basic recipe has many variations, but the honeyed version with dark caramelized crusts is among the most beloved in Japan. It's my favorite too.

CHEF'S TIP: This cake browns quickly because of the honey, but don't worry, it won't burn on the outside before it's cooked through.

¼ cup (1⅞ ounces/52 grams) canola, vegetable, or other neutral oil, plus more for greasing the pan

1½ cups (7⅜ ounces/210 grams) all-purpose flour

½ teaspoon salt

7 large eggs

3 large egg yolks

1½ cups (10½ ounces/300 grams) sugar

¼ cup (3½ ounces/100 grams) honey

Concord Grape Preserves (page 271), optional

1. Preheat the oven to 350°F. Generously grease a 9 × 13-inch cake pan and set aside.

2. Sift together the flour and salt and set aside.

3. Put the eggs, yolks, sugar, and honey in the bowl of an electric mixer and set over a saucepan of simmering water. Whisk constantly until the sugar is completely dissolved and the mixture is warm to the touch, about 10 minutes.

4. Fit the bowl into the mixer and whisk at medium-high speed until the mixture is pale yellow, thick, and completely cool, about 10 minutes. Gently fold in the dry ingredients.

5. In a small bowl, whisk together 1 cup of the batter with the oil until smooth and homogeneous. Add the oil mixture into the remaining batter in a slow, steady stream, folding continuously.

CAKES ■ 37

6. Transfer to the prepared cake pan. Bake for 15 minutes, then turn the heat down to 300°F and bake until a tester inserted in the center comes out clean, about 45 more minutes. Cool completely in the pan on a rack.

7. Serve the cake alone or top each slice with a dollop of Concord Grape Preserves, if desired.

■

STEAMED CAKES

To cook a cake, you bake it, right? Well, what seems obvious in the West isn't always the case in Asia, where cakes are usually steamed. Ovens are still relatively new in Asian homes, and many families must take anything they want baked to the commercial ovens of local bakeries. Microwaves and toaster ovens have grown in popularity, but the stovetop remains the appliance of choice for desserts, cakes included.

Such cakes bear little resemblance to their Western counterparts. Made with rice flour, the traditional Asian cake is a sticky, chewy concoction—for texture, think gumdrop, but a bit softer and with less chew. Of course, the textures and flavors of these cakes can vary widely. Those made in tropical regions often feature coconut, bananas, and pandan leaves, while those made farther north usually feature different varieties of sweetened beans, nuts, or sesame seeds.

The rice cakes with which I am most familiar come from Southeast Asia. The batter is either steamed as a large cake to be cut into individual pieces for serving, as in the Steamed Pandan Layer Cake, or prepared as individual cakes before steaming. These small cakes are often encased in softened banana or pandan leaves for added fragrance and flavor (and a pretty presentation).

Sticky rice cakes are popular throughout Asia not only because they taste great, but because many cultures enjoy them as New Year's treats. The popularity of these traditional sweets, however, hasn't stopped Asian chefs from experimenting with Western-style cakes as well. Cantonese dim sum menus, for example, have long featured delicate sponge cakes made by steaming wheat flour-and-egg batters.

My preferred technique of steaming cakes in the oven is to use a covered bain-marie (that is, a pan filled with hot water). The oven's even heat makes for a foolproof technique that works especially well with classic French desserts, like soufflés.

Steaming is not just an alternative to baking, but a versatile method in its own right. By adding moisture without adding fat, it can create moist, light sweets that are sticky, spongy, or silken. From East to West, these cakes have come a long way.

STEAMED PANDAN LAYER CAKE

Makes one 9-inch round cake, about 24 servings

Asian cakes are often sticky treats that taste more like candy than pastry. Glutinous rice flour lends a rich flavor and a distinctive chewy texture not found anywhere else. I love this particular version of sticky rice cake because of the fragrant pandan, which adds a fresh, floral note and vibrant green color to the cake. The result looks almost like layered Jell-O treats, but the taste is far more sophisticated.

CHEF'S TIP: Pandan leaves, also known as screwpine or bai touy, can be found frozen in Asian markets. Fresh pandan leaves, available only in Asia, impart a brilliant grass green color to desserts. To achieve the same color, you can use pandan extract, also available in Asian markets. Without the extract, the cake will be a calming shade of jade.

2 teaspoons canola, vegetable, or other neutral oil for greasing the pan

½ cup (1⅝ ounces/45 grams) chopped thawed frozen pandan leaves

2½ cups (20 ounces/568 grams) unsweetened coconut milk

1¾ cups (11⅞ ounces/335 grams) sugar

⅔ cup (2¾ ounces/79 grams) tapioca flour

⅔ cup (2¾ ounces/76 grams) glutinous rice flour

3 tablespoons all-purpose flour

2 teaspoons cornstarch

¼ teaspoon salt

A drop of pandan extract, optional

1. Prepare a steamer by filling a large round casserole with water to a depth of 3 inches; the casserole should be at least 11 inches in diameter and have a tightly fitting lid. Put a steamer rack or enough crumpled heavy-duty aluminum foil to support the cake pan on the bottom; the rack or foil should be just above the waterline. Set over medium heat and bring to a steady simmer. Grease a 9-inch round cake pan with the oil and set aside.

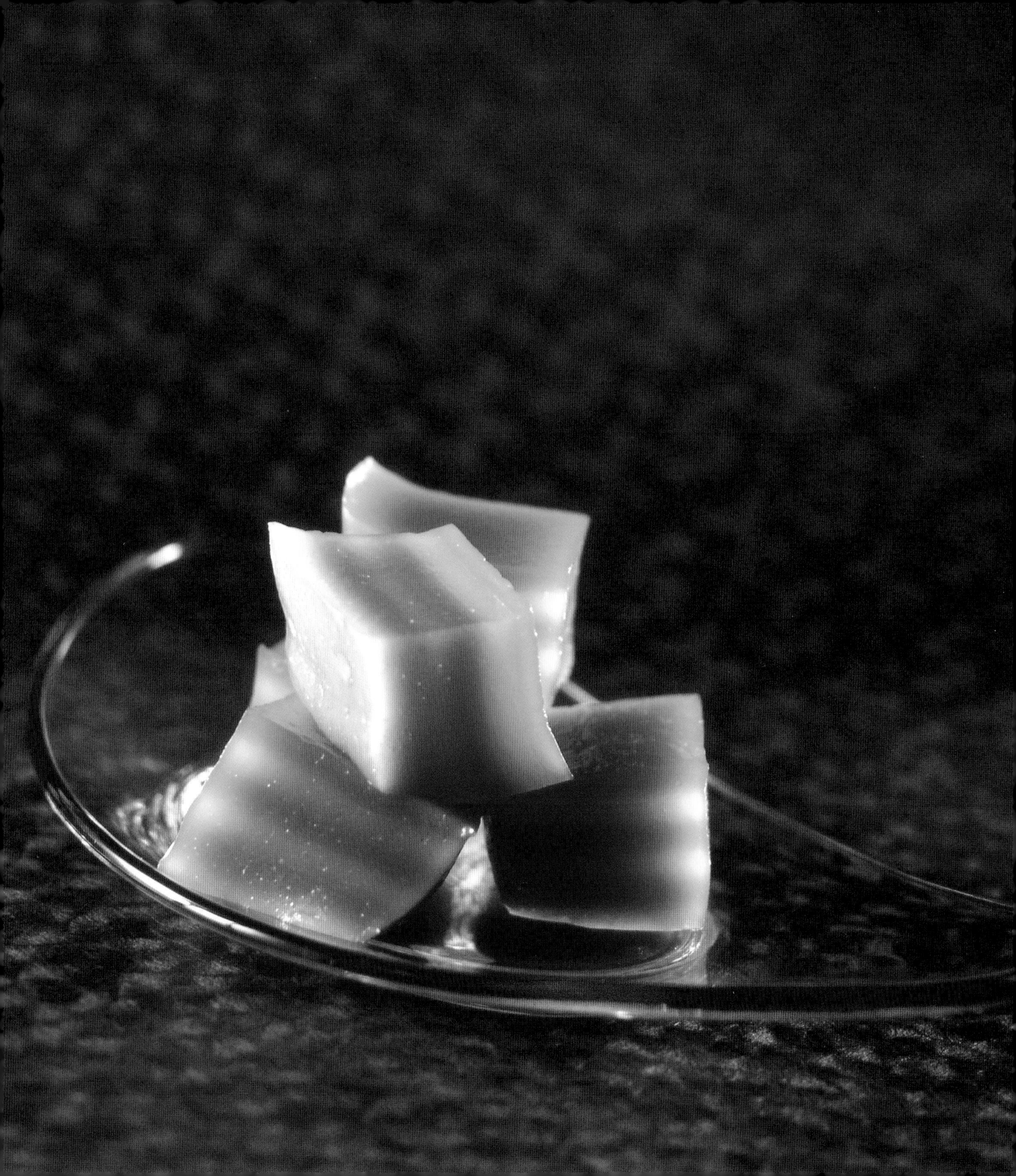

2. Put the pandan leaves in a blender with ¼ cup of the coconut milk and ⅓ cup water. Blend until the pandan leaves are finely chopped. Strain the mixture through a fine-mesh sieve lined with cheesecloth, pressing on the pandan leaves to extract as much liquid as possible. Discard the leaves and set the liquid aside.

3. In a medium bowl, combine the remaining 2¼ cups coconut milk with the sugar and stir until the sugar dissolves; set aside.

4. Mix the three flours, the cornstarch, and the salt together in a large mixing bowl. Add the coconut milk mixture and stir until well blended. Pour half the batter (about 2 cups) into another mixing bowl. Add the pandan liquid and the extract, if using, to one of the bowls and mix well.

5. Pour 1 cup of the green batter into the cake pan, tilting the pan to form an even layer. Carefully set the cake pan on the steamer rack, making sure that the pan sits as evenly as possible. Wrap a thin kitchen towel around the lid, cover the pot tightly, and steam until the cake layer is firm and set, about 4 minutes.

6. Carefully pour 1 cup of the white cake batter on top of the green batter. Pour the batter in from the side so that it will spread into an even layer naturally. Steam, covered, until the white layer is set, about 10 minutes. Repeat with the remaining batter, alternating colors.

7. When the final layer is set, turn off the heat, uncover the pot, and let the cake cool in the casserole until it is cool enough to touch.

8. Remove the cake pan from the casserole, run a knife around the edge, and cut the cake into little squares. (You can eat the trimmings yourself.) It is best served the same day, as it hardens over time.

■

STEAMED ALMOND CAKE

This is a classic Cantonese dim sum treat—a moist and ethereal version of sponge cake. The recipe and the variation below feature popular traditional flavors—almond and pandan, respectively—but vanilla or even coffee extract can also be used.

1 tablespoon canola, vegetable, or other neutral oil for greasing the pan

1¼ cups (6⅞ ounces/194 grams) all-purpose flour

¼ cup (1 ounce/28 grams) almond flour

½ teaspoon baking powder

6 large eggs, separated, at room temperature

1⅓ cups (9⅛ ounces/258 grams) sugar

1½ teaspoons almond extract

1½ teaspoons vanilla extract

¼ teaspoon salt

1. Prepare a steamer by filling a large round casserole with water to a depth of 3 inches; the casserole should be at least 11 inches in diameter and have a tightly fitting lid. Put a steamer rack or enough crumpled heavy-duty aluminum foil to support the cake pan on the bottom; the rack or foil should be just above the waterline. Set over medium heat and bring to a steady simmer. Lightly grease a 9-inch round cake pan or twelve 4-ounce ramekins. Line with parchment paper, grease the paper, and set aside.

2. Sift the all-purpose flour, almond flour, and baking powder together and set aside.

3. Put the egg whites in the bowl of an electric mixer fitted with the whisk attachment and whisk on medium speed until frothy. With the machine running, add half the sugar and continue whisking until medium peaks form. (When you lift the whisk from the mixture, a peak will form and the very tip of the peak will fall back down.) Transfer the whipped whites to another large mixing bowl.

4. Put the egg yolks, almond extract, and vanilla extract in the mixer bowl and whisk at medium speed until well combined, about 2 minutes. With the machine running, add the salt and the remaining sugar and whisk until the mixture is pale yellow, thick, and doubled in volume, about 10 minutes.

5. Add half the whites to the yolks and fold in until completely incorporated. Add half the sifted dry ingredients and fold in gently, then add the remaining dry ingredients and fold in until no traces of flour remain. Add the remaining whites and fold in gently until there are just a few white streaks remaining. Transfer the batter to the cake pan or ramekins.

6. If the water level in the casserole has fallen, replenish it, then turn the heat to medium-high to maintain a strong, steady simmer. Carefully put the cake pan or ramekins on the steamer rack. Wrap a thin kitchen towel around the casserole lid, cover the pot tightly, and steam until a tester inserted in the center comes out clean, about 45 minutes for the cake pan, 20 minutes for the ramekins. Steam the ramekins in batches, if necessary.

7. Remove the lid and let the cake cool in the steamer until you can remove the pan or ramekins without burning yourself. Cut the large cake into slices and serve warm.

Steamed Pandan Cake: Put ½ cup (1⅔ ounces/45 grams) chopped thawed frozen pandan leaves in a blender with 1 tablespoon water and blend until the leaves are finely chopped. Strain through a fine-mesh sieve lined with cheesecloth, pressing on the leaves to extract as much liquid as possible. Substitute the pandan water for the almond extract, and prepare the batter as directed. Use only 4-ounce ramekins for steaming: Lightly grease them, then line them with thawed frozen pandan leaves, overlapping them to cover the bottom and sides of each ramekin and leaving a 1-inch overhang. Lightly grease the pandan leaves, fill the lined ramekins with the batter, and steam as directed above. Lift the pandan baskets out of the ramekins and serve, directing guests to remove the cakes from the leaves before eating.

■

STEAMED YUZU SOUFFLÉS

Inspired by the delicious steamed cake with fresh lemons that Karen DeMasco, pastry chef of New York's Craft, makes, I created my own steamed Asian citrus dessert.

Although I don't use an actual steamer here, the covered water bath achieves the same effect. This soufflé is impossibly delicate and moist, like an airy cheesecake topped with a silky citrus curd. As the soufflé rests and cools to room temperature, the curd naturally separates and creates a fun two-tiered dessert. This soufflé is delicious on its own or with macerated fresh berries.

CHEF'S TIP: Fresh yuzu can sometimes be found in Japanese markets. Frozen or bottled yuzu juice is available in Asian markets and some specialty stores. You can also substitute lemon juice, preferably from Meyer lemons, or a combination of lemon and lime juices.

1 tablespoon unsalted butter, at room temperature, for greasing the ramekins

⅓ cup plus 1 tablespoon (2¾ ounces/80 grams) sugar, plus more for dusting the ramekins

¼ cup (2 ounces/55 grams) cake or all-purpose flour

¾ teaspoon salt

3 large eggs, separated

1 tablespoon grated lemon zest

¼ cup plus 2 tablespoons (3 ounces/84 grams) yuzu juice

1 cup (8 ounces/224 grams) whole milk

1. Preheat the oven to 325°F. Generously butter and lightly sugar eight 4-ounce ramekins or Chinese teacups; set aside.

2. Sift together the flour, salt, and 3 tablespoons sugar and set aside.

3. Put the egg yolks and zest in a large mixing bowl and whisk in the yuzu juice, then the milk. Add the sifted dry ingredients and whisk until well combined, scraping down the sides and bottom of the bowl as necessary.

4. Put the egg whites in the bowl of an electric mixer fitted with the whisk attachment, and whisk until the whites are frothy. With the machine running, slowly add the remaining

3 tablespoons plus 1 teaspoon sugar. Continue whisking until medium-soft peaks form. (When you lift the whisk from the mixture, a peak will form and the tip will fall back down.) Gently fold the egg whites into the yolk mixture a little at a time.

5. Using a ladle, scoop the mixture from the bottom of the bowl and fill the ramekins almost to the brim. Scraping the bottom of the bowl ensures that each serving will have a sufficient amount of yuzu juice. Put the ramekins 1 inch apart in a deep baking or roasting pan. Fill the pan with enough water to come halfway up the sides of the ramekins.

6. Cover the pan with foil, carefully place in the oven, and bake until the soufflés rise ½ inch above the rim of the ramekins, are firm to the touch, and a tester comes out clean, about 30 minutes. Remove the pan from the oven, carefully uncover, and let the soufflés cool in the water until cool enough to touch; they will collapse slightly. Remove the ramekins from the water bath and cool to room temperature on a cooling rack.

7. Serve the soufflés in the ramekins or invert onto serving plates. If they seem stuck, run a paring knife around the edge of each ramekin and then invert.

■

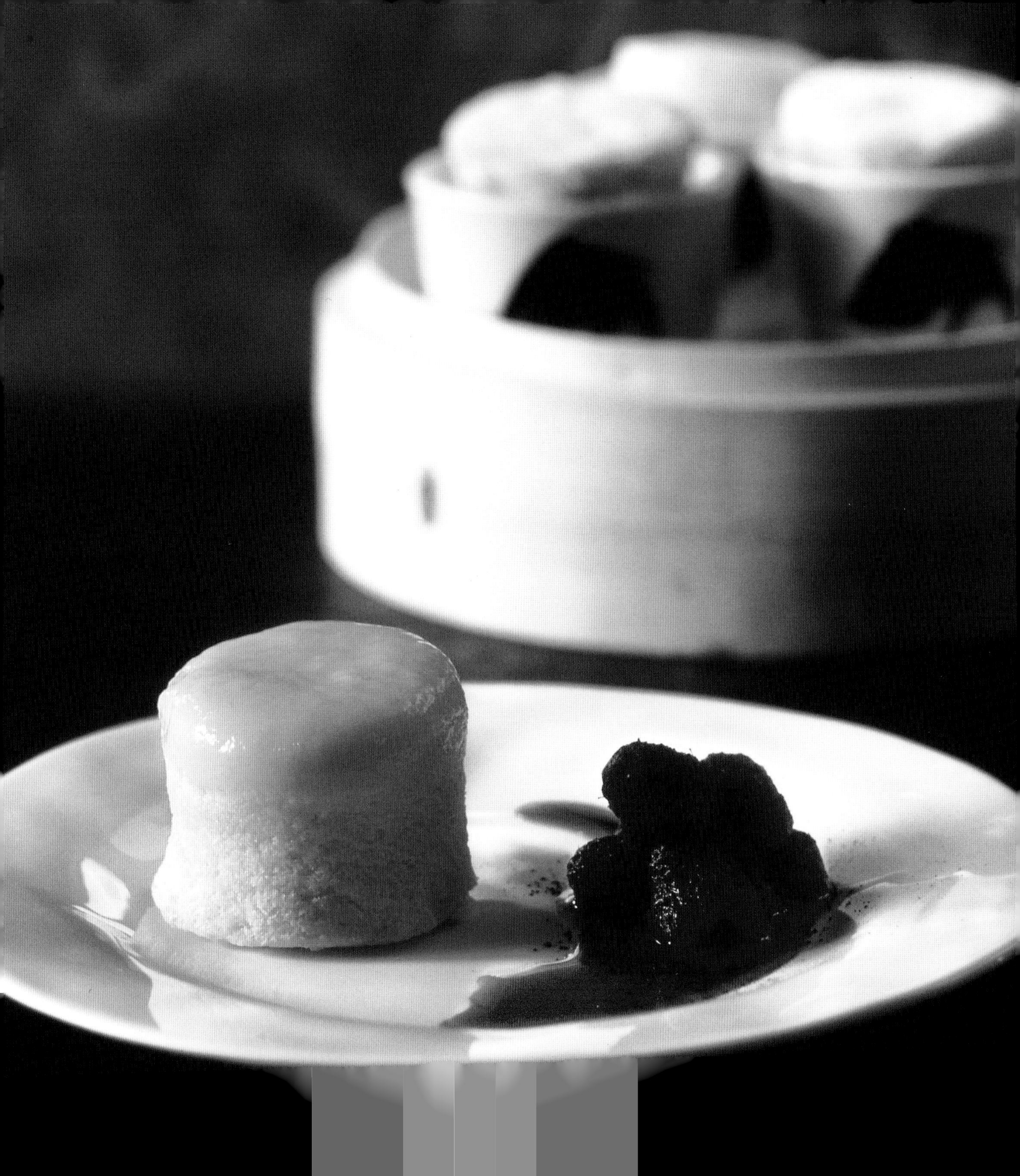

INDIVIDUAL CAKES—
ANY TIME OF DAY

Small, individual cakes are as gorgeous and tasty as their larger counterparts, but they signal something special. It is so satisfying to finish the final crumbs of a whole cake, made especially for you.

Rather than miniaturize the large versions of my cakes, I find my inspiration in the little cakes that are popular throughout Asia. Many of these desserts are actually products of Western imperialism, colonization, and, later, globalization. Particularly in major port cities like Singapore and Hong Kong, indigenous and Western cuisine were blended together so thoroughly that the distinction between local flavors and Western influences is now sometimes indistinguishable.

Formal tea service at many of the emblematic Asian hotels of the colonial era has remained a constant, and the highlight of that service has always been the beautiful small cakes perched on three-tiered silver tea trays. Setting aside colonial rivalries, scones and "pudding" cakes from England sit alongside French tarts and petits fours.

The tea rooms of these hotels also have embraced the culinary trends of the present. Their menus reflect a strong local influence, but they also incorporate aspects of new American cuisine brought across the Pacific by globalization. Star chefs from around the world now learn constantly from each others' work. That soufflé on the menu may be the classic French pouf or the new classic—the compact molten chocolate soufflé cake.

The American food culture has influenced dining on all levels in Asia. Outside the haute cuisine kitchens of four-star hotels are convenience stores, with shelves of pre-packaged American cupcakes and other sweet treats. Over the years, food companies have made variations on classic items to appeal to Asian tastes. I have too. My versions of the formal tea cakes in Asia have fresh, new flavors and my adaptations of fun American treats have sophisticated twists. Simple yet classy, my individual cakes are perfect any time of day.

GINGER DATE PUDDING CAKES
WITH RUM WALNUT TOFFEE SAUCE

To the British, the term "pudding" means "dessert" and encompasses a wide range of sweets, from custards to cakes to trifles. Their moist pudding cakes are known for their warm, hearty flavors, and I love to serve them on cold days. The combination of fresh and candied ginger here adds a nice touch of heat and spice to the fruity sweetness of the dates and the richness of the walnut toffee. This dessert is terrific on its own, with a dollop of crème fraîche, or, of course, with a hot cup of tea.

CHEF'S TIP: To prepare this ahead of time for a party, put the cooled unmolded cakes in a casserole and top with the cooled sauce. Just before serving, reheat the whole thing, covered, in a 350°F oven for 10 minutes.

Ginger Date Pudding Cakes

1 cup plus 2 tablespoons (9 ounces/254 grams) unsalted butter, at room temperature, plus more for greasing the ramekins

6 (5 ounces/143 grams) dried dates, preferably Medjool, pitted, or dried persimmons

One 1-inch piece fresh ginger, cut into ¼-inch slices

¼ teaspoon salt

½ vanilla bean, split lengthwise in half, seeds scraped out, and seeds and pod reserved, or 1 teaspoon vanilla extract

1 teaspoon baking soda

⅔ cup (4⅔ ounces/133 grams) sugar

⅓ cup (1⅝ ounces/45 grams) candied ginger, finely chopped

1 tablespoon grated orange zest

1½ cups (7⅞ ounces/223 grams) all-purpose flour

1 teaspoon baking powder

1 large egg

Rum Walnut Toffee Sauce

1½ cups (5¼ ounces/149 grams) walnut halves

½ cup plus 2 tablespoons (4⅔ ounces/133 grams) unsalted butter

1 cup (8 ounces/227 grams) heavy whipping cream

1⅓ cups (9 ounces/253 grams) packed dark brown sugar

One 1-inch piece fresh ginger, cut into ¼-inch slices

¼ teaspoon salt

½ vanilla bean, split lengthwise in half, seeds scraped out, and seeds and pod reserved, or 1 teaspoon vanilla extract

2 tablespoons dark rum

Sweetened Condensed Milk Chantilly (page 25) or crème fraîche, optional

1. To make the cake: Preheat the oven to 350°F. Generously butter eight 4-ounce ramekins and set aside.

2. Put the dates, ginger slices, salt, vanilla seeds and pod, if using, and 1 cup water in a small saucepan. Bring to a boil over high heat and cook for 10 minutes. Turn the heat to low, stir in the baking soda, and cook for 3 minutes. The mixture will foam and turn an unattractive shade of dark gray; don't worry, the cakes will taste and look fine. Remove from the heat and remove the ginger and vanilla pod from the saucepan; set the mixture aside.

3. Put the butter, sugar, candied ginger, and orange zest in the bowl of an electric mixer fitted with the paddle attachment and beat on medium speed until well mixed, about 2 minutes. Add the dates and their cooking liquid, and mix until the dates are broken into small pieces and everything is well combined, about 2 minutes.

4. With the machine running, add the flour and baking powder. When no traces of flour remain, add the egg and the vanilla extract, if using, and mix just until blended, about 1 minute.

5. Divide the batter among the ramekins. Bake until a tester inserted in the center comes out clean, about 35 minutes. Cool the cakes in the ramekins for 5 minutes, then unmold and cool completely on a rack. (Leave the oven on.)

6. Meanwhile, make the sauce: Put the walnuts on a rimmed baking sheet and toast until golden brown and fragrant, 7 minutes. Remove from the oven and cool completely.

7. Put the butter, cream, brown sugar, ginger, salt, vanilla seeds and pod, if using, and 3 tablespoons water in a medium saucepan and bring to a boil over medium-high heat, whisking occasionally. Reduce the heat slightly and simmer until it is the consistency of a thick sauce, about 15 minutes.

8. Remove the sauce from the heat and remove the ginger slices and vanilla pod. Stir in the toasted nuts, and return the sauce to a boil. Simmer until thick and sticky, about 5 minutes. Remove from the heat and let cool slightly, then stir in the rum and vanilla extract, if using.

9. To serve, place the cakes on serving plates and spoon the warm sauce all around them. Top each one with a dollop of the chantilly, if desired.

AROMATIC COCONUT SOUFFLÉS

I've seen many soufflés in my lifetime but this is one of my favorites. The natural nuttiness and light sweetness of real coconut make these soufflés incredibly aromatic. Your house will smell heavenly as these bake.

CHEF'S TIP: Be sure to thoroughly butter and sugar the ramekins so the soufflés will rise as high as possible.

1 cup (3⅛ ounces/88 grams) finely shredded unsweetened dried coconut

1½ cups (12 ounces/340 grams) unsweetened coconut milk

1 cup (8 ounces/226 grams) heavy whipping cream

½ cup (4 ounces/114 grams) whole milk

2 large eggs, separated

¼ teaspoon salt

¾ cup (5 ounces/143 grams) sugar, plus more for sugaring the ramekins

½ cup plus 1 tablespoon (3⅛ ounces/ 90 grams) all-purpose flour

2 tablespoons unsalted butter, at room temperature, plus more for greasing the ramekins

2 teaspoons vanilla extract

1 large egg white

1. Put the coconut, coconut milk, cream, milk, egg yolks, salt, ½ cup plus 2 tablespoons sugar, and ½ cup of the flour in a medium saucepan, set over medium heat, and cook, whisking constantly, until the mixture thickens and boils. The consistency should be like a very thick batter. Remove from the heat and whisk in the butter and vanilla extract.

2. Let the coconut mixture cool slightly, then strain through a fine-mesh sieve into a large mixing bowl, pressing on the coconut to extract all the liquid. Set aside to cool completely.

3. Preheat the oven to 425°F. Generously butter eight 4-ounce ramekins, taking care to butter the rims, and lightly sugar, tapping out any excess. Refrigerate the ramekins until you are ready to fill them.

4. Put the egg whites in the bowl of an electric mixer fitted with the whisk attachment. Whisk until the whites are frothy, then, with the machine running, slowly add the remaining 2 tablespoons sugar. Continue whisking until medium peaks form. (When you

lift the whisk from the mixture, a peak will form and the very tip of the peak will fall back down.)

5. Whisk the cooled coconut cream until it loosens and has a near liquid consistency. Add all the whites to the cream and fold in very gently until there are just a few white streaks remaining. Sift the remaining 1 tablespoon flour over the mixture and fold in gently until no traces of flour remain.

6. Divide the batter among the ramekins. Bake until puffed and light golden brown on top, about 20 minutes. Serve immediately.

■

COCONUT "TWINKIE" CUPCAKES WITH LEMON FILLING

Makes 12 cupcakes

I love the concept of Twinkies, but I can do without the artificial taste. So, I've put together two of my favorite flavors in a little filled cupcake that's neither too dry nor excessively sweet. These are a great way to celebrate a friend's birthday.

CHEF'S TIP: Fill these cupcakes with anything you like. If you don't have time to make the lemon curd filling, fill them with marmalade and top them with whipped cream.

Lemon Filling

½ cup (4 ounces/113 grams) fresh lemon juice

2 tablespoons unsalted butter, at room temperature

½ cup (4 ounces/113 grams) heavy whipping cream

½ cup (3⅔ ounces/104 grams) sugar

3 large egg yolks

1 vanilla bean, split lengthwise in half, seeds scraped out, and seeds and pod reserved, or 2 teaspoons vanilla extract

½ teaspoon salt

Coconut Cupcakes

1 tablespoon unsalted butter, at room temperature, for greasing the ramekins

½ cup (3½ ounces/98 grams) sugar, plus more for sugaring the ramekins

½ cup (2½ ounces/72 grams) all-purpose flour

½ cup (1½ ounces/42 grams) finely shredded unsweetened dried coconut

3 large eggs, separated, at room temperature

1 large egg yolk, at room temperature

1 tablespoon grated lemon zest

¼ teaspoon salt

1 teaspoon vanilla extract

1. To make the lemon filling: Put all of the ingredients in a double boiler or in a heatproof bowl set over a saucepan of barely simmering water. Whisk constantly until the mixture becomes very thick, like jam, about 15 minutes. Remove from the heat, put a piece of plastic wrap directly on the surface of the curd, and refrigerate until completely chilled, about 2 hours.

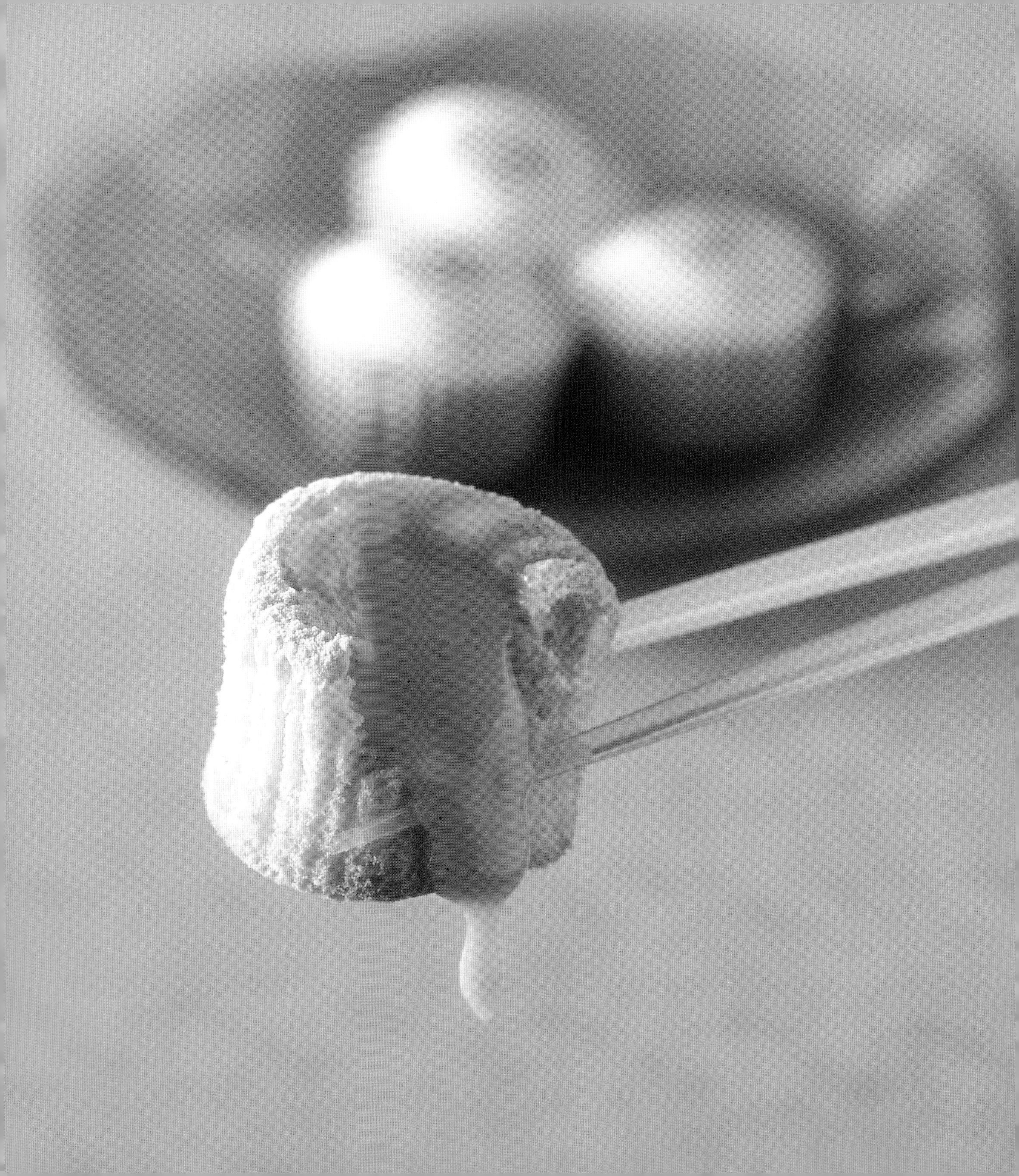

2. Meanwhile, make the coconut cupcakes: Preheat the oven to 350°F. Generously butter and sugar twelve 4-ounce ramekins or a 12-cup muffin tin; set aside.

3. Sift the flour into a large mixing bowl and stir in the coconut. Set aside.

4. Put the egg whites in the bowl of an electric mixer fitted with the whisk attachment and whisk at medium-high speed until frothy. With the machine running, slowly add ⅓ cup of the sugar and continue whisking until medium-soft peaks form. (When you lift the whisk from the mixture, a peak will form and the top of the peak will fall back down.) Transfer the whipped whites to another large bowl.

5. Put the egg yolks and lemon zest in the electric mixer bowl and whisk at medium speed until the yolks break, then add the salt and the remaining 2 tablespoons plus 2 teaspoons sugar and continue whisking until the yolks are pale yellow, thick, and doubled in volume, about 10 minutes.

6. Add the vanilla to the yolk mixture and whisk until well incorporated. Add one-third of the whipped whites to the yolks and stir well. Carefully fold in the remaining whites just until incorporated, trying to make sure they do not lose volume. Fold in half the flour mixture, then fold in the remaining flour until no traces of flour remain.

7. Divide the batter among the ramekins or muffin cups. If using ramekins, put them on a baking sheet. Bake for 4 minutes, then rotate the pan and bake until a tester comes out clean and the tops are puffed and golden brown, about 5 minutes more. Remove from the oven and cool for 5 minutes in the ramekins or pan, then unmold and cool completely on a rack. The cakes will deflate as they cool.

8. Transfer the chilled lemon filling to a pastry bag fitted with a small plain tip. Poke a hole in the top of each cupcake with the tip of the pastry bag, and slowly pipe in the curd until it begins to squirt out the opening. You will be able to feel when the cupcake is filled. Or, if you do not have a pastry bag, use a small paring knife to poke a hole in the top of each cupcake. Put the lemon curd in a large Ziploc bag, snip off the tip of one of the corners to make a small hole, and use the bag to pipe the curd into the cupcakes. Serve the same day.

■

DRAGON DEVIL'S FOOD CUPCAKES

I adapted this Asian-inspired cupcake from a recipe created by my friend Elizabeth Falkner, chef-owner of Citizen Cake in San Francisco. She makes some of the best cupcakes I've ever had. We even came up with an Asian-inspired name for this cupcake to describe its exotic flavor. The chocolate frosting here, with its smoky spiced tea and warm bourbon, is to die for. This cupcake is not kid's play—its rich, complex flavors will wow the most sophisticated gourmet.

Devil's Food Cupcakes

½ cup (4 ounces/113 grams) unsalted butter, at room temperature, plus more for greasing the pan

1 cup (5 ounces/144 grams) cake or all-purpose flour

2 tablespoons unsweetened cocoa powder, preferably Dutch processed

½ teaspoon baking powder

½ teaspoon baking soda

1 teaspoon ground cinnamon

½ cup (3⅓ ounces/95 grams) sugar

¾ cup (3¾ ounces/108 grams) packed light brown sugar

½ teaspoon salt

2 large eggs

½ cup (4 ounces/113 grams) buttermilk, at room temperature

3 ounces (90 grams) bittersweet chocolate, roughly chopped

Chocolate Frosting

2 teaspoons Lapsang souchong or other black Chinese tea leaves

1 whole star anise

3 tablespoons bourbon

4 ounces (120 grams) bittersweet chocolate, roughly chopped

¼ cup (2 ounces/56 grams) heavy whipping cream

2 tablespoons honey

3 tablespoons unsalted butter, at room temperature

¼ cup plus 2 tablespoons (1½ ounces/42 grams) confectioners' sugar, sifted

¼ teaspoon salt

¼ cup (1⅜ ounces/40 grams) dried cherries

1. To make the cupcakes: Preheat the oven to 350°F. Lightly butter a 12-cup muffin tin (to anchor the paper liners) and line with cupcake liners. Set aside.

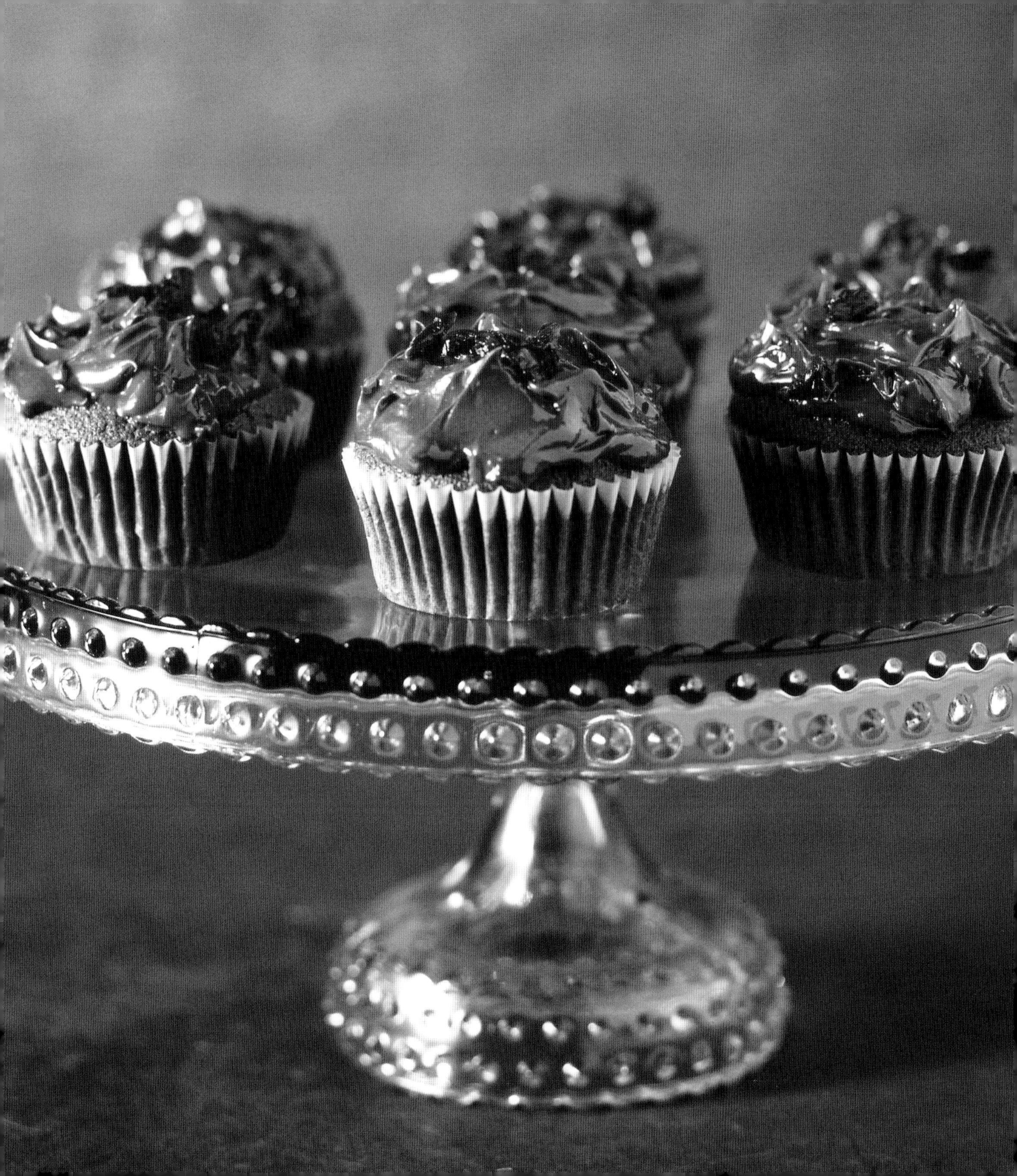

2. Sift together the flour, cocoa powder, baking powder, baking soda, and cinnamon and set aside.

3. Put the butter, both sugars, and the salt into the bowl of an electric mixer fitted with the paddle attachment and beat on medium speed until the mixture is light and fluffy, about 5 minutes. With the machine running, add the eggs one at a time, and mix until well incorporated, about 2 minutes.

4. Scrape down the sides and bottom of the bowl, turn the speed to low, and add one-quarter of the dry ingredients. When no traces of flour remain, add one-third of the buttermilk and mix until incorporated. Continue adding the flour mixture and the buttermilk alternately, ending with flour. Scrape down the sides and bottom of the bowl and mix in the chopped chocolate.

5. Divide the batter among the muffin cups; each cup should be three-quarters full. Bake until a tester comes out clean, about 30 minutes. Remove the cupcakes from the muffin tin and cool completely on a cooling rack.

6. Meanwhile, make the frosting: Put the tea, star anise, bourbon, and 2 tablespoons water into a small saucepan and bring to a boil. Turn the heat to medium-low and simmer for 30 seconds. Remove from the heat and steep, uncovered, for 20 minutes.

7. Meanwhile, put the chocolate into the bowl of an electric mixer fitted with the paddle attachment. Put the heavy cream, honey, and 2 tablespoons water in a small saucepan, stir well, and set over medium heat. As soon as bubbles begin to form around the edges, remove from the heat and pour over the chocolate. Let the mixture sit for 1 minute, then mix slowly until the chocolate has dissolved and the ganache is smooth.

8. Strain the steeped tea through a fine-mesh sieve into the chocolate ganache, pressing on the tea leaves to extract as much liquid as possible. Mix on medium speed until well combined. Add the butter, confectioners' sugar, and salt and continue mixing until well blended and creamy.

9. Spread the frosting on top of the cooled cupcakes. Arrange the dried cherries decoratively on top and serve.

■

CHOCOLATE CAKES WITH MATCHA TRUFFLE CENTERS

Makes 8 individual cakes

You've probably had molten chocolate cake in your neighborhood restaurant, but *this* version has a green tea and white chocolate truffle inside. The interior melts while the cake bakes and then oozes out like hot chocolate sauce when served. The combination of tea and chocolate—yin and yang—is very common in Asia. The tea cuts through the sweetness of the white chocolate and lends an earthy flavor to the cake.

CHEF'S TIP: Serve this cake straight from the oven. You can make the truffles or assemble the cakes ahead of time. If you choose to do the latter, bake the cakes directly from the refrigerator—do not bring to room temperature first.

Matcha Truffles

4 ounces (120 grams) white chocolate, roughly chopped

2 tablespoons unsalted butter

3 tablespoons heavy whipping cream

⅛ teaspoon salt

1 tablespoon matcha (green tea powder)

Chocolate Cakes

5½ tablespoons (2¾ ounces/77 grams) unsalted butter, plus more for greasing the ramekins

1 tablespoon all-purpose flour, for flouring the ramekins

5½ ounces (165 grams) bittersweet chocolate, chopped

4 large eggs, separated, at room temperature

¼ teaspoon salt

3 tablespoons sugar

2 teaspoons cornstarch

1. To make the truffles: Combine the white chocolate, butter, cream, and salt in a double boiler or in a heatproof bowl set over a saucepan of gently simmering water and heat, stirring occasionally, until the chocolate and butter are completely melted and smooth. Whisk in the matcha until fully incorporated. Transfer the ganache to a shallow dish and refrigerate, uncovered, until firm.

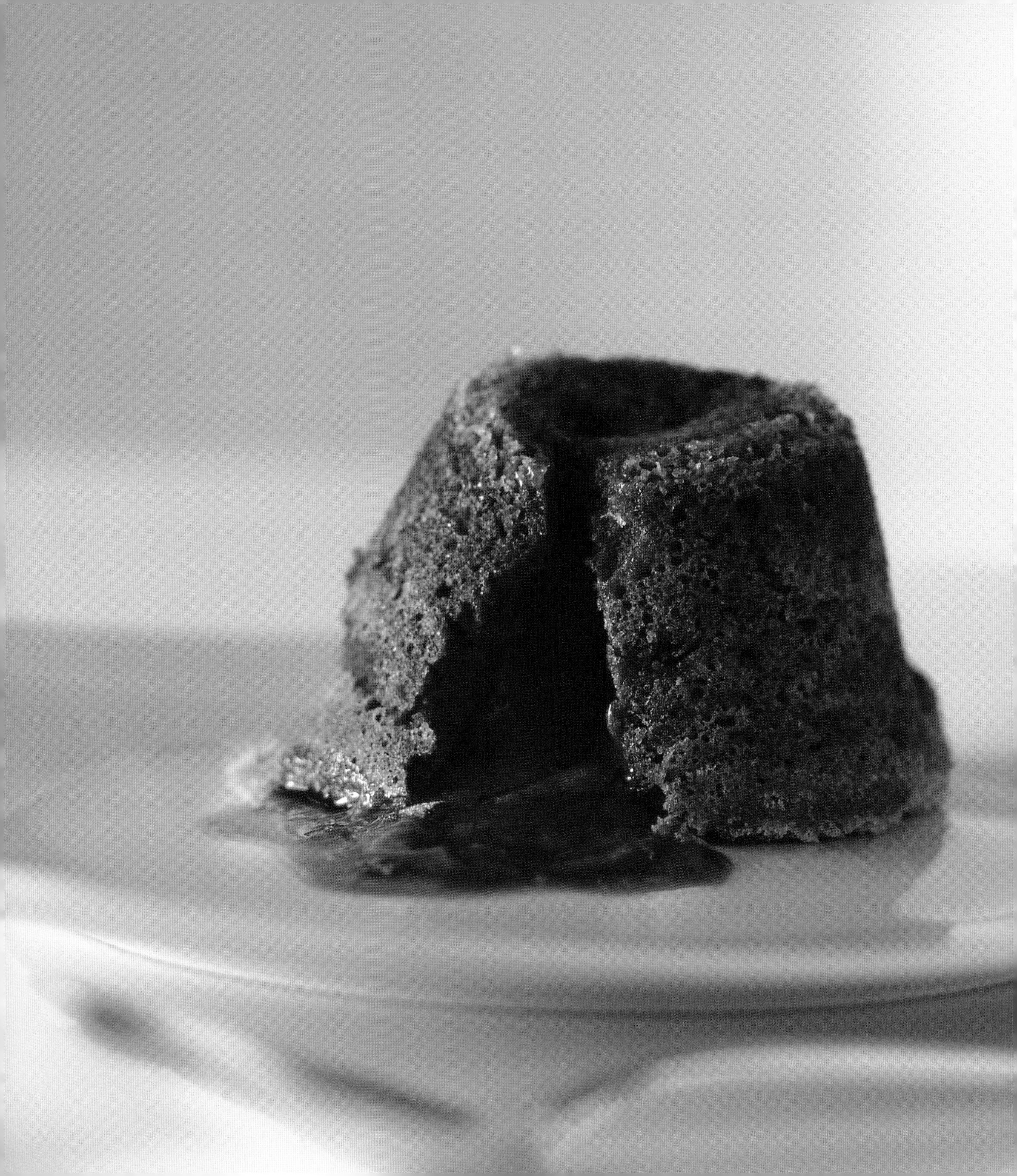

2. When the ganache is almost set, make the chocolate cakes: Preheat the oven to 425°F. Generously butter and flour eight 4-ounce ramekins and set aside.

3. Melt the butter and chocolate in a double boiler or in a heatproof bowl set over a saucepan of gently simmering water, stirring occasionally, until completely melted and smooth. Remove from the heat.

4. Put the yolks, salt, and half the sugar in a large mixing bowl and whisk just until blended. Add the melted chocolate mixture, whisk well, and set aside.

5. Put the egg whites in the bowl of an electric mixer fitted with the whisk attachment and whisk at medium-high speed until frothy. With the machine running, slowly add the remaining sugar and continue whisking until medium peaks form. (When you lift the whisk from the mixture, a peak will form and the very tip of the peak will fall back down.) Whisk in the cornstarch until incorporated.

6. Whisk half the whites into the yolk mixture until fully incorporated, then gently fold in the remaining whites. Divide the batter evenly among the ramekins.

7. Use a 1-inch diameter ice cream scoop or a measuring spoon to scoop the white chocolate mixture into eight 1-inch balls. Press a ball into the center of each ramekin and use the back of a spoon to smooth the batter over the truffle until it is covered.

8. Bake until the cakes are a dark chocolatey brown and dry to the touch, about 7 minutes; they should have risen about ½ inch above the rim of the ramekins. Cool for 1 minute in the ramekins, then invert onto serving plates and serve.

■

THE CHINESE BAKERY: LAYER CAKES

The Chinese bakery is one of my favorite food institutions. Whether you're in Hong Kong, Taipei, Shanghai, New York, San Francisco, or Los Angeles, you'll find the same style of bakery. Only the size of these shops varies—there are sprawling emporiums featuring rows upon rows of baked goods in gleaming glass cases, and then there are those with just enough room for you and one long counter. Whether the bakery is part of a multinational chain or is a local mom-and-pop joint, the sweet treats remain nearly the same.

Because baking is a relatively new concept in Chinese cuisine, many of the items have decidedly Western roots. The ubiquitous lemon, chocolate, and coffee rolls, for example, are an adaptation of the British and American jelly roll (also known as a Swiss roll). But many Chinese bakery products also reflect influences from other parts of Asia. Buns filled with sweet red beans are similar to Japanese red adzuki bean treats; puff pastry turnovers filled with curry taste a lot like samosas; and sweet coconut breads have strong hints of Thailand and the Philippines.

The unifying theme of Chinese bakery items is their light flavor and texture. A far cry from the heavier, buttery goods found in most American bakeries, Chinese bakery treats have a distinctive feathery texture and a measured sweetness. I liven up the Chinatown sweets I grew up on with more aggressive flavors and a slightly more substantial crumb.

And I make them look good. The traditional white whipped cream topping just doesn't do it for me. I prefer instead artist Wayne Thiebaud's vision of the perfect layer cake. Stacked tall and perfectly symmetrical, layer cakes should have clean icing lines with a warm color palette that is at once daring and elegant. Hints of subtle detail, not garish flourishes, are the key to creating a truly beautiful layer cake.

YUZU JELLY ROLL

Makes 2 small cake rolls, about 8 servings

Every Chinatown bakery has rows of jelly roll cakes along the counter. Often the cakes don't taste as good as they look. I decided to scrap the usual bland buttercream filling and make a yuzu curd instead. If you can't find yuzu juice, lemon juice is a fine substitute, as is raspberry jam. This version is smaller in size than those bakery cakes you might have seen—I think it looks *and* tastes better this way.

CHEF'S TIPS: If you're intimidated by the rolling process described below, you can still enjoy the flavors of this cake. Cut the sheet cake crosswise into thirds, spread the curd on each section, and layer into a 3-tiered rectangular cake. Cut into 1-inch slices and enjoy.

You can also make this cake ahead of time and freeze the wrapped cake for up to 2 weeks. Defrost, unwrapped, at room temperature before serving.

Yuzu Curd

1¼ cups (10 ounces/282 grams) yuzu juice or fresh lemon juice

⅓ cup (2⅔ ounces/75 grams) unsalted butter, at room temperature

3 tablespoons heavy whipping cream

1⅓ cups (8⅞ ounces/250 grams) sugar

5 large eggs

5 large egg yolks

½ teaspoon salt

½ gelatin sheet, soaked in cold water until softened and drained, or ¼ teaspoon powdered gelatin, softened in 2 teaspoons cold water

Lemon Chiffon Cake

Nonstick cooking spray

5 large eggs, separated

1 cup (7 ounces/196 grams) sugar

2 large egg yolks

1½ tablespoons grated lemon zest

¼ teaspoon salt

1½ teaspoons fresh lemon juice

¾ cup (4¼ ounces/119 grams) all-purpose flour

1. To make the yuzu curd: Put all the ingredients except the gelatin in a double boiler or in a large heatproof bowl set over a saucepan of gently simmering water. Cook, whisking constantly, until the mixture becomes very thick, like jam, about 15 minutes. Add the softened gelatin and whisk until dissolved. Remove from the heat, put a piece of plastic wrap directly on the surface of the curd, and refrigerate until completely chilled, 2 hours.

2. Meanwhile, make the lemon chiffon cake: Preheat the oven to 300°F. Spray a 12 × 17-inch rimmed baking sheet with nonstick cooking spray, line with parchment paper, and spray the paper.

3. Put the egg whites in the bowl of an electric mixer fitted with the whisk attachment and whisk at medium-high speed until frothy. With the machine running, slowly add ⅔ cup of the sugar and continue whisking until medium-soft peaks form. (When you lift the whisk from the mixture, a peak will form and the tip of the peak will fall back down.) Transfer the whipped whites to a large bowl.

4. Put the egg yolks and zest in the mixer bowl and whisk at medium speed until the yolks break. Add the salt and the remaining ⅓ cup sugar and continue whisking until the yolks are pale yellow, thick, and doubled in volume, about 15 minutes. Add the lemon juice and whisk until well incorporated.

5. Add one-third of the whipped whites to the yolks and mix well, then carefully fold in the remaining whites until incorporated, trying to not lose any volume. Sift in half the flour and fold in gently, then sift in the remaining flour and fold gently until no traces of flour remain.

6. Transfer the batter to the prepared baking sheet and tap the pan lightly against the counter to remove any air bubbles. Spray a 12 × 17-inch sheet of parchment paper and put it, sprayed side down, on the batter. Gently smooth out the parchment to remove any air pockets between the paper and the batter. Bake for 4 minutes, then rotate the pan and bake until a tester comes out clean, about 4 minutes more. Remove from the oven, immediately peel off the top sheet of parchment paper, and cool in the pan on a rack.

7. Lay two 12 × 17-inch sheets of parchment paper on your work surface. Invert the cake onto one of them and peel off the bottom sheet of parchment. Cut the cake lengthwise in half. Flip one half of the cake right side up onto the other sheet of parchment, and turn over the other piece of cake so that both cake halves are right side up on individual sheets of parchment paper. Turn one of the cakes so that the long cut side is facing you. Spread half the chilled curd ⅛ inch thick over the entire surface. Slide your fingers under the long side of the parchment closest to you, lift the cake with it, and begin rolling the cake as tightly as

possible, as you would a slippery sleeping bag. When you've completed the first rotation, give the cake a little squeeze along the length of the parchment to keep the roll tight, then continue until the cake is completely rolled. Be sure to not roll the parchment into the cake—just use it as a rolling aid. The finished roll will be about 3 inches in diameter. Wrap the parchment paper tightly around the roll, then wrap the whole roll tightly in plastic wrap, twisting the ends to seal them. Repeat with the other cake. Refrigerate for at least 2 hours to set.

8. Cut into 1½-inch slices and serve.

Raspberry Jelly Roll: Substitute 1½ cups (17 ounces/480 grams) raspberry jam for the yuzu curd.

■

GREEN TEA CREAM AND FRESH FRUIT CAKE

Makes one 8-inch square cake, about 10 servings

The smooth green tea cream filling is as smoky and flavorful as green tea ice cream, so you don't need to use very much between the layers of cake. Diced fresh fruit in the cream makes this cake light and refreshing. Use mild-flavored orange-colored fruits, such as persimmons or papaya, which contrast nicely with the sage-colored cream.

CHEF'S TIPS: If you do not have time to refrigerate the cake, you can freeze the assembled cake for half an hour to make it easier to invert and unmold.

If you are short on time, you can also forgo the green tea polka dots. They are primarily decorative and don't dramatically affect the flavor of the cake.

White Cake	Green Tea Cream
Nonstick cooking spray	2 cups (16 ounces/454 grams) heavy whipping cream
¾ cup (3 ounces/85 grams) cake or all-purpose flour	¼ cup (2 ounces/57 grams) whole milk
¼ teaspoon salt	2 tablespoons vanilla extract
4 large eggs, separated, at room temperature	¼ cup (⅞ ounce/24 grams) matcha (green tea powder)
1 cup (7 ounces/196 grams) sugar	⅔ cup (4½ ounces/126 grams) sugar
1 large egg yolk	2 tablespoons fresh lemon juice
2 teaspoons matcha (green tea powder)	1½ cups diced ripe Fuyu persimmons

1. To make the cake: Preheat the oven to 350°F. Spray a 12 × 17-inch rimmed baking sheet with nonstick cooking spray, line with a nonstick baking mat or parchment paper, and spray the paper. Set aside.

2. Sift the flour and salt together and set aside.

3. Put the egg whites in the bowl of an electric mixer fitted with the whisk attachment and whisk on medium speed until frothy. With the machine running, add ⅔ cup of the sugar

in a slow, steady stream. Continue whisking until medium peaks form, about 12 minutes. (When you lift the whisk from the bowl, a peak will form and the very tip will fall back down.) Transfer the whipped egg whites to a large bowl.

4. Put the egg yolks into the mixer bowl and whisk on medium speed until the yolks break. With the machine running, add the remaining ⅓ cup sugar in a slow, steady stream and continue to whisk until the mixture is pale yellow, thick, and doubled in volume, about 15 minutes.

5. Add half the egg whites to the yolks and stir well until fully incorporated. Add the remaining whites and fold gently until there are only a few white streaks remaining. Add the sifted flour mixture and fold gently until no traces of flour remain.

6. Put ¼ cup of the batter in a small bowl and mix in the green tea powder until evenly green. Refrigerate the remaining cake batter until ready to use. Make decorative dots on the prepared sheet pan with the green tea batter. Lay a cake stencil with ½-inch ovals on the prepared sheet pan and spread the batter evenly over the stencil. If you cannot find a cake stencil, use a pastry bag fitted with a plain ¼-inch tip to make ½-inch dots. Freeze or refrigerate until the dots feel dry.

7. Spread the reserved chilled cake batter over the chilled dots in an even layer. Work quickly to avoid smearing the dots. Bake for 4 minutes, then rotate the pan and bake until a tester comes out clean, about 5 more minutes. Cool in the pan for 5 minutes, then invert onto a cooling rack, peel off the parchment paper, and cool completely.

8. To make the cream: Put all the ingredients in the bowl of an electric mixer fitted with the whisk attachment. Whisk on medium speed until medium-soft peaks form. (When you lift the whisk from the bowl, a peak will form and the tip will fall back down.) Refrigerate until ready to use.

9. To assemble the cake: Line an 8-inch square cake pan with plastic wrap, leaving a 10-inch overhang on all sides. Trim 1 inch from the long side of the cake to make a 12 × 16-inch rectangle. Cut a 4-inch-wide strip from one long side of the cake so that you have one 4 × 16-inch rectangle and one 8 × 16-inch rectangle. Cut both rectangles crosswise in half so that you end up with two 8-inch squares and two 4 × 8-inch rectangles.

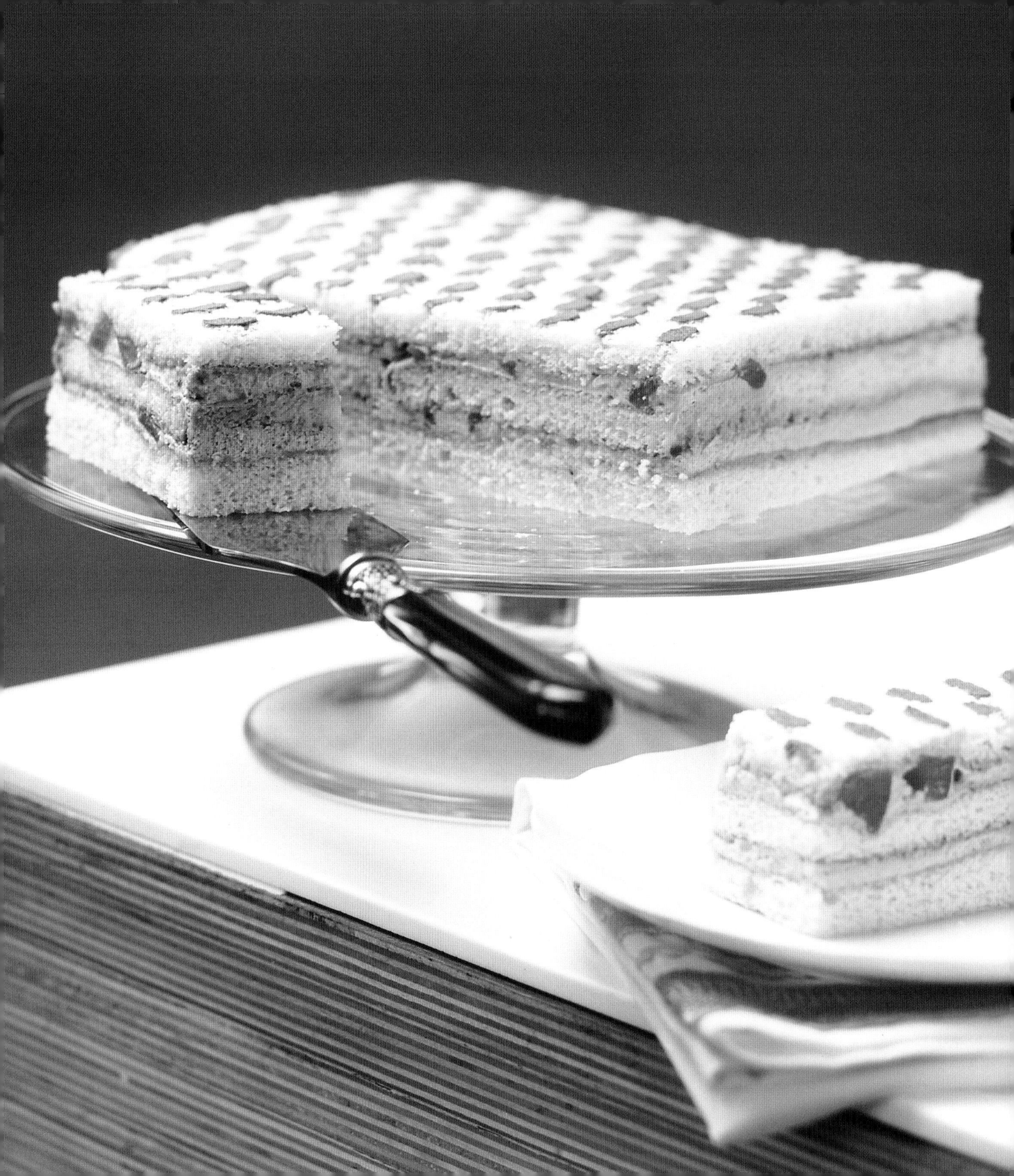

10. Put one of the 8-inch squares, green dot side down, in the bottom of the cake pan. Spread half of the cream on the cake and scatter half the persimmons on top. Arrange the 2 cake rectangles side by side on top of the cream and press down gently. Spread the remaining cream on the rectangles and top with the remaining persimmons. Place the second cake square, dot side up, on top. Fold over the overhanging plastic wrap, cover completely with another sheet of plastic wrap, and refrigerate until set, at least 4 hours.

11. When ready to serve, remove the plastic wrap and carefully invert the cake onto a serving plate. Slice and serve immediately.

■

CARROT CAKE WITH LIME–CREAM CHEESE FROSTING

Makes one 10-inch round cake, about 12 servings

If you've ever been intimidated by the prospect of creating a tall frosted carrot cake, try this underconstructed version. I don't frost the sides, allowing the pretty layers of burnt orange cake and creamy white frosting to show. Between the incredibly moist cake layers is my version of cream cheese frosting. Instead of the usual lemon flavoring, I spike mine with lime for a bit more punch. Speaking of punch, although kids will love this cake, the rum-soaked raisins make it a decidedly adult treat. Note that it's even better the next day, whenever you eventually wake up.

CHEF'S TIPS: This cake can be made without the rum—substitute an equal amount of water in the recipe below.

You can decorate the top of the cake with a dozen thin strips of carrot blanched in simple syrup. Bring 1 cup water and 1 cup sugar to a boil, stirring occasionally. Add ¼ cup carrot strips and return to a boil. Remove from the heat. Drain the carrot and dry completely on a cooling rack.

Carrot Cake

1 cup (8 ounces/226 grams) unsalted butter, at room temperature, plus more for greasing the pan

2 cups (10¼ ounces/290 grams) all-purpose flour

2 teaspoons baking powder

2 teaspoons baking soda

1⅓ cups (7 ounces/200 grams) packed light brown sugar

½ cup (3½ ounces/100 grams) sugar

½ teaspoon ground cinnamon

½ teaspoon freshly grated nutmeg

½ teaspoon salt

4 cups (25⅔ ounces/728 grams) finely shredded carrots

4 large eggs, lightly beaten

½ cup (4 ounces/113 grams) canola, vegetable, or other neutral oil

Lime–Cream Cheese Frosting

1 cup (4¾ ounces/136 grams) raisins

½ cup (4 ounces/113 grams) dark rum

12 ounces (336 grams) cream cheese, at room temperature

⅔ cup (4⅔ ounces/133 grams) sugar

½ teaspoon salt

1 tablespoon grated lime zest

1 tablespoon fresh lime juice

1⅔ cups (13⅜ ounces/380 grams) sour cream, at room temperature

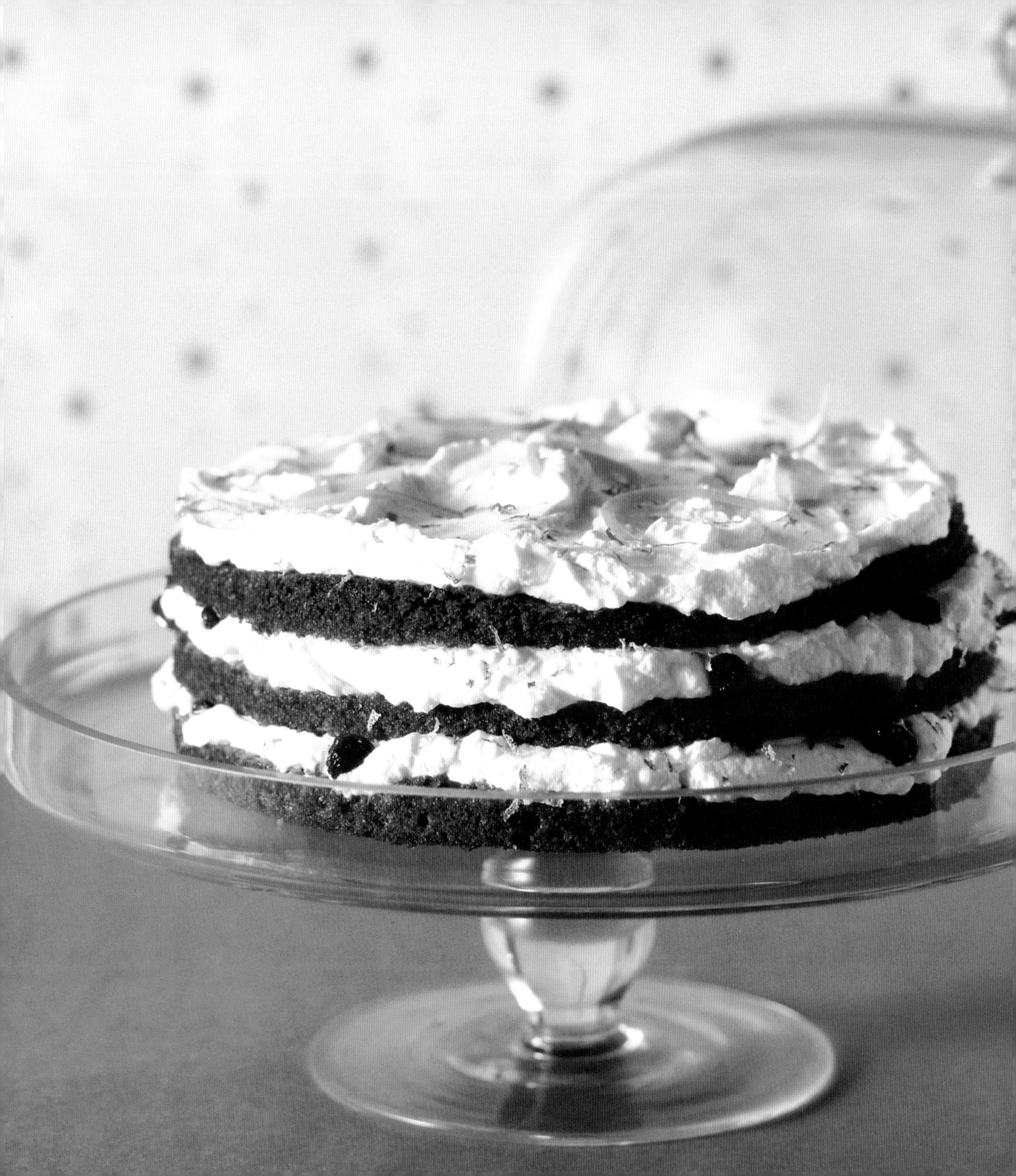

1. To make the carrot cake: Preheat the oven to 350°F. Butter a 10-inch round cake pan, line the bottom with parchment paper, and butter the parchment paper. Set aside.

2. Sift together the flour, baking powder, and baking soda and set aside.

3. Put the butter, brown sugar, sugar, cinnamon, nutmeg, and salt into the bowl of an electric mixer fitted with the paddle attachment and beat on medium-high speed until the mixture is light and fluffy, about 10 minutes. Scrape down the sides and bottom of the bowl. Turn the speed to low and slowly add the sifted dry ingredients, mixing until no traces of flour remain. Add the carrots and mix until evenly distributed, then turn the speed to medium-low and add the eggs, mixing until incorporated. Fold in the oil.

4. Pour the batter into the prepared pan. Bake until a tester inserted in the center comes out clean, about 1 hour. Cool in the pan for 5 minutes, then invert onto a cooling rack, peel off the parchment paper, and cool completely.

5. Meanwhile, make the cream cheese frosting: Put the raisins in a small bowl and cover with the rum. Soak at room temperature for at least 30 minutes. (The raisins can be soaked for as long as overnight.)

6. Put the cream cheese, sugar, and salt into the bowl of the mixer fitted with the paddle attachment. Beat on medium-high speed until the mixture is light and fluffy, about 7 minutes. Fold in the lime zest, lime juice, and sour cream until incorporated. Cover and refrigerate until cold and stiff enough to spread, about 30 minutes.

7. Using a long serrated knife, cut the cake horizontally into 3 even layers. Place the bottom layer on a cake plate and spread one-third of the frosting evenly over it. Scatter half the raisins on top, and set another cake layer on top. Frost with half of the remaining frosting, scatter the remaining raisins on top, and set the last cake layer on top. Frost the top layer, and refrigerate the cake until set, at least 1 hour, or as long as overnight. Serve chilled.

■

MALTED CHOCOLATE LAYER CAKE

Makes one 8-inch square cake, about 10 servings

This cake has a winning triumvirate of flavors—chocolate, malt, and coffee. Asian bakers often combine these flavors in subtle, sophisticated chocolate desserts. This impeccably elegant creation is every bit a match for any "death-by-chocolate" American-style cake.

CHEF'S TIP: The cake is beautiful as is, but you can further decorate it by sifting Ovaltine or cocoa powder over the entire surface of the cake or by pressing Walnut Cookie (page 104) crumbs onto its sides.

Chocolate Cake

½ cup plus 2 tablespoons (1⅔ ounces/45 grams) unsweetened cocoa powder, preferably Dutch-processed

3 tablespoons all-purpose flour

2 tablespoons cornstarch

5 large eggs, separated

⅔ cup (4⅜ ounces/125 grams) sugar

4 large egg yolks

1 teaspoon salt

¼ cup (1¾ ounces/50 grams) canola, vegetable, or other neutral oil

3 tablespoons buttermilk

Malted Chocolate Mousse

¾ cup (6 ounces/168 grams) whole milk

½ cup (3½ ounces/98 grams) sugar

¼ teaspoon salt

¼ cup (1⅓ ounces/37 grams) Horlicks powder

6 large egg yolks

2 gelatin sheets, soaked in cold water until softened and drained, or 1¼ teaspoons powdered gelatin, softened in 1 tablespoon cold water

5 ounces (150 grams) bittersweet chocolate, finely chopped

1 cup (8 ounces/226 grams) heavy whipping cream

Vietnamese Coffee Buttercream

½ cup (4 ounces/113 grams) unsalted butter, at room temperature

½ cup (2 ounces/55 grams) confectioners' sugar

¼ teaspoon salt

¼ cup plus 1 tablespoon (1½ shots) Vietnamese drip coffee or espresso

2 tablespoons sweetened condensed milk

½ teaspoon vanilla extract

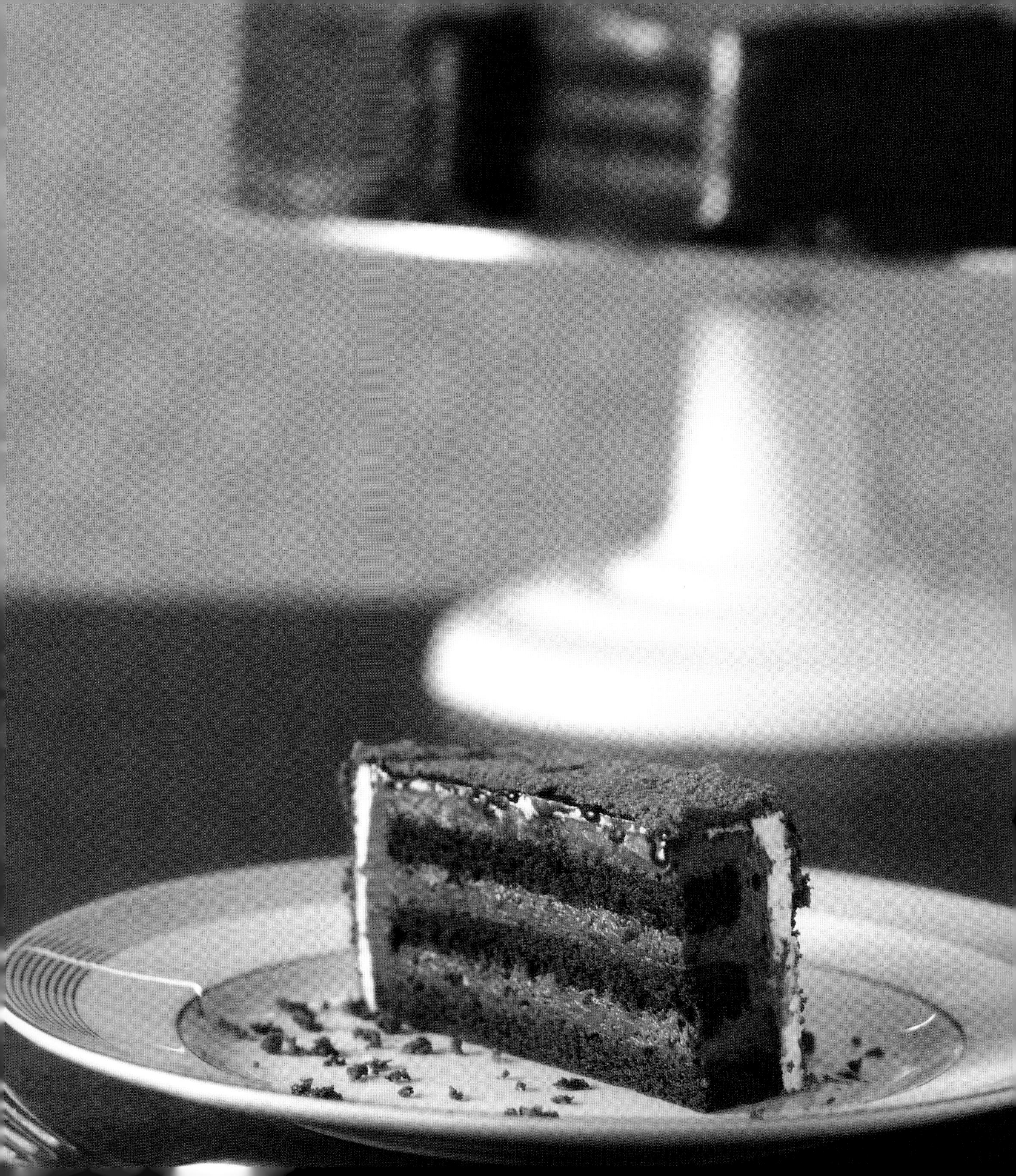

1. To make the chocolate cake: Preheat the oven to 350°F. Spray an 11 × 17-inch rimmed baking sheet with nonstick cooking spray, line with parchment paper, and spray the paper. Set aside.

2. Sift the cocoa, flour, and cornstarch together and set aside.

3. Put the egg whites in the bowl of an electric mixer fitted with the whisk attachment and whisk at medium-high speed until frothy. With the machine running, slowly add ⅓ cup of the sugar and continue whisking until medium-soft peaks form. (When you lift the whisk from the mixture, a peak will form and the top of the peak will fall back down.) Transfer the whipped whites to a large bowl.

4. Put the yolks in the electric mixer bowl and whisk on medium speed until the yolks break. With the machine running, add the salt and the remaining ⅓ cup sugar in a slow, steady stream. Continue whisking until the mixture is pale yellow, thick, and doubled in volume, about 12 minutes.

5. Whisk half the whites into the yolk mixture until fully incorporated, then gently fold in the dry ingredients until no traces of flour or cocoa remain. Add the remaining whites to the mixture and fold gently until only a few white streaks remain. Whisk the oil and buttermilk together until smooth and homogenous, then fold into the batter until completely incorporated.

6. Spread the batter evenly in the baking sheet. Bake for 5 minutes, then rotate the pan and bake until a tester comes out clean, about 5 more minutes. Cool completely in the pan on a rack.

7. Meanwhile, make the mousse: Put the milk, sugar, and salt in a small saucepan, stir well, and set over medium heat. Warm just until bubbles form around the edges, then whisk in the Horlicks until completely dissolved. Remove from the heat.

8. Put the yolks in a large mixing bowl and whisk until the yolks break. Add the warmed Horlicks mixture in a steady stream while whisking constantly. Return the mixture to the saucepan and cook over low heat, stirring constantly, for 2 minutes. Remove from the heat and add the softened gelatin. Stir until the gelatin melts, then stir in the chocolate until it melts completely. Let the mixture cool to room temperature, at least 1 hour.

9. Once the chocolate has cooled, put the cream into the bowl of an electric mixer fitted with the whisk attachment. Whisk at medium speed until medium peaks form. (When you lift the whisk from the cream, a peak will form, and the very tip will fall back down.) Fold the cream into the chocolate mixture.

10. To assemble the cake: Line an 8-inch square cake pan with plastic wrap, leaving a 10-inch overhang on all sides. Trim 1 inch from the long side of the cake to make a 12 × 16-inch rectangle. Invert the cake onto a large work surface and peel off the parchment paper. Cut a 4-inch-wide strip from one long side so that you have one 4 × 16-inch rectangle and one 8 × 16-inch rectangle. Cut both rectangles crosswise in half so that you end up with two 8-inch squares and two 4 × 8-inch rectangles.

11. Put one of the 8-inch squares in the bottom of the cake pan. Spread half of the mousse on top, and arrange the 2 cake rectangles side by side on top of the mousse. Spread the remaining mousse on the rectangles, and top with the remaining cake square. Fold over the overhanging plastic wrap, cover with another sheet of plastic wrap, and refrigerate until set, at least 4 hours or up to 1 day.

12. Once the cake is set, make the buttercream: Put the butter into the bowl of an electric mixer fitted with the paddle attachment and beat on medium-high speed until light and fluffy, about 2 minutes. Mix in the confectioners' sugar and salt. Scrape down the sides and bottom of the bowl and add the coffee, condensed milk, and vanilla. Turn the speed to medium-high and mix until smooth and creamy, about 4 minutes.

13. Invert the cake onto a cake platter and unwrap. Use an offset spatula or butter knife to spread the buttercream evenly over the entire surface of the cake. Refrigerate again to set the buttercream, at least 30 minutes. Serve chilled.

■

CHEESECAKES

Cheesecakes have not been popular for long in Asia. The ultra-rich and creamy texture of cream cheese is so foreign to the Asian palate that it has only recently become available in Asia.

The one exception to this is Japan. Traditional Japanese food, of course, is known for its light, clean flavors—not what you think of when you think cheesecake. But in modern-day Japan, Western food is as common as Japanese, and cheesecake is often the choice for dessert.

Some perceptive Japanese cook discovered that, by using tofu, cheesecake could be made lighter without sacrificing its inherent goodness. Over time, tofu cheesecake has become something of a nouveau national dessert in Japan.

Japanese tofu cheesecakes are usually made with silken tofu, which itself is made from sweet fresh soybeans that are gently simmered until they are as smooth as silk. The resulting dairy-free, no-bake creations are great for a nation filled with lactose-intolerant adults who don't have ovens. But, convenience aside, the rich, sweet flavors and the airy, smooth texture puts most traditional cheesecakes to shame.

I'm bringing this American-influenced Japanese dessert back to America, with tofu in tow. Putting cream cheese and tofu together into one cheesecake makes for a rich and light dessert with subtle and complex flavor.

GRAND MARNIER TOFU CHEESECAKE

Makes one 8-inch square or round cheesecake, about 10 servings

This cheesecake has all the richness of traditional American-style cheesecake but with a distinctive fresh flavor. Although traditional Japanese versions use only tofu, I prefer combining the tofu with cream cheese and citrus juice and zest. Grand Marnier is popular in Asia, and the orange liqueur adds a sophisticated note.

CHEF'S TIP: This cheesecake is wonderful served with an assortment of fresh berries that have been tossed with sugar and lemon juice.

Ginger Graham Cracker Crust

½ cup (4 ounces/113 grams) unsalted butter, melted, plus more for greasing the pan

11 (6⅛ ounces/174 grams) graham crackers, crushed into fine crumbs, about 1½ cups

1½ cups (8 ounces/224 grams) packed dark brown sugar

½ teaspoon ground cinnamon

½ teaspoon ground ginger

¼ teaspoon salt

Grand Marnier Tofu Filling

19 ounces (538 grams) silken tofu

1½ teaspoons fresh lemon juice

½ cup (4 ounces/113 grams) heavy whipping cream

1 teaspoon salt

5 gelatin sheets, soaked in cold water until softened and drained, or 2¼ teaspoons powdered gelatin, softened in ¼ cup (2 ounces/56 grams) cold water

12 ounces (341 grams) cream cheese, at room temperature

¾ cup plus 1 tablespoon (5½ ounces/156 grams) sugar

3 tablespoons grated orange zest

1 tablespoon grated lemon zest

2 tablespoons Grand Marnier

1. To make the graham cracker crust: Preheat the oven to 300°F. Lightly butter an 8-inch square or round glass or ceramic baking dish and set aside.

2. Put the graham crackers, brown sugar, cinnamon, ginger, and salt into a mixing bowl. Mix well, then add the melted butter and mix with your hands until the crumbs are evenly moistened. Transfer the mixture to the prepared baking dish and press into an even layer on the bottom.

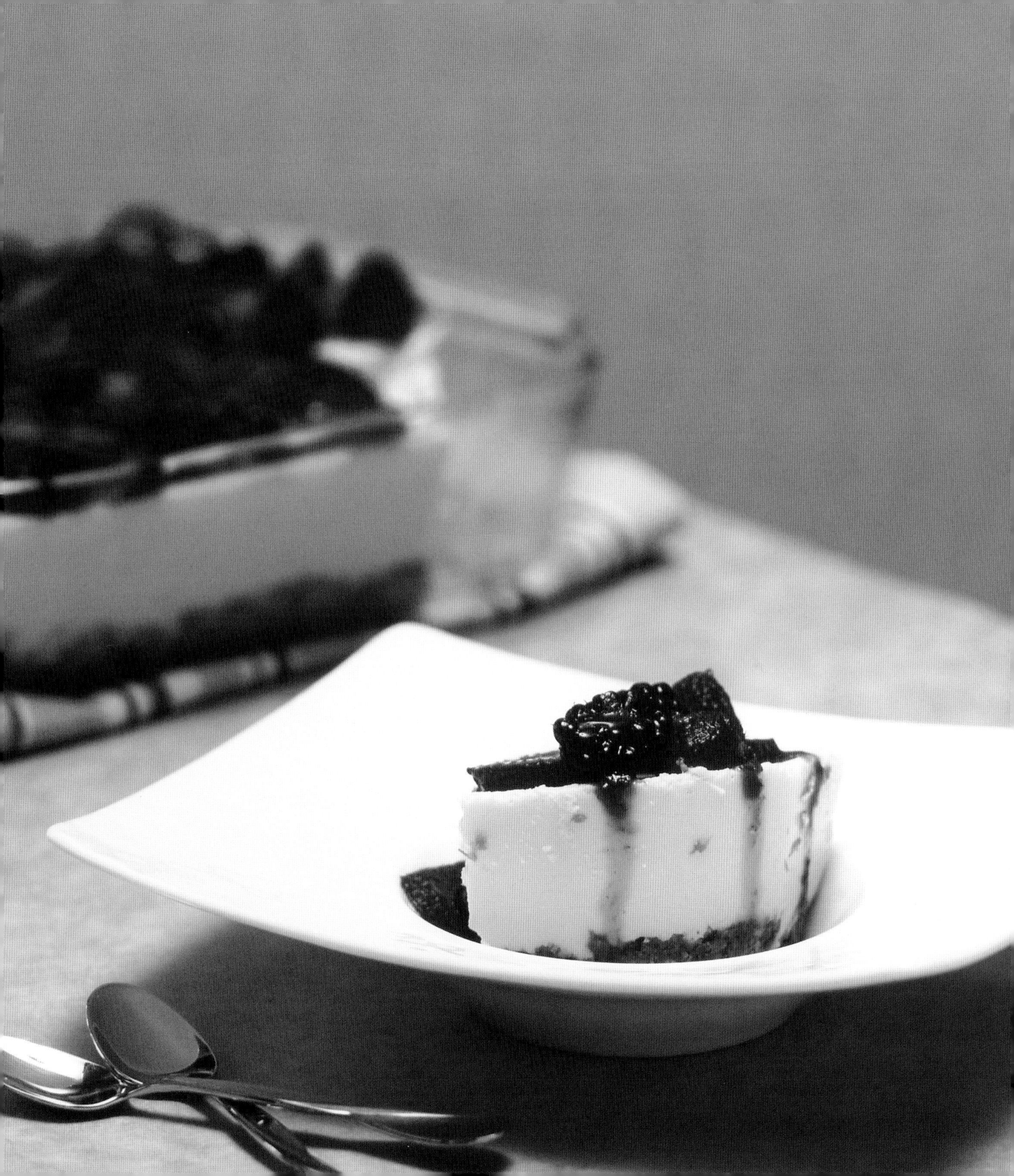

3. Bake the crust until golden brown, about 25 minutes. Remove from the oven and cool completely.

4. To make the cheesecake filling: Put the tofu and lemon juice in a blender and blend until smooth. Set aside.

5. Put the cream and salt in a medium saucepan and warm over medium heat until bubbles begin to form around the edges. Stir in the softened gelatin until completely dissolved. Remove from the heat.

6. Put the cream cheese, sugar, and orange and lemon zests into the bowl of an electric mixer fitted with the paddle attachment. Mix on medium speed until light and fluffy, about 10 minutes. Scrape down the sides and bottom of the bowl, add the Grand Marnier, and mix on medium speed until smooth, about 1 minute. Gently fold in the gelatin cream and tofu mixture until well incorporated.

7. Pour the filling into the cooled crust. Refrigerate, uncovered, until set, at least 4 hours, or, preferably, overnight. Serve chilled.

■

KABOCHA SQUASH CHEESECAKE WITH WALNUT CRUST

Makes one 9-inch cheesecake, about 10 servings

In November 2004, just a week before Thanksgiving, Melissa Clark featured this recipe in the *New York Times*. Shortly thereafter, a flood of orders for the cheesecake came in to Spice Market, but it wasn't even on the menu. I had no intention of making whole cheesecakes for sale, but customers persisted. I gladly changed my mind when I saw how happy it made people to take home a tasty and exotic variation on an old favorite.

Kabocha Squash Filling

One 3-pound (1,361 grams) kabocha squash

8 ounces (226 grams) cream cheese, at room temperature

1 cup (7 ounces/200 grams) sugar

1½ teaspoons ground cinnamon

1 teaspoon ground ginger

⅓ teaspoon freshly grated nutmeg

½ teaspoon salt

1½ teaspoons brandy

2 large eggs, at room temperature

Walnut Crust

¼ cup (2⅛ ounces/60 grams) unsalted butter, melted, plus more for greasing the pan

½ cup (2 ounces/60 grams) walnuts

½ cup (2½ ounces/72 grams) packed light brown sugar

11 (6⅛ ounces/174 grams) graham crackers, crushed into fine crumbs, about 1½ cups

2 teaspoons grated lime zest

½ teaspoon ground cinnamon

⅛ teaspoon ground ginger

¼ teaspoon salt

Sweetened Condensed Milk Chantilly (page 25), optional

1. To make the filling: Prepare a steamer by filling a large round casserole with water to a depth of 3 inches; the casserole should be able to hold the squash comfortably and have a tightly fitting lid. Put a steamer rack or enough crumpled heavy-duty aluminum foil to support the squash on the bottom; the rack or foil should be just above

the waterline. Set over medium heat and bring to a steady simmer. Put the whole squash on the rack, cover the pot, and steam until a knife pierces the flesh easily, about 1 hour.

2. Remove from the heat, uncover the pot, and cool the squash in the steamer until cool enough to handle.

3. Meanwhile, make the crust: Preheat the oven to 325°F. Lightly butter a 9-inch springform pan, line with parchment paper, and butter the paper. Set aside.

4. Spread the walnuts on a rimmed baking sheet and toast, shaking the pan occasionally, until fragrant, about 15 minutes. Cool completely. Turn the oven down to 300°F.

5. Put the walnuts and ¼ cup of the brown sugar in the bowl of a food processor and pulse until the walnuts are coarsely ground. (You can also crush the walnuts by hand, gently pounding them with a heavy skillet or rolling pin.) Transfer the walnuts to a mixing bowl and add the graham cracker crumbs, lime zest, cinnamon, ginger, salt, and the remaining ¼ cup brown sugar. Mix well, then add the melted butter and mix with your hands until everything is evenly moistened. Transfer the mixture to the prepared pan and press into an even layer on the bottom.

6. Bake the crust until golden brown, about 12 minutes. Cool completely. Leave the oven on.

7. When the squash is cool enough to handle, remove it from the steamer, cut it in half, and scoop out and discard the seeds and strings. Scoop out 2½ cups of the squash flesh into a small bowl. Reserve any remaining squash for another use.

8. Put the cream cheese, sugar, cinnamon, ginger, nutmeg, and salt into the bowl of a food processor and process, scraping down the sides and bottom of the bowl occasionally, until the mixture is light and smooth. Add the squash and process again, scraping down the sides and bottom of the bowl occasionally, until smooth. Add the brandy and eggs and process just until they are incorporated. Transfer to a bowl and finish mixing with a rubber spatula.

9. Transfer the filling to the cooled crust. Bake until the center is set but still slightly jiggly, about 1 hour. Cool completely and unmold.

10. Serve the cheesecake with the condensed milk chantilly, if desired.

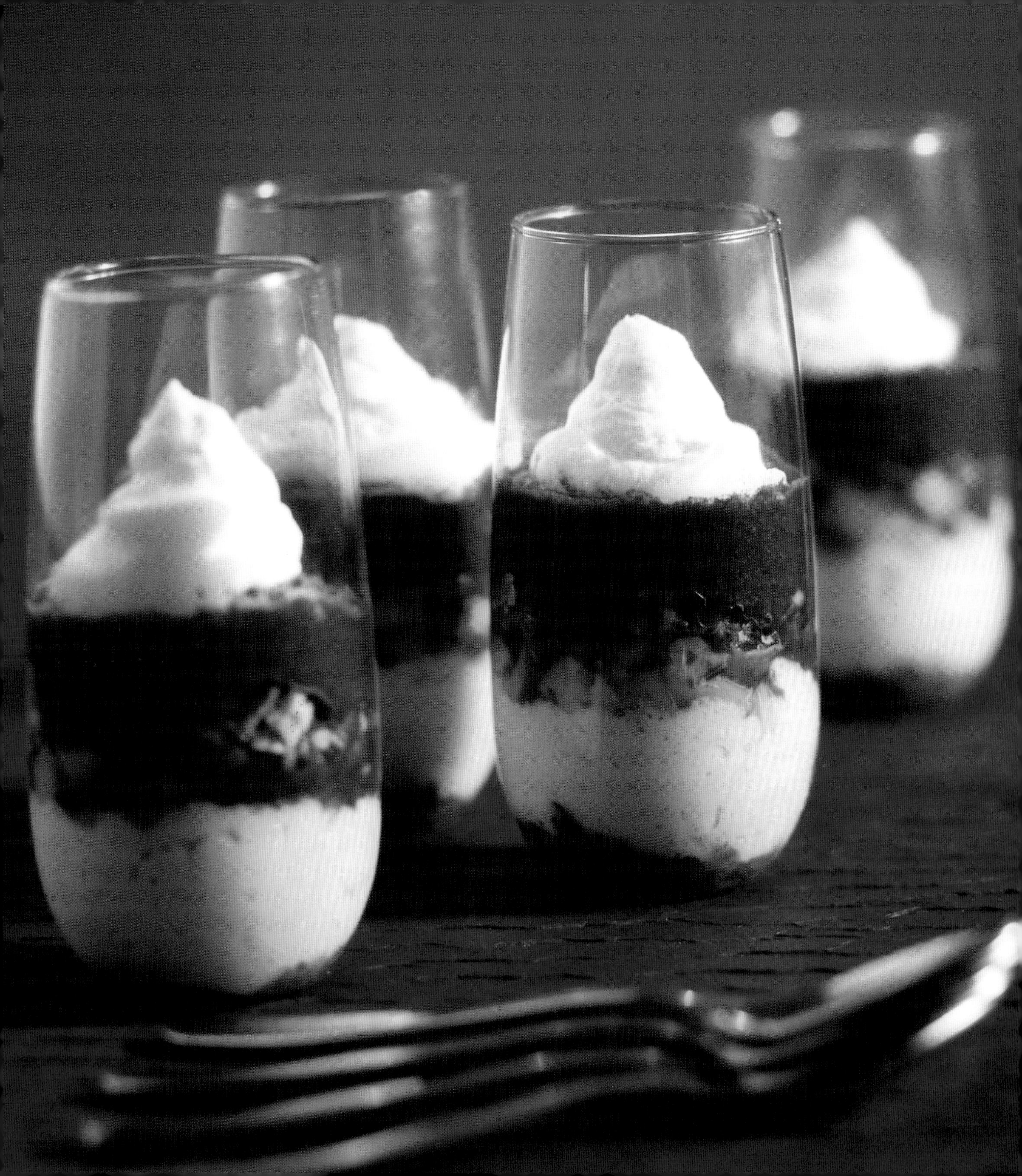

CHOCOLATE-MANGO CHEESECAKE PARFAIT WITH CHOCOLATE MACADAMIA COOKIE CRUMBS

Makes 8 servings

This dessert began as an inventively flavored but traditionally shaped cheesecake created by my friend Vicki Wells, pastry chef to all Bobby Flay's restaurants. When paired with chocolate, the sweet mango adds a surprisingly rich and exotic taste, while the layers of creamy orange and dark chocolate make for a stunning presentation.

CHEF'S TIP: You can find canned Indian mango puree—preferably the Ratna brand of Alphonso mangoes—in Indian and some gourmet markets. Or make your own by pureeing mango flesh in a blender until smooth. Be sure to use ripe, sweet mangoes. If necessary, mix a few teaspoons of sugar into the puree to sweeten it.

Chocolate Macadamia Cookie Crumbs

3 tablespoons macadamia nuts, toasted

⅓ cup (2 ounces/56 grams) sugar

½ cup (2½ ounces/71 grams) all-purpose flour

3 tablespoons unsweetened cocoa powder, preferably Dutch-processed

⅛ teaspoon salt

6 tablespoons (3 ounces/85 grams) unsalted butter, cut into ½-inch cubes and chilled

1 large egg

⅓ teaspoon vanilla

Mango Cream Cheese

12 ounces (340 grams) cream cheese, at room temperature

½ cup (2⅞ ounces/80 grams) sugar

¼ teaspoon salt

3 tablespoons crème fraîche

½ cup (4¼ ounces/120 grams) canned Indian mango puree or fresh mango puree

1 teaspoon fresh lime juice

Mango Chocolate Ganache

3½ ounces (92 grams) bittersweet chocolate, roughly chopped

3½ ounces (92 grams) milk chocolate, roughly chopped

1½ cups (12 ounces/339 grams) heavy whipping cream

½ cup (4¼ ounces/120 grams) canned Indian mango puree or fresh mango puree

¼ teaspoon salt

1 ripe mango, peeled, seeded, and cut into ¼-inch dice

½ Thai chile, seeded, deveined, and minced, optional

Sweetened Condensed Milk Chantilly (page 25)

1. To make the cookie crust: Preheat the oven to 350°F. Line an 8-inch square cake pan with parchment paper and set aside.

2. Put the macadamias and half the sugar in the bowl of a food processor. Pulse until coarsely ground, then add the flour, cocoa, salt, and the remaining sugar and pulse until well mixed. Add the butter and pulse until the mixture resembles small peas. Add the egg, vanilla, and ½ teaspoon water and pulse just until the mixture comes together. Transfer the dough to the lined cake pan and press it into a thin, even layer with your fingers.

3. Bake until the dough is cooked through and hard, about 12 minutes. Cool completely in the pan.

4. Break the cookie into large pieces and transfer to the food processor. Process until ground into fine crumbs. Set aside.

5. To make the mango cream cheese: Put the cream cheese, sugar, and salt in the bowl of an electric mixer fitted with the paddle attachment and mix on medium speed until light and fluffy, about 5 minutes. Scrape down the sides and bottom of the bowl and add the crème fraîche, mango puree, and lime juice. Mix on medium speed until well incorporated. Set aside.

6. To make the mango chocolate ganache: Put the chopped chocolates in a heatproof bowl and set aside. Put the cream, mango puree, and salt in a small saucepan, stir well, and set over medium-high heat. As soon as bubbles form around the edges of the pan, pour the mixture over the chocolate. Let the mixture sit for 3 minutes, then whisk gently until smooth.

7. To assemble the parfaits: Divide the cookie crumbs among eight tall glasses. Top with the mango cream cheese, diced mango, Thai chile, if desired, and, finally, the chocolate ganache. Top with the chantilly, if desired, and serve immediately.

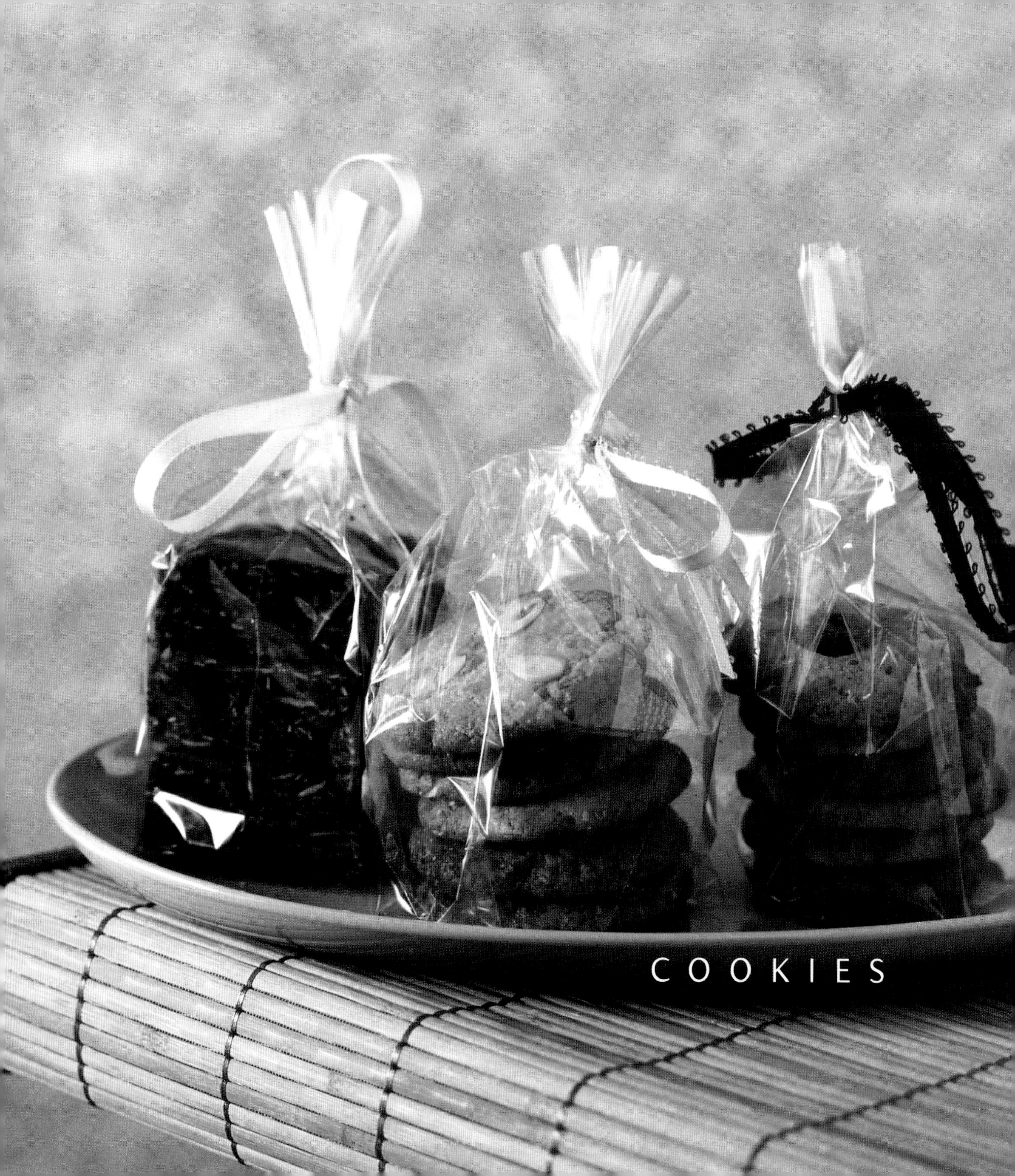

COOKIES

Giving cookies as gifts always brightens someone's day. The trick, of course, is to make unique cookies. Part of the challenge is to accommodate competing loyalties to various cookie styles—crunchy versus chewy, crisp versus cakey, chunky versus smooth. I include examples of each style here. What ties them all together is a desire to make a classic cookie new. Using Asian-inspired techniques and ingredients, break out of your cookie rut.

Cookies are also the best dessert with which to experiment as a baker. Many people are afraid that if they stray too far from a standard dessert recipe, the whole thing will fall apart. Cookies—as befits the ultimate comfort dessert—give the baker a wider margin for error. As a general rule, more butter and sugar relative to the dry ingredients makes a cookie crisper. More flour relative to butter makes a cookie chewier, and more eggs makes a cookie cakey. As for flavors, you can mix and match your favorite spices and extracts to come up with your own creations.

DROP COOKIES

Although cookies are prevalent in Asia, drop cookies—mounds of batter baked in the oven—are not. Asian cookies are often deep-fried or cooked in heavy cast-iron molds, and they are rarely baked. When I moved to America as a child, I fell in love with drop cookies. I adored the crisp, cakey textures of these oddly shaped home-style treats. The only thing missing was, well, the flavor. I appreciated the subtle tastes of butter and vanilla extract, but I wanted something a little more assertive.

A good friend provided the inspiration. Floyd Cardoz, chef of Tabla restaurant in New York and a leader in Indian cooking, taught me a trick that is a foundation of Indian cuisine: "bloom" spices in fat. The heady, aromatic spices common in Indian cuisine are best when cooked in, or combined with, butter or oil. The fat brings out their inherent flavor in a controlled way that carries through to the final product.

Suprisingly, cookie dough is a perfect medium for this technique. The first step in making drop cookies is creaming the butter, usually with sugar, until the mixture is light and fluffy. Adding spices and other aromatics at this stage instead of sifting them with the dry ingredients enhances their flavor while allowing the cookies to maintain their distinctive textures.

To further enhance the cookies' flavor, I zor as long as overnight, before baking. As the dough rests, the flavors develop even more. You can shape the dough into balls (or a log for cutting) before wrapping tightly and chilling. This technique allows you to bake a few cookies at a time or a whole batch.

Finally, if you want to experience these spiced cookies at their fullest, eat them warm, as heat brings out heat. Otherwise, let them cool completely to enjoy subtle and interesting twists on your standard favorites.

COCONUT CHOCOLATE CHIP COOKIES

Makes 3 dozen cookies

Everyone has a favorite chocolate chip cookie recipe and this is mine. The cooks at Spice Market loved it too. Whenever I made pretty packages of these cookies for the diners, the bags would mysteriously disappear from the kitchen throughout the day.

CHEF'S TIP: Creaming the butter with the coconut maximizes the cookies' distinctive nuttiness, which provides a great backdrop for the rich, deep flavor of bittersweet chocolate. Be sure to use unsweetened coconut here—not only does it taste much better than the sweetened variety, it also makes these cookies crumbly and crisp.

1⅓ cups (4 ounces/113 grams) finely shredded unsweetened dried coconut

2 cups (11 ounces/310 grams) all-purpose flour

1½ teaspoons baking powder

1 cup (8 ounces/226 grams) unsalted butter, at room temperature

1 cup plus 1 tablespoon (6 ounces/169 grams) packed dark brown sugar

¾ cup plus 2 tablespoons (6 ounces/169 grams) sugar

½ teaspoon salt

2 large eggs

2 teaspoons vanilla extract

2½ cups (11⅞ ounces/336 grams) bittersweet pistoles (page 14), bittersweet chocolate chips, or roughly chopped bittersweet chocolate

1. Preheat the oven to 300°F.

2. Spread the coconut on a large rimmed baking sheet and bake until golden brown and fragrant, about 7 minutes. Set aside to cool completely.

3. Sift together the flour and baking powder and set aside.

4. Put the butter, both sugars, the salt, and cooled toasted coconut into the bowl of an electric mixer fitted with the paddle attachment. Mix on medium speed until light and fluffy, about 3 minutes. With the machine running, add the eggs one at a time, and then add the vanilla. Turn the mixer speed to low and add half the flour mixture. When

incorporated, add the remaining flour and mix until no traces of flour remain. Stir in the chocolate chips. If you have time, cover the dough tightly and chill for at least 2 hours, or up to 3 days, before baking.

5. When ready to bake, preheat the oven to 325°F. Line two baking sheets with parchment paper.

6. Scoop the cookie dough into 1-inch balls and put 2 inches apart on the baking sheets. Bake until brown and crisp, about 12 minutes. Transfer to a cooling rack to cool. The cookies can be stored in an airtight container for up to 3 days.

GINGER OATMEAL RAISIN COOKIES

Makes 3 dozen cookies

My mom is the only person I know who hates cookies. But after years of labor, I've finally created a cookie that she enjoys. She loves the heady ginger aroma, the subtle heat of cayenne, and the soft, chewy texture. And because it contains oatmeal and raisins, she considers it a "healthy" dessert that she can indulge in guilt-free.

CHEF'S TIP: If you want an even chewier cookie, underbake it slightly—just until the top is dry and golden, about 8 minutes. For a crisper cookie, simply bake a little longer, about 12 minutes.

1½ cups (8¼ ounces/233 grams) all-purpose flour

1½ teaspoons baking powder

1½ teaspoons baking soda

1 cup (8 ounces/226 grams) unsalted butter, cut into 1-inch cubes and chilled

⅔ cup (4 ounces/114 grams) packed light brown sugar

½ cup (4 ounces/114 grams) sugar

2 tablespoons candied ginger, finely chopped, plus more for garnish if desired

1½ teaspoons ground cinnamon

¼ teaspoon salt

¼ teaspoon cayenne pepper, optional

2 large eggs

1 tablespoon whole milk

2 teaspoons vanilla extract

2 cups (6 ounces/170 grams) old-fashioned rolled oats

1¼ cups (6 ounces/170 grams) raisins, preferably golden

1. Sift together the flour, baking powder, and baking soda and set aside.

2. Put the butter, both sugars, the ginger, cinnamon, salt, and cayenne, if desired, into the bowl of an electric mixer fitted with the paddle attachment. Beat on medium speed until light and fluffy, about 4 minutes. With the machine running, add the eggs one at a time, then add the milk and vanilla. As soon as the liquids are incorporated, stop the mixer and scrape down the sides and bottom of the bowl.

3. Turn the mixer speed to low and add half the flour mixture. When it is incorporated, add the remaining flour and mix until no traces of flour remain. Stir in the oats and raisins. If you have time, cover the dough and let chill for at least 2 hours, or up to 3 days, before baking.

4. When ready to bake, preheat the oven to 325°F. Line two baking sheets with parchment paper.

5. Scoop the cookie dough into 1-inch balls and put 2 inches apart on the baking sheets. Use your palm to slightly flatten each ball, then sprinkle the tops with chopped candied ginger, if desired.

6. Bake the cookies until lightly golden brown, about 10 minutes. Transfer to a cooling rack to cool completely. The cookies can be stored in an airtight container for up to 3 days.

PEANUT BUTTER COOKIES

Makes 3 dozen cookies

Most peanut butter cookies are too heavy, one-dimensional, and cloyingly sweet to my taste. Increasing the cookies' nuttiness and flavor by using a brown butter and decreasing the usual amount of flour resulted in peanut butter cookies with a crunchy exterior, chewy center, and layers of nutty flavors. The fleur de sel brings out the natural sweetness of the peanuts and adds sophistication to these humble cookies.

CHEF'S TIP: Avoid overbaking these cookies. Remove them from the oven as soon as they are lightly browned for a rich peanut buttery taste.

1½ cups (8 ounces/228 grams) unsalted peanuts

1¼ cups (10 ounces/284 grams) unsalted butter

2 cups (11 ounces/310 grams) all-purpose flour

1½ teaspoons baking soda

1 cup (8 ounces/228 grams) peanut butter, preferably all-natural

1⅓ cups (8 ounces/228 grams) packed light brown sugar

1¼ cups (8 ounces/228 grams) sugar

½ teaspoon salt

2 large eggs

1 teaspoon vanilla extract

2 teaspoons fleur de sel or other mild sea salt, such as Maldon

1. Preheat the oven to 325°F. Toast the peanuts until fragrant, about 7 minutes. Let cool completely.

2. Put the butter in a medium saucepan and set over medium heat. Cook, stirring and scraping the bottom of the pan occasionally, until the solids separate out and the butter has browned and smells nutty, about 10 minutes. Set aside to cool to room temperature, 30 minutes.

3. Line two baking sheets with parchment paper and set aside.

4. Sift together the flour and baking soda and set aside.

5. Put the peanut butter, both sugars, the salt, and cooled brown butter and peanuts in the bowl of a food processor. Process until the peanuts are coarsely ground, then add the eggs and vanilla and process until well blended. Scrape down the sides and bottom of the bowl, add the flour mixture, and process just until no traces of flour remain.

6. Scoop the cookies into 1-inch balls and put 2 inches apart on the baking sheets. Flatten the balls with the palm of your hand into 1½-inch rounds, and sprinkle the tops with the fleur de sel.

7. Bake until lightly golden, about 12 minutes. Cool on the baking sheets for 2 minutes, then transfer to a cooling rack to cool completely. The cookies can be stored in an airtight container for up to 3 days.

SPICED COCONUT BROWNIES

The combination of chocolate and coconut has long been a favorite pairing of mine. When used as the foundation for a brownie, the result is a chewy square with long-lasting flavor—not unlike a great candy bar. In this recipe, unsweetened coconut replaces some of the flour for a rich, decadent brownie that tastes more chocolatey than most. A pinch of cayenne pepper goes a long way in this simple but sophisticated bittersweet treat.

CHEF'S TIPS: You need to cool these brownies for at least 1 hour before enjoying them warm and at least 2 hours before you can cut them cleanly into squares. Also, if you eat the spiced brownies too soon after baking, the heat of the cayenne pepper may be overpowering.

Nonstick cooking spray

4 cups (12 ounces/340 grams) finely shredded unsweetened dried coconut

1 cup (5½ ounces/155 grams) all-purpose flour

1 tablespoon baking powder

2¼ cups (18 ounces/510 grams) unsalted butter

18 ounces (510 grams) bittersweet chocolate, roughly chopped

7 ounces (198 grams) unsweetened chocolate, roughly chopped

2 teaspoons salt

¼ teaspoon cayenne pepper, optional

7 large eggs, at room temperature

2⅓ cups (16⅛ ounces/458 grams) sugar

1 tablespoon vanilla extract

1 cup (7 ounces/198 grams) semisweet chocolate chips

1. Preheat the oven to 350°F. Spray a 12 × 17-inch rimmed baking sheet with nonstick cooking spray, line with parchment paper, and spray again. Set aside.

2. Spread the coconut on another rimmed baking sheet and toast in the oven until light brown and fragrant, about 7 minutes. Set aside to cool.

3. Meanwhile, sift together the flour and baking powder and set aside.

4. Combine the butter, bittersweet chocolate, unsweetened chocolate, salt, and cayenne, if desired, in a double boiler or in a heatproof bowl set over a saucepan of gently simmering

water and melt the butter and chocolate, stirring occasionally. When completely melted and smooth, remove from the heat.

5. Put the eggs in the bowl of an electric mixer fitted with the whisk attachment and whisk at medium speed until frothy. With the machine running, add the sugar and continue to whisk until the mixture is pale yellow, thick, and doubled in volume, about 8 minutes. Mix in the vanilla. Turn the mixer speed to low, add the melted chocolate in a slow, steady stream, and whisk for 2 minutes. Remove the bowl from the mixer and fold in the flour mixture, then the cooled toasted coconut and chocolate chips.

6. Spread the batter evenly into the prepared pan. Bake for 15 minutes, then rotate the pan and bake until a tester comes out barely clean, about 10 minutes more. The surface should be dry to the touch. Cool in the pan on a rack, for at least 2 hours if possible. The brownies can be stored in an airtight container for up to 1 week.

■

SPICED CHOCOLATE KRINKLES

Makes 3 dozen cookies

These chewy chocolate cookies are wonderfully aromatic, perfect for enjoying after dinner, serving at holiday parties or giving as seasonal gifts. The rich chocolate and spices give them familiarity and warmth; putting those things together supplies an extra little thrill.

CHEF'S TIP: Don't be tempted to make these cookies bigger. They look more appealing when small and the flavors and texture are best enjoyed in a single bite.

2 tablespoons canola, vegetable, or other neutral oil

1 ounce (28 grams) bittersweet chocolate, chopped

1 teaspoon grated fresh ginger

¼ teaspoon ground ginger

¼ teaspoon ground cardamom

⅛ teaspoon cayenne pepper

⅛ teaspoon salt

⅓ cup (2 ounces/54 grams) all-purpose flour

2 tablespoons almond flour or coconut powder

2 tablespoons unsweetened cocoa powder

½ teaspoon baking powder

1 large egg

½ cup (3¾ ounces/106 grams) sugar

½ teaspoon vanilla extract

½ cup (2 ounces/55 grams) confectioners' sugar

1. Put the oil, chocolate, both gingers, the cardamom, cayenne, and salt in a double boiler or in a heatproof bowl set over a saucepan of gently simmering water and melt the chocolate, stirring occasionally. Remove from the heat, transfer to a bowl if necessary, and cool completely.

2. Sift together the flours, cocoa powder, and baking powder and set aside.

3. When the chocolate mixture has cooled to room temperature, add the egg, sugar, and vanilla extract and stir just until combined. Gently fold in the flour mixture until well incorporated. Transfer the dough to a large sheet of plastic wrap, flatten into a 1-inch-thick disk, and wrap tightly in the plastic. Chill until hard, at least 2 hours or up to 5 days.

4. When ready to bake, preheat the oven to 375°F. Line two baking sheets with parchment paper.

5. Put the confectioners' sugar in a small bowl. Pinch off a piece of dough, form it into a ½-inch ball, roll in the confectioners' sugar until well coated, and place on a prepared baking sheet. Repeat with the remaining dough, putting the coated balls 1 inch apart on the baking sheets.

6. Bake the cookies until the tops look cracked and are dry to the touch, about 10 minutes. Transfer to a cooling rack to cool completely. The cookies can be stored in an airtight container for up to 2 days.

■

PISTACHIO ROSE
THUMBPRINT COOKIES

Some of the flavors and spices of India are almost indistinguishable from those of Persia, and for good reason. When the Moghuls entered India in the sixteenth century, they brought along Persian culinary influences, which mingled with the indigenous cooking of northern India. Rich nuts, like pistachio, and heady aromatics, like rose, became staples. As for me, I've found that taking one tradition—American thumbprint cookies—and combining it with another—Indian pistachio and rose flavors—makes for one excellent cookie.

CHEF'S TIP: If you can't find rose jam, which is available in Indian and Middle Eastern markets and some gourmet shops, substitute another fruit jam. Choose one that is not too sweet.

1¼ cups (6¼ ounces/177 grams) all-purpose flour

¾ teaspoon baking powder

1 cup (4⅓ ounces/122 grams) unsalted shelled pistachios

¾ cup (6 ounces/169 grams) unsalted butter, at room temperature

4 ounces (113 grams) cream cheese, at room temperature

2 tablespoons grated orange zest

¾ cup plus 1 tablespoon (6 ounces/157 grams) sugar

¼ teaspoon salt

1 large egg

1 tablespoon fresh orange juice

3 tablespoons rose jam or other fruit jam

1. Sift the flour and baking powder together and set aside.

2. Put the pistachios into the bowl of a food processor and process to a fine powder; do not overprocess, or the nuts will become pistachio butter. (You can also crush the nuts by putting them in a heavy-duty plastic bag and pounding with a heavy skillet.)

3. Put the pistachios, butter, cream cheese, orange zest, sugar, and salt into the bowl of an electric mixer fitted with the paddle attachment and beat on medium speed until the

mixture is light and fluffy, about 5 minutes. Scrape down the sides and bottom of the bowl. Turn the machine to medium speed and mix in the egg and orange juice. Turn the speed to low and add the flour mixture in two additions, mixing just until no traces of flour remain.

4. Line two baking sheets with parchment paper. Form the dough into 1-inch balls and put 2 inches apart on the baking sheets. Refrigerate, uncovered, until firm, at least 30 minutes.

5. When ready to bake, preheat the oven to 350°F.

6. Use your thumb to make a ½-inch-deep indentation in the center of each ball. Fill each thumbprint with ¼ teaspoon jam, and bake until lightly browned, about 10 minutes. Transfer to a cooling rack to cool completely. The cookies can be stored in an airtight container for up to 2 days.

■

CHINESE-AMERICAN COOKIES

Whether Chinatown is the suburban sprawl of Monterey Park, the narrow streets of New York, or the hilly roads of San Francisco, the food, especially the cookies, remains the same. In every Chinatown around the world, if you don't get fortune cookies with your check, you'll get crumbly almond cookies. The cookies taste good, which would be reason enough to look forward to them at every Chinatown meal. But the real story is that Chinatowns around the world were originally settled largely by Cantonese immigrants and remain strongly Cantonese to this day. Although only one tiny corner of vast China, the Canton region has been hugely influential in the spread of Chinese culture throughout the world. Covering a stretch of the country's southern coastline with several important ports, it was an early hub of trade and commerce—first with South and Southeast Asia, and later with the Western world. It soon began exporting its own people to other countries, including America. The first Cantonese settlers came as railroad workers in the nineteenth century, but the largest wave of immigration from Canton and Hong Kong came in the twentieth century.

Cantonese settlers, known for being smart people, quickly learned that Americans loved their cookies and they invented Chinese versions for their restaurants. Almond cookies, with their lovely glaze, and fortune cookies, thin and crisp (and, of course, fortuitous), are synonymous with Chinese-American restaurants. The inventors and origins of both cookies are disputed, although California is the most likely birthplace. Regardless of where they came from, they are now as American as apple pie.

Obviously, times have changed in American Chinatowns. Immigrants from all over China, Taiwan, and Southeast Asia have slowly transformed Chinatown cuisine. Sichuan eateries, dishing up fiery stir-fries, sit next to Shanghainese soup dumpling joints and Taiwanese pearl tea shops. Vietnamese pho noodle houses pop up daily. Authentic and regional Chinese food is in demand. But the reality is that Cantonese Chinatown cuisine is authentic in its own right.

CHINESE ALMOND COOKIES

Makes 3 dozen cookies

These are a staple in traditional Chinese-American restaurants. The store-bought ones tend to be hard and tasteless, but these are wonderfully light, with a crisp edge and a chewy center. The traditional cookies are also a dull dark yellow from an egg yolk wash. I use an egg white wash to get the same glazed effect but with a creamy shimmer. The slivered almonds on top add a nice crunch and a fresh toasted nut flavor.

1¾ cups (9⅔ ounces/272 grams) all-purpose flour

1 cup plus 2 tablespoons (7⅜ ounces/210 grams) sugar

½ teaspoon baking soda

1¼ cups (4⅔ ounces/132 grams) almond flour

1 cup (8 ounces/226 grams) unsalted butter, cut into ½-inch cubes and chilled

½ teaspoon salt

1 large egg

1 teaspoon almond extract

½ cup (2⅛ ounces/60 grams) slivered almonds

1 large egg white, beaten

1. Sift together the flour, sugar, and baking soda and set aside.

2. Put the almond flour, butter, and salt into the bowl of an electric mixer fitted with the paddle attachment and beat on medium speed until the mixture resembles cornmeal, about 3 minutes. With the machine running, add the egg and almond extract and mix until well incorporated. Turn the speed to low and add the flour mixture. Mix just until no traces of flour remain.

3. Transfer the dough to a large sheet of plastic wrap, flatten into a 1-inch-thick disk, and wrap tightly in the plastic. Refrigerate until hard, at least 30 minutes or up to 3 days.

4. When ready to bake, preheat the oven to 325°F. Line two baking sheets with parchment paper.

5. Form the dough into ½-inch balls and put 1 inch apart on the baking sheets. Use the palm of your hand to press the balls into 1-inch circles. Press 4 slivered almonds into each cookie, arranging them decoratively to form an X. Brush the tops of the cookies with the egg white.

6. Bake the cookies until golden and crisp around the edges, about 15 minutes. Cool completely on the baking sheets on a cooling rack. The cookies can be stored in an airtight container for up to 3 days.

WALNUT COOKIES

Makes 3 dozen cookies

Before fortune cookies soared in popularity in the 1950s, egg-glazed almond cookies (see the preceding recipe) came with the check at many Chinese restaurants. This is another take on that culinary icon. Chinese chefs consider walnuts to be classier than almonds; I don't know about all that, but they sure taste great here.

In addition to eating these cookies plain, I crush them into tiny crumbs for my Vietnamese Coffee Tapioca "Affogato" (page 266), to decorate frosted cakes, like the Malted Chocolate Layer Cake (page 73), or to top ice cream sundaes.

CHEF'S TIP: Starting the dough by creaming butter with walnuts to make walnut butter makes for an even more aromatic and nutty cookie.

2 cups (5 ounces/140 grams) walnuts

1⅓ cups (7⅓ ounces/207 grams) all-purpose flour

1 teaspoon baking powder

1 teaspoon baking soda

1 cup (8 ounces/226 grams) unsalted butter, at room temperature

⅓ cup (2⅔ ounces/75 grams) sugar

½ teaspoon salt

⅓ cup (2⅔ ounces/75 grams) packed light brown sugar

1 large egg

1½ teaspoons vanilla extract

1. Preheat the oven to 300°F.

2. Put the walnuts on a baking sheet and toast until golden and fragrant, about 10 minutes, stirring once. Remove from the oven and cool completely.

3. Sift the flour, baking powder, and baking soda together and set aside.

4. Put the butter, sugar, salt, and ½ cup of the walnuts in the bowl of an electric mixer fitted with the paddle attachment. Beat on medium speed, scraping down the sides of the bowl once or twice, until the walnuts break up and the mixture is light and fluffy, about 5 minutes. With the machine running, add the eggs one at a time and then the vanilla, mixing until fully incorporated. Turn the speed to low and add the flour mixture, mixing

just until no traces of flour remain. Cover the bowl and refrigerate for at least 4 hours, or up to 3 days.

5. When ready to bake, preheat the oven to 325°F. Line two baking sheets with parchment paper.

6. Form the dough into 1-inch balls and put 2 inches apart on the baking sheets. Use your palm to flatten each ball slightly, and gently press a walnut half into the center of each cookie. Bake until lightly golden brown, about 10 minutes. Transfer to a cooling rack to cool completely. The cookies can be stored in an airtight container for up to 3 days.

■

CHOCOLATE FORTUNE COOKIES

Makes 3 dozen cookies

Jean-Georges Vongerichten wanted fortune cookies—good ones—for his Chinese restaurant 66. With no staff and only two days to go before the restaurant was to open, I called my colleague Johnny Iuzzini for help. He showed me how to shape these delicate tuile disks into the iconic Chinese-American treat. That's right—an Italian kid who grew up in New York showed me, a Chinese-Thai kid who grew up in Asia, how to make fortune cookies.

CHEF'S TIP: If you are inserting fortunes into these cookies, be sure to use inks that will not bleed when heated, as the cookies will be hot when you fold them.

¾ cup (4 ounces/115 grams) all-purpose flour

¾ cup (3⅛ ounces/90 grams) confectioners' sugar

¼ cup plus 3 tablespoons (1⅛ ounces/32 grams) unsweetened cocoa powder

½ cup (4 ounces/113 grams) unsalted butter, at room temperature

3 tablespoons corn syrup

⅛ teaspoon salt

4 large egg whites

36 fortunes written on 3 × ¼-inch strips of paper, optional

1. Sift together the flour, confectioners' sugar, and cocoa powder and set aside.

2. Put the butter, corn syrup, and salt into the bowl of an electric mixer fitted with the paddle attachment and beat on medium speed just until well combined, about 3 minutes. Turn the speed to low and add the flour mixture, then the egg whites, mixing until the dough comes together, about 5 minutes. Transfer to a large sheet of plastic wrap, flatten into a 1-inch-thick disk, and wrap tightly in the plastic. Refrigerate for at least 2 hours or up to 3 days.

3. When ready to bake, preheat the oven to 350°F. Set out a tuile cookie pan or empty egg carton to use as a cooling rack for the cookies. You will also need a 4-inch round cookie stencil. To make your own, take the plastic lid of a large yogurt or similar container and cut off the rimmed edge. Using a razor blade or similar instrument, cut a 4-inch circle out of the center of the lid, taking care not to cut through the edge of the lid.

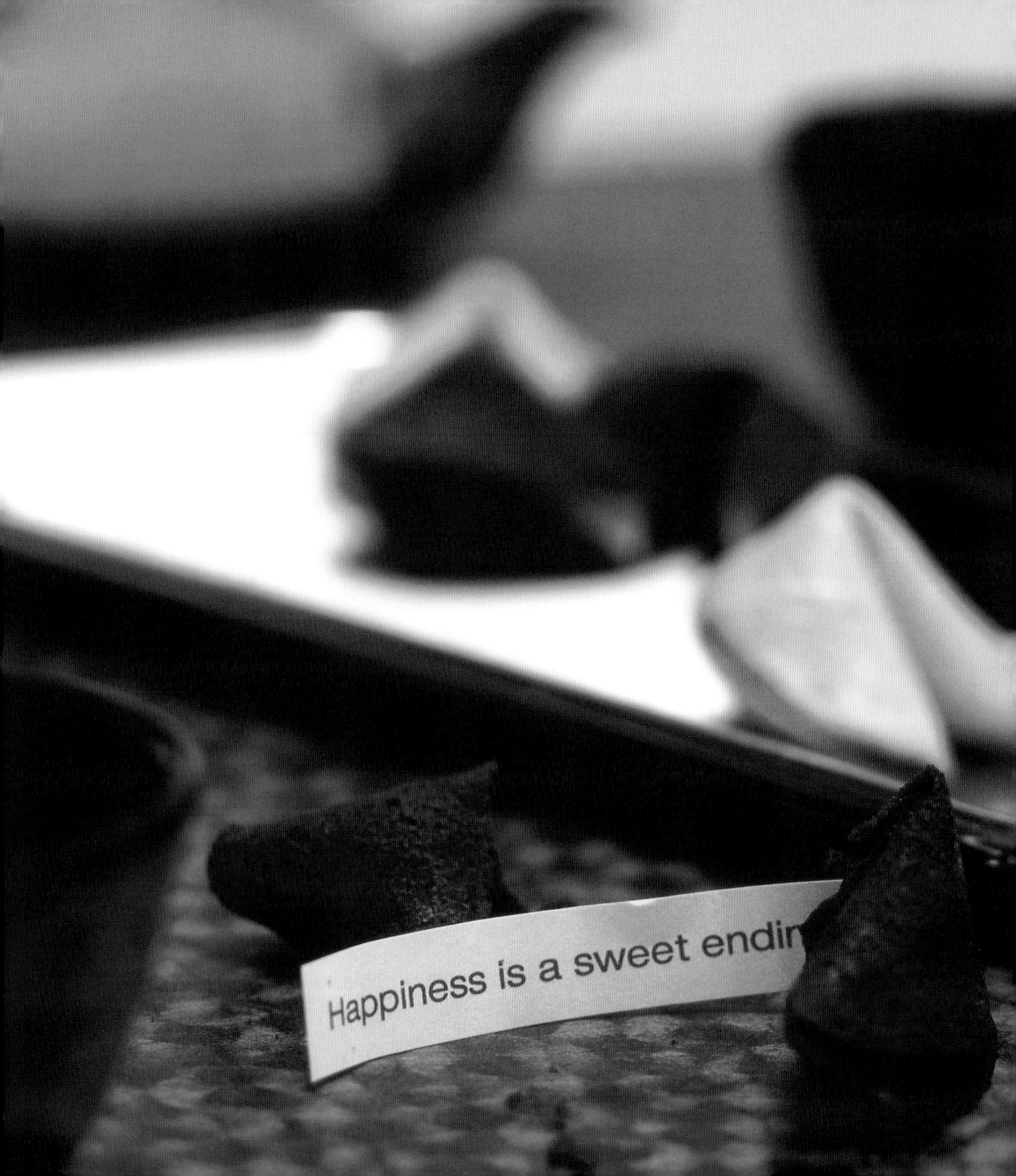
Happiness is a sweet endin

4. Set the cookie stencil on a nonstick baking mat and use a small offset spatula or a table knife to spread 2 teaspoons of dough evenly inside the stencil, spreading the dough into a very thin, smooth circle, about $\frac{1}{16}$ inch thick. Continue making the circles, setting them 1 inch apart, until the mat is full.

5. Transfer the mat to a baking sheet and bake until the tops of the cookies are dry, about 5 minutes. Remove the pan from the oven and, working very quickly, shape the cookies: one at a time, set a paper fortune, if desired, in the center of the cookie, fold the cookie in half, and, holding the cookie with the folded edge facing up, bring the 2 pointed ends upward so that they come together above the folded edge. The cookies should still be hot to the touch as you work; if they cool too much before you fold them, they will break. If necessary, you can reheat them in the oven for about 30 seconds to make them pliable again. Set the cookies in the tuile pan or egg carton to cool, so that they will hold their shape, and cool completely. Repeat with the remaining batter. The cookies can be stored in an airtight container for up to 1 week.

■

ALMOND FORTUNE COOKIES

Almond, symbolic for purity in the Chinese culture, is also one of the most loved flavors when it comes to Chinese cuisine. And it is also the original flavor for fortune cookies, which remain a classic.

CHEF'S TIP: Bake the cookies just until the batter is dry to the touch and slightly browned at the edges. Overbaking will cause the cookie to be brittle and difficult to fold.

⅔ cup (3⅓ ounces/95 grams) all-purpose flour

¾ cup (3⅛ ounces/87 grams) almond flour

2 tablespoons unsalted butter, at room temperature

1 cup (3¾ ounces/107 grams) confectioners' sugar

2 tablespoons grated orange zest

⅛ teaspoon salt

2 large egg whites

36 fortunes written on 3 × ¼-inch strips of paper, optional

1. Sift the flours together and set aside.

2. Put the butter, confectioners' sugar, orange zest, and salt in the bowl of an electric mixer fitted with the paddle attachment and beat on medium speed until well combined, about 3 minutes. Turn the speed to low and add the flour mixture, then the egg whites, mixing until the dough comes together, about 5 minutes. Transfer to a large sheet of plastic wrap, flatten into a 1-inch-thick disk, and wrap tightly in the plastic. Refrigerate for at least 2 hours or up to 3 days.

3. When ready to bake, preheat the oven to 350°F. Set out a tuile cookie pan or empty egg carton to use as a cooling rack for the cookies. You will also need a 4-inch round cookie stencil. To make your own, take the plastic lid of a large yogurt or similar container and cut off the rimmed edge. Using a razor blade or a similar instrument, cut a 4-inch circle out of the center of the lid, taking care not to cut through the edge of the lid.

4. Set the cookie stencil on a nonstick baking mat and use a small offset spatula or a table knife to spread 2 teaspoons of dough evenly inside the stencil, spreading the dough into a very thin, smooth circle, about 1/16 inch thick. Continue making the circles, setting them 1 inch apart, until the mat is full.

5. Transfer the mat to a baking sheet and bake until the tops of the cookies are dry, about 5 minutes. Remove the pan from the oven and, working very quickly, shape the cookies: one at a time, set a paper fortune, if desired, in the center of the cookie, fold the cookie in half, and, holding the cookie with the folded edge facing up, bring the 2 pointed ends upward so that they come together above the folded edge. The cookies should still be hot to the touch as you work; if they cool too much, they will break. If necessary, you can re-heat them in the oven for about 30 seconds to make them pliable again. Set the cookies in the tuile pan or egg carton to cool, so that they will hold their shape, and cool completely. Repeat with the remaining batter. The cookies can be stored in an airtight container for up to 1 week.

■

CHOCOLATE-COVERED "POCKY" STICKS

Makes 32 sticks

Pocky is a popular and beloved Japanese snack food: thin cookie sticks covered in milk chocolate or other delectable coatings. (There's even an extra-dark-chocolate version called Men's Pocky.) I wanted to re-create this iconic treat for the home cook, so I called my dear friend Sherry Yard, the pastry chef at Spago in Beverly Hills. This recipe, which she developed just for me, is actually a sweet variation on her standard breadstick. While Sherry prefers a strawberry–white chocolate coating (bright pink is her trademark color), these are covered in bittersweet chocolate.

¼ cup (2⅞ ounces/80 grams) sweetened condensed milk

1 cup (5½ ounces/155 grams) all-purpose flour

½ teaspoon baking powder

2 tablespoons sugar

⅛ teaspoon ground cardamom

⅛ teaspoon salt

¼ cup (2 ounces/57 grams) unsalted butter, at room temperature

1 large egg white, beaten

3½ ounces (99 grams) bittersweet chocolate, chopped

1 ounce (28 grams) milk chocolate, chopped

1. Mix the sweetened condensed milk with 2 tablespoons water and set aside.

2. Put the flour, baking powder, sugar, cardamom, and salt into the bowl of an electric mixer fitted with the paddle attachment. Mix on low speed until well mixed. Add the butter and mix until the mixture resembles cornmeal, about 5 minutes. With the machine running, add the condensed milk mixture all at once and continue mixing until it is fully incorporated and the dough forms a ball around the paddle, 5 minutes. Transfer to a large sheet of plastic wrap, pat into a 1-inch-thick disk, and wrap tightly in the plastic. Refrigerate for 20 minutes.

3. Preheat the oven to 300°F. Line two large baking sheets with parchment paper and set aside.

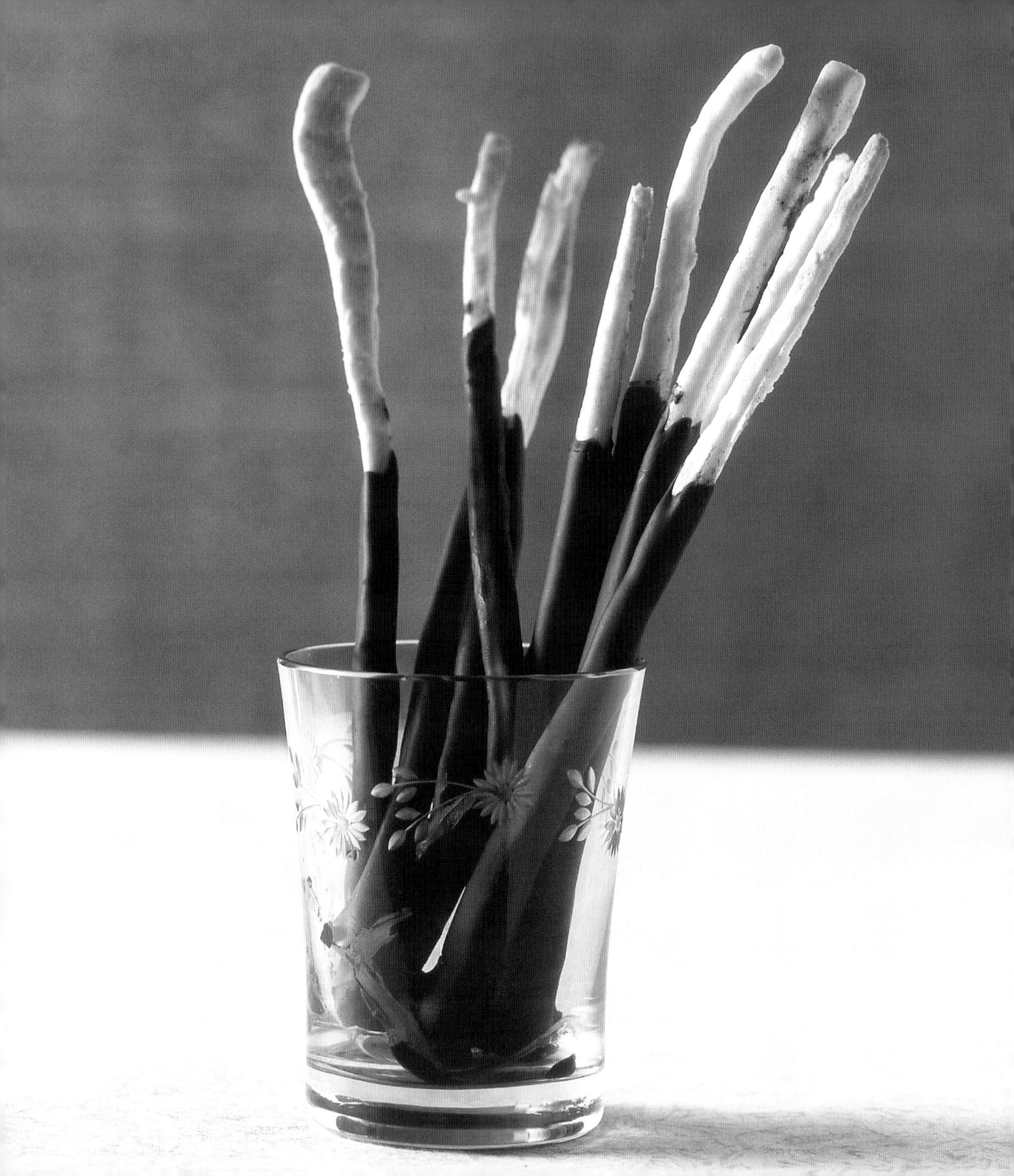

4. Divide the dough into quarters and divide each quarter into 8 pieces. Roll one piece into a ball, then stretch it and roll it under your palms into a 10-inch stick, about ¼ inch in diameter. Transfer the stick to a lined baking sheet and repeat with the remaining dough, setting the sticks ½ inch apart. Refrigerate the sticks, uncovered, for 10 minutes.

5. Brush the sticks with the egg white, and bake until golden brown and crisp, about 25 minutes. Cool completely on the pans set on a rack.

6. Melt the bittersweet chocolate in a double boiler or heatproof bowl set over a saucepan of very hot water, stirring just until smooth. Add the milk chocolate and continue stirring until the mixture is completely melted and smooth. Transfer the chocolate mixture to a long, shallow dish.

7. Lay out a sheet of parchment or foil. Dip the cooled cookie sticks into the chocolate, leaving a couple of inches uncovered, and place on the parchment paper or foil. The chocolate will harden as it cools. The cookie sticks can be stored in an airtight container for up to 2 days.

CHOCOLATE KUMQUAT
SPRING ROLLS

Makes 3 dozen spring rolls, about 10 servings

Spring rolls are the quintessential Asian appetizer, but I have adapted the concept to dessert. When cooked, these rolls are like cylindrical molten cakes with warm chocolate oozing out of an impossibly thin and crisp "pastry" shell. The kumquats not only cut through the richness with their distinct citrus tartness, but also are a symbol of good fortune, as *kum* is a homonym for "gold" in Chinese.

CHEF'S TIP: Make sure you use thin spring roll wrappers, which can be found in Asian markets, not egg roll wrappers.

5 kumquats, cut into ¼-inch slices and seeded, juices reserved

½ cup plus 1 tablespoon (4½ ounces/127 grams) heavy whipping cream

⅛ teaspoon salt

8¼ ounces (233 grams) bittersweet chocolate, finely chopped

1 large egg yolk

1 tablespoon Grand Marnier

1 tablespoon unsalted butter, softened

Thirty-six 5-inch square spring roll wrappers

1 large egg, lightly beaten

Canola, vegetable, or other neutral oil for deep-frying

1. Put the kumquat slices and their juices into a small saucepan, add the cream and salt, and warm over medium heat just until bubbles form around the edges of the pan. Remove from the heat.

2. Put the chocolate into the bowl of a food processor and pour the hot kumquat cream over it. Let sit for 2 minutes, then process until the mixture becomes smooth and shiny. Add the egg yolk, Grand Marnier, and butter and process to combine.

3. Line an 8½ × 4½-inch loaf pan with plastic wrap. Pour the chocolate mixture into the pan and transfer to the freezer. Freeze, uncovered, until completely hard.

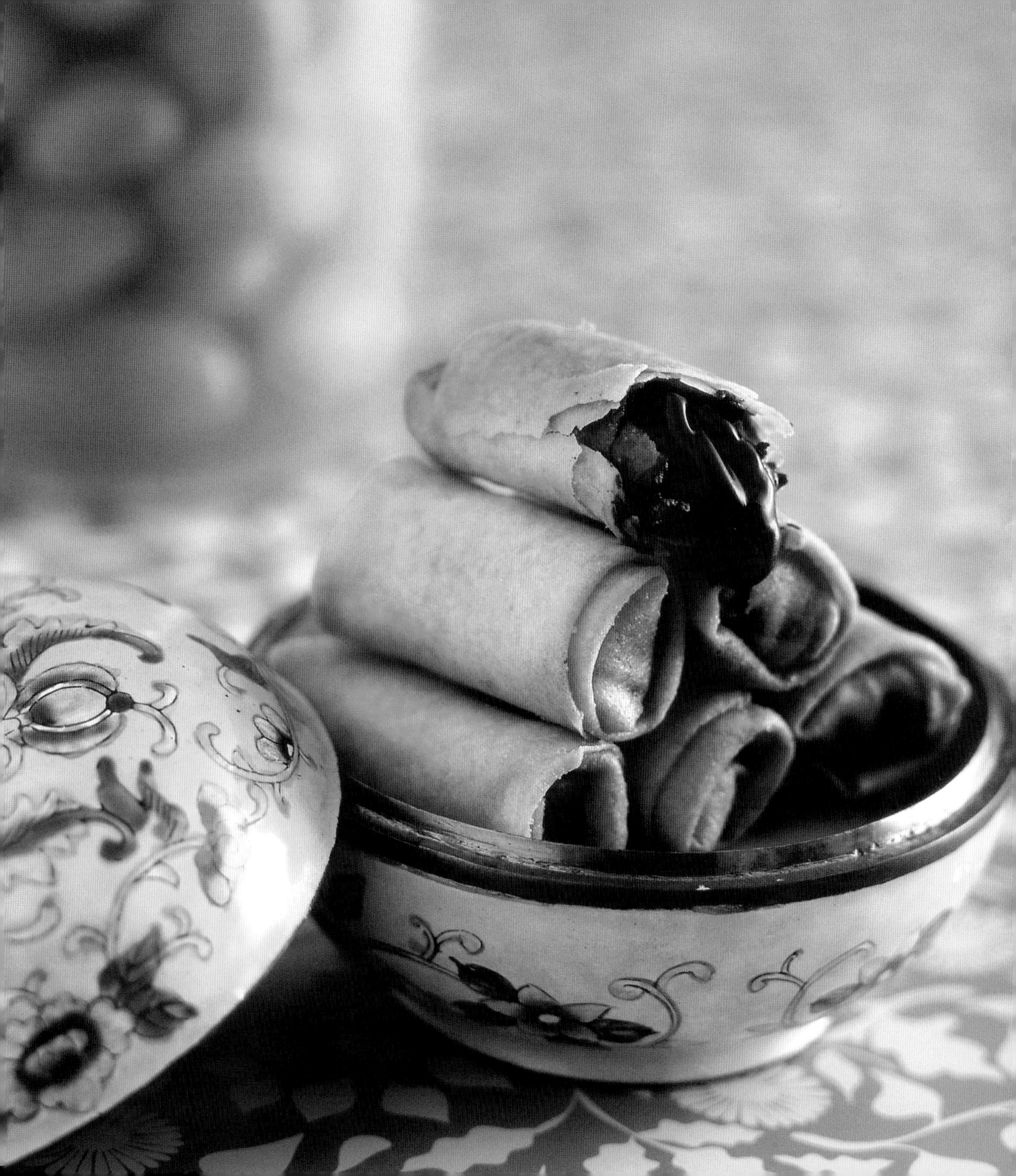

4. Unmold the chocolate bar and peel off the plastic wrap. Cut the bar lengthwise in half, then cut each half crosswise into ½-inch slices. You should have 36 chocolate bars.

5. Lightly brush the entire surface of a spring roll wrapper with a bit of the beaten egg. Turn the wrapper so that you see a diamond, and lay a chocolate bar across the end closest to you so that the ends of the bar meet the edges of the wrapper to form a triangle. Take the corner of the wrapper closest to you and wrap it around the chocolate, then roll the chocolate away from you one full rotation. Tightly fold the sides in toward the center, then continue to roll up to the end of the wrapper, making sure the end is tightly sealed. Set on a baking sheet. Repeat with the remaining wrappers and chocolate. Freeze the spring rolls for at least 10 minutes or up to 2 days; take them out only when you are ready to fry them.

6. Fill a saucepan with oil to a depth of 2 inches and heat to 350°F. When the oil is ready (a tiny pinch of flour will sizzle), add a few spring rolls, taking care to not crowd the pan, and cook, turning occasionally and adjusting the heat as necessary to maintain 350°F, until golden brown, about 4 minutes. Drain on paper towels and cook the remaining rolls. Serve warm.

■

CREAM PUFFS

Cream puffs were recently introduced in Asia and they have become a huge sensation. Bakery shops completely devoted to cream puffs (like American doughnut shops) have cropped up across Japan and now all over Asia. Japanese bakers have adapted the original French pâte à choux into versions with crisp exteriors and light, soft centers filled with Asian-flavored creams. Here's my version.

½ cup (4 ounces/113 grams) unsalted butter

½ cup (4 ounces/113 grams) whole milk

2 tablespoons sweetened condensed milk

¼ teaspoon salt

1 cup (5½ ounces/155 grams)

all-purpose flour, sifted

5 large eggs

1 large egg yolk

1 cup (8 ounces/226 grams) heavy whipping cream

Ginger Pastry Cream (page 132)

1. Preheat the oven to 400°F. Line two baking sheets with parchment paper and set aside.

2. Put the butter, milk, sweetened condensed milk, ½ cup plus 2 tablespoons water, and salt in a saucepan and bring to a boil over medium-high heat, stirring occasionally. Add the flour and cook, stirring constantly with a heatproof spatula, scraping the bottom of the pan and folding the dough over and over, until it is smooth and just starts to stick to the bottom of the saucepan, about 7 minutes.

3. Transfer the dough to the bowl of an electric mixer fitted with the paddle attachment. Mix the dough on medium speed for 1 minute to allow the steam to escape and the dough to cool slightly. With the machine running, add 4 eggs and the yolk one at a time, mixing until well incorporated, about 2 minutes. Turn the mixer speed to high and mix for 10 seconds.

4. Transfer the dough to a pastry bag fitted with a ½-inch-diameter plain piping tip. Pipe out 1-inch-wide 1-inch-tall rounds 2 inches apart onto the prepared baking sheets; try to

form a peak at the top of each. Lightly beat the remaining egg and brush on the tops of the puffs.

5. Bake for 10 minutes, then lower the temperature to 350°F and bake until the puffs are risen and golden brown, about 20 more minutes. Resist the temptation to peek in at the puffs as they bake or they may fall. Remove from the oven and cool completely on the pans set on a rack.

6. Meanwhile, put the cream in the bowl of an electric mixer fitted with the whisk attachment and whisk until medium peaks form. (When you lift the whisk from the mixture, a peak will form and the very tip of the peak will fall back down.) Gently fold in the pastry cream until fully incorporated and refrigerate until ready to use.

7. When ready to serve, cut the puffs horizontally in half. Spoon or pipe 2 tablespoons of the pastry cream onto the bottom half of each puff, sandwich with the tops, and serve immediately.

Strawberry Cream Puffs: Fold ¼ cup strawberry jam into the whipped cream mixture.

Green Tea Cream Puffs: Substitute Green Tea Cream (page 66) for the whipped cream mixture.

■

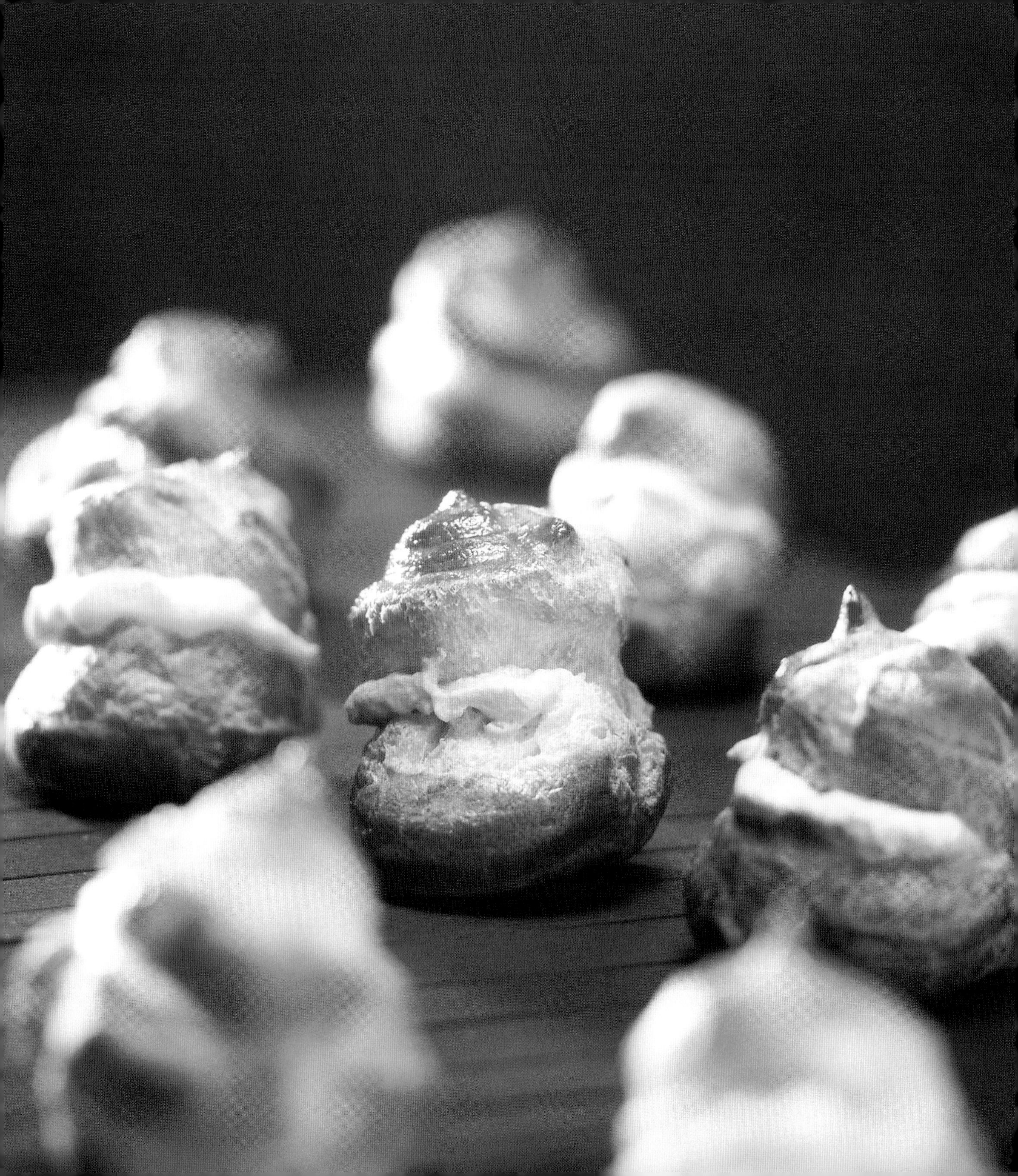

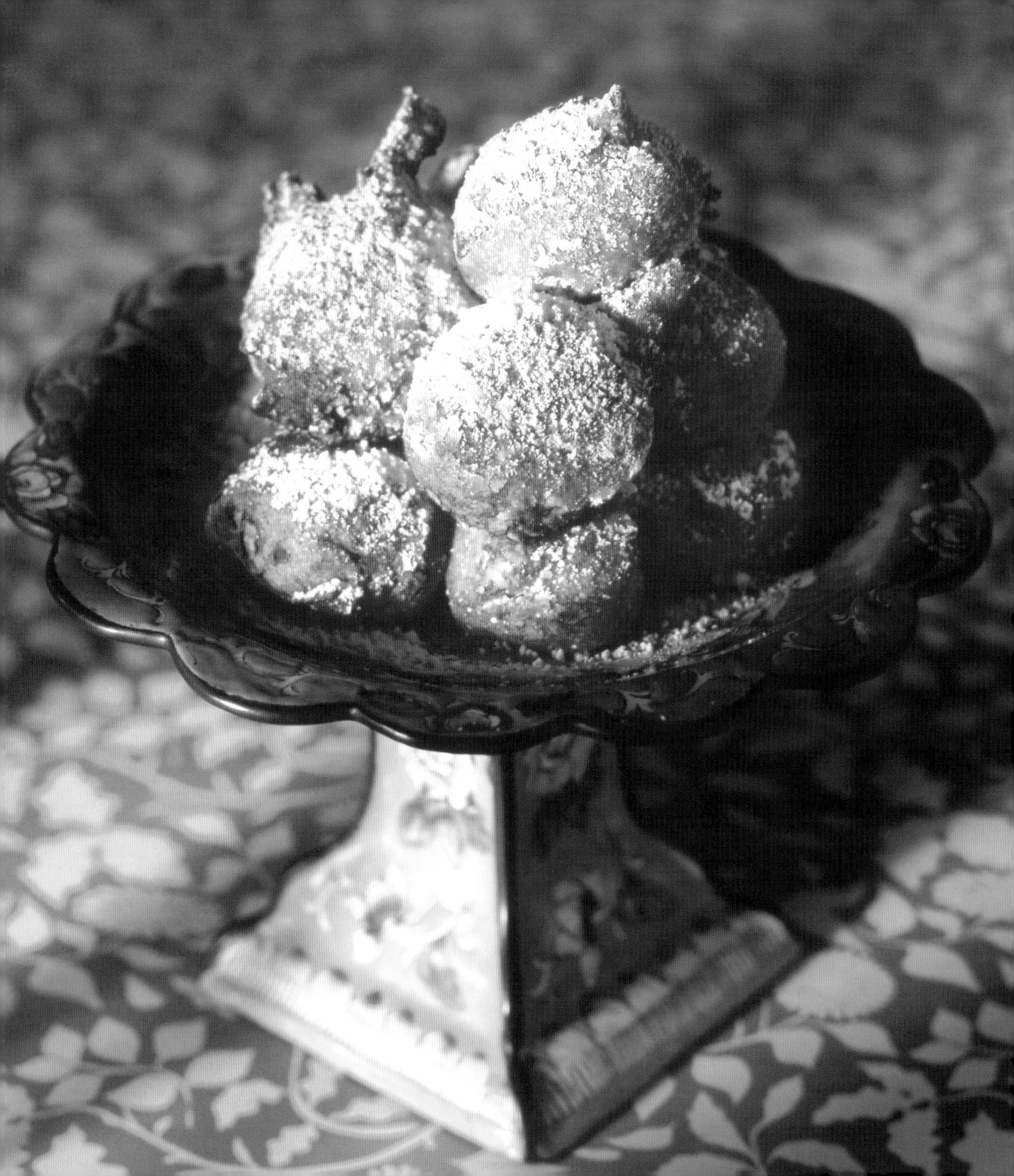

SWEET POTATO DOUGHNUTS
WITH ROAST APPLE FILLING

Makes 2 dozen doughnuts

When I first tested these, I decided to make two batches—one baked, one fried. The fried batch was very good (what fried dough isn't?), but the baked batch was even better. The dough was lighter and airier, and the apple filling was both crunchy and juicy. Neither too rich nor too heavy, these doughnuts remind me of the sweet buns in Asian bakeries. I love serving them for breakfast or with afternoon tea.

CHEF'S TIP: Be sure to brush the molds generously with butter to prevent the dough from sticking.

Sweet Potato Doughnuts

1 medium (12¼ ounces/343 grams) sweet potato, peeled and cut into 1-inch slices

1 tablespoon active dry yeast

⅓ cup (3 ounces/83 grams) evaporated milk

⅓ cup (2⅓ ounces/67 grams) buttermilk

⅔ cup (5 ounces/143 grams) sugar, plus more for sugaring the molds

1¾ cups (9⅜ ounces/266 grams) all-purpose flour

3 tablespoons unsalted butter for greasing the molds

Roast Apple Filling

2 apples, preferably Granny Smith, peeled, cored, and cut into 1-inch chunks

2 teaspoons fresh lemon juice

2 tablespoons sugar

¼ teaspoon ground cinnamon

2 teaspoons unsalted butter

2 teaspoons vanilla extract

1. To make the doughnuts: Fill a large saucepan fitted with a steamer basket or rack with water to a depth of 3 inches. Bring the water to a gentle simmer and add the sweet potato to the steamer basket. Cover and steam until a knife pierces through the flesh easily, about 20 minutes. Remove from the heat and cool slightly.

2. Mash the sweet potato with a fork until smooth. Set aside.

3. Sprinkle the yeast over ¼ cup warm water (110°F) and let sit until foamy, about 10 minutes.

4. Transfer the mashed sweet potato to the bowl of an electric mixer fitted with the paddle attachment and add the evaporated milk, buttermilk, and ⅓ cup water. Mix on medium speed until well incorporated, about 3 minutes. Add the sugar and mix until dissolved, about 5 minutes. Turn the mixer speed to low and add the foamy yeast, then add the flour ½ cup at a time. Once all the flour has been incorporated, mix for 1 minute more. Cover the bowl with plastic wrap and let the dough rise in a warm place until nearly doubled in bulk, about 1 hour.

5. Meanwhile, make the filling: Toss the apples with the lemon juice, sugar, and cinnamon. Set a large skillet over medium heat for 3 minutes, then add the apples and butter. Cook, stirring occasionally, until the apples are browned and slightly softened, about 30 minutes. Stir in the vanilla extract and set aside to cool completely.

6. Generously butter twenty-four 4-ounce ramekins or two 12-cup muffin tins, then sprinkle the molds lightly with sugar. Fill each mold with 3 tablespoons of the soft, wet dough, then press a piece of roasted apple into the center of each. Gently gather the dough together to cover the apple and pinch the top seam tightly. Cover lightly with plastic wrap and let rise for 30 minutes.

7. Meanwhile, preheat the oven to 350°F.

8. Uncover the doughnuts and bake until puffed and golden brown, about 20 minutes. Serve warm.

Kabocha Squash Beignets: Omit the butter and sugar for the molds. In the doughnut recipe, omit the Roast Apple Filling and substitute 1⅓ cups (12¼ ounces/343 grams) mashed Kabocha squash (see page 18) for the sweet potato and pumpkin spiced ale for the buttermilk. You will need canola, vegetable, or other neutral oil for deep-frying. Fill a saucepan with oil to a depth of 3 inches and heat to 350°F. When the oil is ready (a tiny pinch of flour will sizzle), shape the risen dough into 2-inch balls and gently drop into the oil; cook about 5 at a time—do not crowd the pan. Cook until puffy and golden brown, about 2 minutes, then turn and cook for another minute. Remove the cooked beignets with a slotted spoon and drain on paper towels. Roll the hot beignets in sugar, if desired, and serve warm.

■

PIES AND TARTS

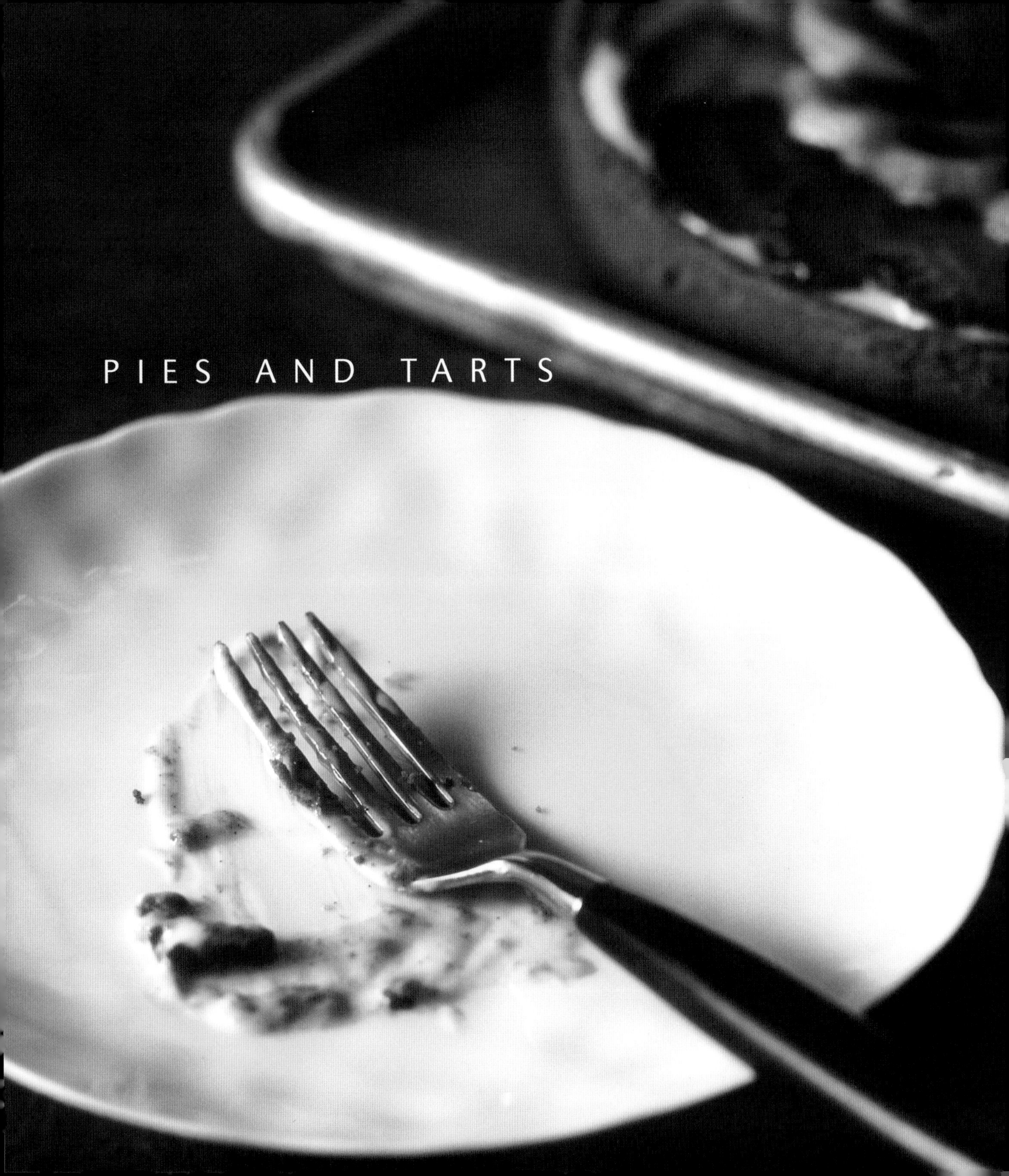

Pies and tarts can signal a special occasion or make an ordinary event feel special. It's not that they're particularly fancy, though a decorated tart is quite elegant. It's that there's always an element of surprise. No matter how tried and true certain combinations are, the crust can always be spiced differently and the fillings varied according to season.

Perhaps that sense of anticipation and excitement is why pies and tarts are universally loved. Will it be sweet or tangy? Moist or crumbly? Most pie and tart crusts look the same, so it's rarely possible to discern their true flavor and texture before you taste them. The same is true for pastry creams and certain other fillings. That's why I often slip Asian flavors into these things—a buttery dough enlivened with finely ground toasted jasmine rice, or a light cream sharply flavored with lime.

Interestingly, while many efforts to incorporate Asian flavors into Western desserts started on this side of the Pacific, this one began in Asia. In fact, it's not so much a fusion trend as it is a long-standing tradition in Asian desserts. Custard tarts, known as *dahn taht,* are a standard dim sum item, and *kuey taht* or "tangerine pies" are popular holiday cookies that are usually made during Chinese New Year, especially in Southeast Asia.

The recipes that follow not only present innovative flavors and techniques for old classics, they also introduce classics from the other side of the world. Constructing a pie or tart may seem like a lot of work, but think of it as simply baking a shell and filling it. You can make the shell ahead of time—even freeze it in the pan—and bake it whenever you're ready. In fact, freezing the dough and baking it straight from the freezer actually keeps the crust light and crisp. Likewise, pastry creams can always be refrigerated and spread chilled.

THE SOUTH AND THE EAST:
CONNECTIONS WITH PIES AND MORE

Pies are essentially tender, flaky bowls of dough filled with something sweet. In southern China and Southeast Asia, piecrusts are commonly made with lard. This used to be true in America too, and many Southern cooks still won't use anything else. As unappetizing as it might seem to some, lard definitely makes the best piecrusts, lending them a fullness of flavor that butter just can't touch some of the recipes that follow give you the option of using either butter or lard.

Two of the pies included here—the Coconut Cream Pie and the Banana Cream Pie—are known in both the American South and Southeast Asia. I use jasmine rice or ginger to give the crusts an Asian twist, but American palates will find something they recognize and love.

Tarts are less common in the American South than in Southeast Asia, but even here I've made the East-West connection. In creating the Chocolate and Vietnamese Coffee Tart, I realized that the closest American analogue to Vietnam's famously dark coffee is New Orleans's café au lait, which is made with chicory coffee and mixed with sugar and hot milk. Either coffee works well in this decadent and elegant dish.

BANANA CREAM PIE

If I had to choose a favorite pie, it would be creamy, custardy banana cream pie. Here, fresh and candied ginger add a nice kick, balanced by sweet milk chocolate. Chocolate and banana are meant for each other, but the thin layer of milk chocolate lining the crust also keeps the crust nice and crisp. This pie is perfect on its own, or garnish it with milk chocolate shavings by running a vegetable peeler along a bar of chocolate.

CHEF'S TIP: If you don't have pastry or cake flour, substitute another ½ cup (2¾ ounces/77 grams) all-purpose flour and add ½ teaspoon lemon juice with the ice water to keep the crust tender and flaky.

Gingered Pie Pastry

1 cup (5½ ounces/155 grams) all-purpose flour, plus more for rolling

½ cup (2¾ ounces/79 grams) pastry or cake flour (see Chef's Tip)

1 tablespoon plus 1 teaspoon sugar

¼ teaspoon ground ginger

⅛ teaspoon ground cinnamon

¾ teaspoon salt

½ cup (4 ounces/113 grams) unsalted butter or lard, cut into ½-inch cubes and chilled

Banana Cream Filling

3⅓ ounces (93 grams) milk chocolate, chopped

1 cup (8 ounces/226 grams) heavy whipping cream

Ginger Pastry Cream (page 132)

5 ripe bananas, peeled and cut into ¼-inch slices

1 tablespoon finely chopped candied ginger, plus more for garnish, optional

Milk chocolate for shaving, optional

1. To make the pastry: Put the flours, sugar, ginger, cinnamon, and salt into a large mixing bowl and mix well. Cut in the butter using a pastry cutter or your fingers until the mixture resembles cornmeal. Gently knead the dough, adding ice water 1 tablespoon at a time, until you can squeeze the mixture into a ball. On a temperate dry day, you will need about ¼ cup water. Form the dough into a ball, press it into a 1-inch-thick disk, and wrap tightly in plastic wrap. Chill until firm, at least 1 hour.

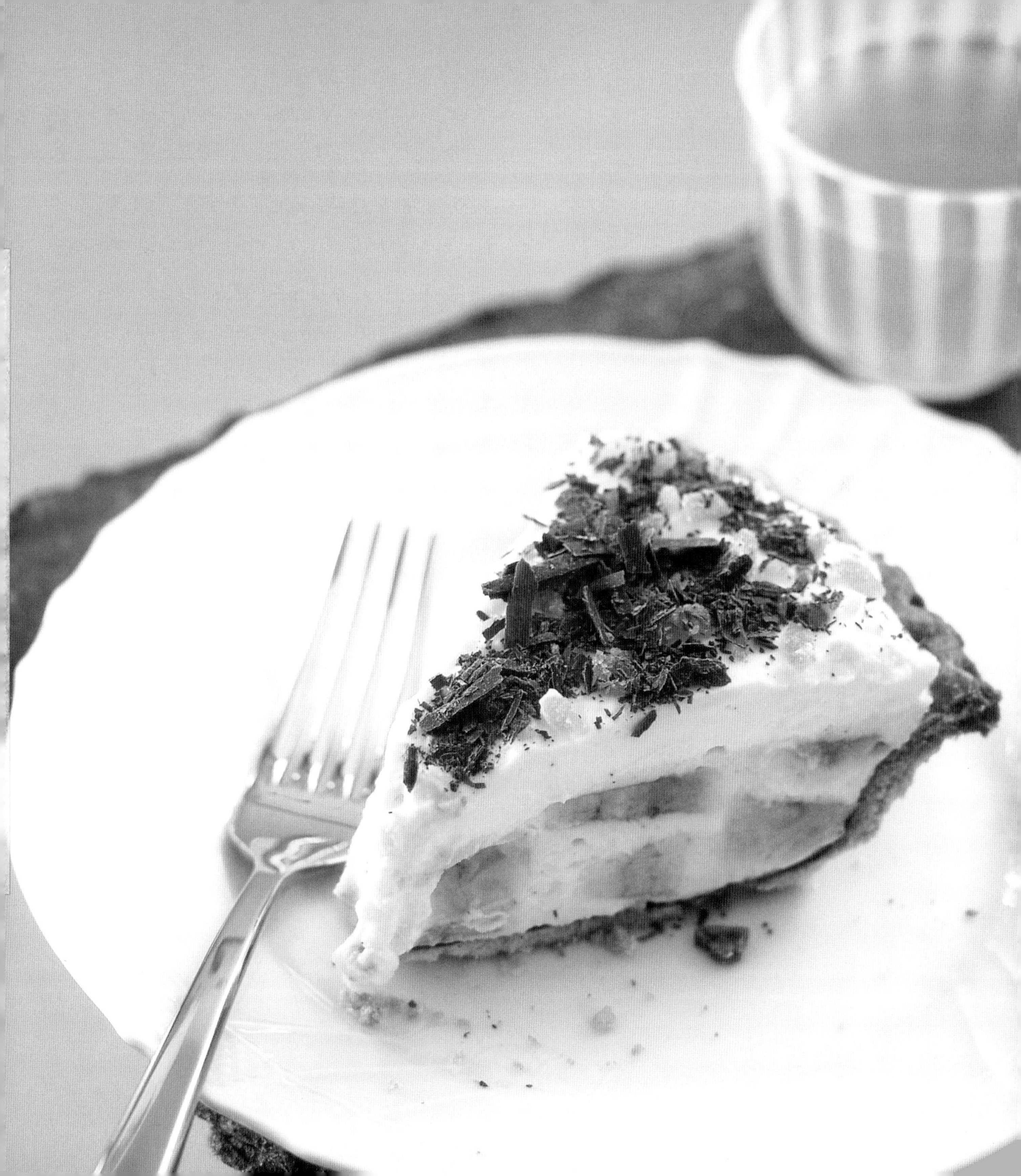

2. Lightly flour a work surface and a rolling pin. Roll the dough into a 12-inch circle, ¼-inch thick, rotating the circle a quarter turn with each roll. Lightly flour the dough and loosely roll it around the rolling pin, then unroll it into a 9-inch glass or ceramic pie dish and press gently into the dish. Trim any excess dough and decoratively crimp the edge, if desired. Loosely cover with plastic wrap and freeze until hard, at least 30 minutes.

3. Preheat the oven to 425°F.

4. Line the dough with parchment paper and fill with pie weights or dried beans. Bake for 10 minutes. Turn the heat down to 325°F and bake for another 15 minutes. Remove the pie weights and parchment paper and bake the crust until browned and dry to the touch, about 20 minutes more. Remove from the oven and cool completely.

5. To make the filling: Melt the chocolate in a double boiler or heatproof bowl set over a larger pan of hot water. As soon as the chocolate melts, stir well, pour into the cooled piecrust, and spread evenly in a thin layer. Let the chocolate cool and harden.

6. Put the heavy cream in the bowl of an electric mixer fitted with the whisk attachment and whisk on medium speed until medium peaks form. (When you lift the whisk from the mixture, a peak will form and the very tip of the peak will fall back down.) Fold one-third of the whipped cream into the pastry cream to lighten it. Then fold in another third. Set the remaining whipped cream aside.

7. Spread half of the pastry cream mixture in the piecrust. Top with a layer of half the sliced bananas and half the chopped ginger. Repeat with another layer of pastry cream, bananas, and ginger, then spread the reserved whipped cream decoratively on top of the pie. Garnish with the candied ginger and shaved milk chocolate on top, if desired. Refrigerate for at least 2 hours or up to 6 hours before serving.

■

COCONUT CREAM PIE WITH TOASTED JASMINE RICE CRUST

Toasted and ground jasmine rice is a common seasoning in Southeast Asian savory salads and grilled meats. Although it may seem like an unusual pastry ingredient, it is ideal for piecrusts. Like cornmeal, the toasted and ground rice adds an earthy aroma and a fantastic crunch that is perfect with the soft coconut cream filling.

CHEF'S TIPS: Make sure the butter is cold before cutting it into the dry ingredients. Freeze it for 10 minutes if it isn't completely chilled.

You can find coconut powder in most Asian markets. If you can't find it, you can make your own by grinding finely shredded unsweetened dried coconut into a powder with a food processor. In a pinch, you can substitute all-purpose flour.

Toasted Jasmine Rice Crust

¼ cup (1¾ ounces/49 grams) raw jasmine rice

1¼ cups (6⅜ ounces/180 grams) all-purpose flour, plus more for rolling

¼ cup (¾ ounce/21 grams) coconut powder

1 tablespoon sugar

¾ teaspoon salt

½ cup (4 ounces/113 grams) unsalted butter or lard, cut into ½-inch cubes and chilled

½ teaspoon rice vinegar

Coconut Cream Filling

1 cup (3⅛ ounces/88 grams) finely shredded unsweetened dried coconut, plus more for garnish

1½ cups (13¼ ounces/375 grams) coconut milk

1 cup (8 ounces/227 grams) heavy whipping cream

½ cup (4 ounces/113 grams) whole milk

2 large eggs

¾ cup (5 ounces/141 grams) sugar

½ cup (2½ ounces/72 grams) all-purpose flour

¼ teaspoon salt

2 tablespoons unsalted butter

2 teaspoons vanilla extract

1. To make the crust: Put the rice in a medium skillet, set over medium heat, and toast, shaking the pan occasionally, until the rice is fragrant and golden brown, about 10 minutes. Transfer to a sheet of parchment paper or a plate to cool completely, then put in a coffee grinder and grind to a very fine powder.

2. Put the rice powder, flour, coconut powder, sugar, and salt in the bowl of a food processor and process until well mixed, about 30 seconds. Add the butter and pulse until the mixture resembles small peas, about 10 times. Add the vinegar and 3 tablespoons ice water and pulse just until the dough sticks together when pinched, about 7 times. If necessary, add up to another tablespoon of ice water and pulse 2 or 3 times. (You can also mix the dry ingredients in a large bowl, cut in the butter with a pastry cutter or your fingers, and stir in the vinegar and water until the dough comes together.) Form the dough into a ball, press into a 1-inch-thick disk, and wrap tightly in plastic wrap. Chill until firm, at least 1 hour.

3. Lightly flour a work surface and a rolling pin. Roll the dough to a ¼-inch thickness, rotating the circle a quarter turn with each roll. Lightly flour the dough and loosely roll it around the rolling pin, then unroll it into a 9-inch glass or ceramic pie dish and press gently into the dish. Trim any excess dough and decoratively crimp the edge, if desired. Loosely cover with plastic wrap and freeze until hard, at least 30 minutes.

4. Preheat the oven to 425°F.

5. Line the pie shell with parchment paper and fill with pie weights or dried beans. Bake for 10 minutes, then lower the heat to 325°F and bake for 15 minutes. Remove the pie weights and parchment and bake about twenty minutes more, or until the crust is dry and a deep golden brown. Cool completely. Turn the oven down to 300°F.

6. Meanwhile, make the coconut filling: Spread the coconut on a rimmed baking sheet and toast in the oven, stirring once, until golden brown and fragrant, about 10 minutes. Remove from the oven and cool completely.

7. Put the coconut milk, cream, whole milk, eggs, sugar, flour, and salt in a medium saucepan, set over medium heat, and bring slowly to a boil, whisking constantly. The mixture should have thickened to a pastry cream consistency, somewhere between a thin batter and a thick liquid. Stir in the butter until melted, then remove from the heat and stir in the vanilla and toasted coconut.

8. Transfer the pastry cream to a large bowl, cover the surface directly with a sheet of plastic wrap, and let it set and thicken at room temperature, about 1 hour. (If you are preparing this ahead of time, refrigerate the cream until ready to use.)

9. Spread the pastry cream evenly into the pie shell, garnish with shredded coconut, if desired, and serve.

■

FRUIT TART WITH GINGER PASTRY CREAM

Ginger is used in Asian desserts as frequently as vanilla is used in Western desserts—it's as aromatic and flavorful, but far less expensive. When combined with creamy fillings, ginger cuts through the richness for an alluring spiciness that tingles the tongue. You can use ginger pastry cream as a base for any fruit tart but I like the sweet-sour ones, such as berries, kiwis, and citrus fruits.

Gingered Tart Dough

1 cup plus 2 tablespoons (6½ ounces/183 grams) all-purpose flour, plus more for rolling

¼ cup (⅞ ounces/23 grams) almond flour

⅔ cup (2½ ounces/69 grams) confectioners' sugar

¼ teaspoon ground ginger

⅛ teaspoon salt

½ cup (4 ounces/113 grams) unsalted butter, cut into ½-inch cubes and chilled

1 large egg yolk

¼ teaspoon vanilla extract

Ginger Pastry Cream

3 large egg yolks

⅓ cup (2½ ounces/71 grams) sugar

3 tablespoons cornstarch

1 cup (8 ounces/227 grams) whole milk

One 1-inch piece fresh ginger, sliced

⅛ teaspoon salt

½ teaspoon vanilla extract

2 tablespoons unsalted butter

2 pints raspberries

2 kiwis, peeled and cut into ¼-inch slices

2 tablespoons apricot jam

1. Preheat the oven to 350°F.

2. To make the dough: Put the all-purpose flour, almond flour, confectioners' sugar, ginger, and salt in the bowl of a food processor. Pulse a few times to mix, then add the butter and pulse until the mixture resembles small peas, about 15 times. With the machine running, add the egg yolk and vanilla extract and process just until the dough begins to clump into large pieces, about 20 seconds.

3. Form the dough into a ball, press it into a 1-inch-thick disk, and wrap tightly in plastic wrap. Chill until firm, at least 1 hour. The dough will keep for up to 2 days in the refrigerator or up to 1 month, well wrapped, in the freezer. If frozen, thaw in the refrigerator before use.

4. Lightly flour a work surface and a rolling pin. Roll the dough to a ⅛-inch thickness, rotating the circle a quarter turn with each roll. Lightly flour the dough and loosely roll it around the rolling pin, then unroll it into a 10-inch tart pan with a removable bottom or a 10-inch tart ring set on a parchment paper–lined baking sheet and press it up against the sides. Trim off any excess.

5. Line the tart shell with parchment paper and fill with pie weights or dried beans. Bake for 10 minutes. Remove the pie weights and parchment paper and bake until the dough is golden brown and dry to the touch, about 13 minutes more. Cool completely on a rack.

6. Meanwhile, make the pastry cream: Whisk the egg yolks, sugar, and cornstarch together in a medium bowl until the sugar is dissolved; set aside. Put the milk, ginger, and salt in a small saucepan and warm over medium-high heat until bubbles form around the edges, about 5 minutes. Remove from the heat and add the warm milk to the egg yolks in a slow, steady stream, whisking constantly. Return the mixture to the saucepan, set over low heat, and cook, whisking constantly and vigorously, until the mixture thickens, about 5 minutes. The cream should stick to the bottom of the saucepan and form a ribbon on the surface when you lift the whisk. Remove from the heat and stir in the vanilla and then the butter until melted and smooth. Transfer the pastry cream to a large bowl, cover the surface directly with plastic wrap, and let it set and thicken at room temperature, about 2 hours. (If you are preparing this ahead of time, refrigerate the cream until ready to use.)

7. Unmold the tart shell and transfer to a serving plate. Remove the ginger from the pastry cream, and spread the cream evenly into the shell, smoothing the top with an offset spatula or a table knife. Arrange the fruit decoratively on top. Mix the jam with 2 teaspoons water, and brush this glaze over the top of the tart. Serve.

PINEAPPLE MASCARPONE TART

Each bite of this tart captures the spiced heat of the gingered crust, the tangy yet mellowing influence of the cheese, the zing of fine lime zest, and the smoky sweetness of the roasted pineapple bits.

All-purpose flour for rolling

Gingered Tart Dough (page132)

Pineapple Mascarpone Filling

1 cup (8 ounces/226 grams) heavy whipping cream

½ cup (4 ounces/114 grams) mascarpone cheese

¼ cup (1⅞ ounces/53 grams) sugar

1 tablespoon grated lime zest

2 teaspoons fresh lime juice

2 teaspoons dark rum, optional

1 recipe Palm Sugar–Roasted Pineapple (page 215)

1. Preheat the oven to 350°F.

2. Lightly flour a work surface and a rolling pin. Roll the dough to a ⅛-inch thickness, rotating the circle a quarter turn with each roll. Lightly flour the dough and loosely roll it around the rolling pin, then unroll it into a 10-inch tart pan with a removable bottom or a 10-inch tart ring set on a parchment paper–lined baking sheet and press it up against the sides. Trim off any excess.

3. Line the tart shell with parchment paper and fill with pie weights or dried beans. Bake for 10 minutes. Remove the pie weights and parchment paper and bake until the dough is golden and dry to the touch, about 10 minutes. Cool completely on a rack.

4. To make the filling: Put the cream in the bowl of an electric mixer fitted with the whisk attachment and whisk at medium speed until medium peaks form, about 7 minutes. (When you lift the whisk from the cream, a peak will form and the very tip of the peak will fall back down.) Transfer to another bowl.

5. Put the mascarpone cheese, sugar, lime zest, lime juice, and rum in the mixer bowl. Mix with the paddle attachment on medium speed until everything is well combined and the sugar is dissolved, about 4 minutes. Add one-third of the whipped cream and vigorously mix until the texture becomes pasty. Add the remaining cream and fold in very gently until fully incorporated.

6. Spread the mascarpone mixture evenly into the cooled tart shell. Top decoratively with the pineapple and serve.

■

THAI TEA WHITE CHOCOLATE TART

Makes one 8-inch tart, about 10 servings

Since Thai tea is often mixed with sweetened condensed milk to achieve its distinctive flavor and color, it makes sense to pair Thai tea with white chocolate here. The strong tea cuts through the sweetness of the chocolate for a light, balanced ganache filling.

CHEF'S TIP: Thai tea leaves are available at many Asian markets and tea shops. If you cannot find them, substitute jasmine tea.

Lime Tart Pastry

½ cup plus 1 tablespoon (4⅜ ounces/125 grams) unsalted butter, at room temperature

2 teaspoons grated lime zest

¾ cup (3 ounces/85 grams) confectioners' sugar

¼ teaspoon salt

1 large egg

½ teaspoon vanilla extract

1⅔ cups (8⅞ ounces/250 grams) all-purpose flour, plus more for rolling

Thai Tea White Chocolate Ganache

18 ounces (511 grams) white chocolate, finely chopped

¼ cup (2 ounces/56 grams) unsalted butter, at room temperature

¼ cup (¾ ounce/20 grams) loose Thai tea leaves

⅔ cup (5½ ounces/156 grams) heavy whipping cream

1 cup (8 ounces/226 grams) evaporated milk

2 tablespoons corn syrup

¼ teaspoon salt

1 teaspoon orange blossom water, optional

1. To make the tart dough: Put the butter, lime zest, sugar, and salt in the bowl of an electric mixer fitted with the paddle attachment. Mix on medium speed until the mixture resembles cornmeal, about 3 minutes. With the machine running, add the egg and vanilla and mix until incorporated. Scrape down the sides and bottom of the bowl. Turn the speed to medium-low and slowly add the flour, about one-third at a time, mixing just until no traces of flour remain. Form the dough into a ball, press into a 1-inch-thick disk, and wrap tightly in plastic wrap. Chill until firm, at least 1 hour.

2. Preheat the oven to 350°F.

3. Lightly flour a work surface and a rolling pin. Roll the dough to a ⅛-inch thickness, rotating the circle a quarter turn with each roll. Lightly flour the dough and loosely roll it around the rolling pin, then unroll it into an 8-inch tart pan with a removable bottom or an 8-inch tart ring set on a parchment paper–lined baking sheet and press it up against the sides. Trim off any excess.

4. Line the tart shell with parchment paper and fill with pie weights or dried beans. Bake for 10 minutes. Remove the pie weights and parchment paper and bake until the dough is golden and dry to the touch, about 5 minutes more. Cool completely on a rack.

5. To make the ganache: Put the chocolate and butter in a large mixing bowl. Put the tea leaves, cream, corn syrup, evaporated milk, and salt in a small saucepan, set over medium-high heat, and warm, stirring constantly, until bubbles form around the edges, about 5 minutes.

6. Strain the tea mixture through a fine-mesh sieve lined with cheesecloth onto the chocolate. Squeeze the tea leaves in the cheesecloth to extract as much liquid as possible. Gently stir the chocolate-tea mixture until the chocolate is completely melted, then stir in the orange blossom water, if using. Immediately pour the mixture into the cooled tart shell and let it set completely at room temperature before serving.

■

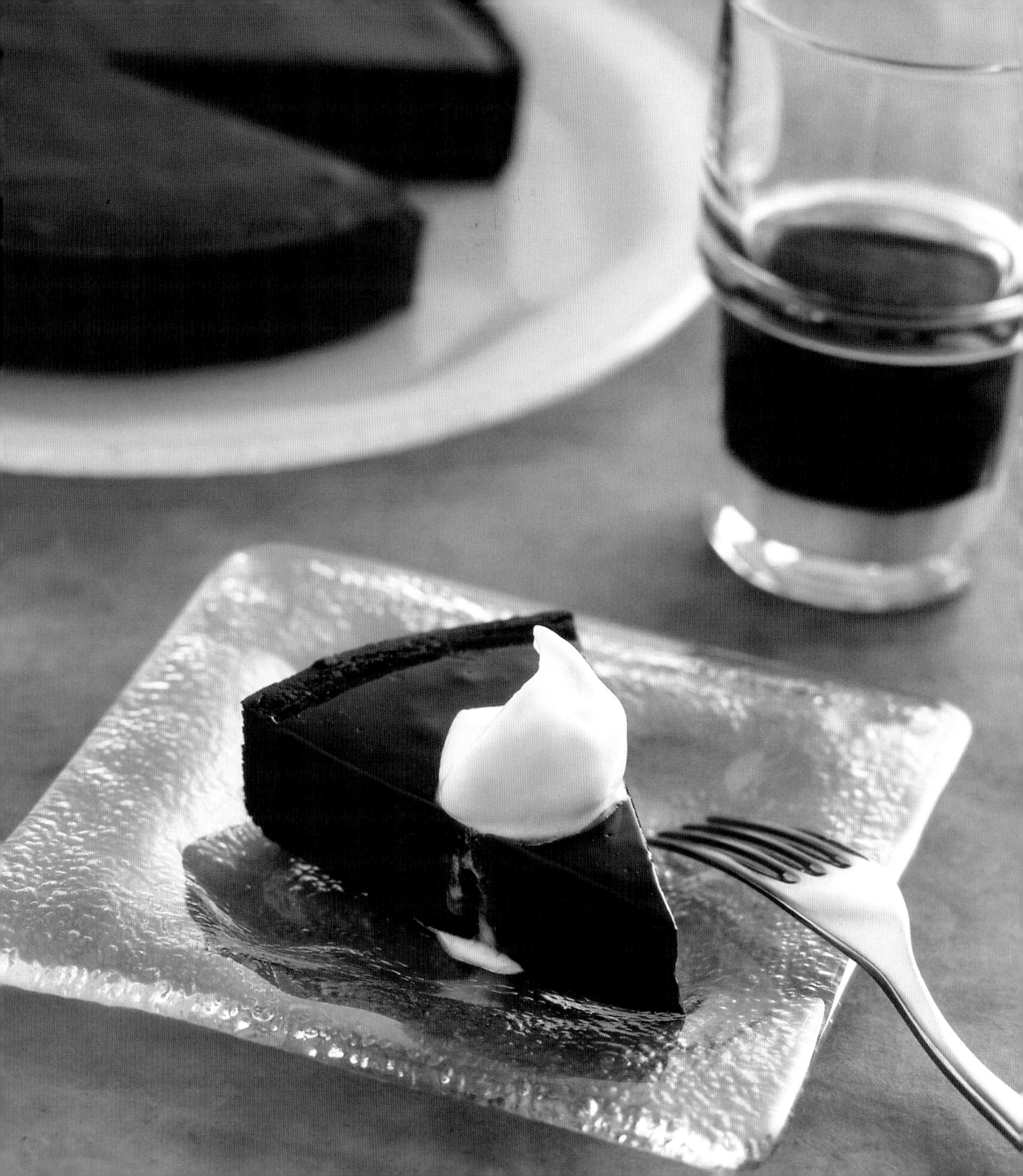

CHOCOLATE AND VIETNAMESE COFFEE TART

This is one of the most requested recipes by diners and food writers among the desserts served at Spice Market. People just love the way the coffee cuts through the richness of the chocolate and imparts exotic, smoky overtones. Limiting the sugar added to the tart itself allows the chocolate flavor to really come through. For an added treat, top each slice with a little scoop of Condensed Milk Ice Cream (page 266).

CHEF'S TIP: Substitute Sweetened Condensed Milk Chantilly (page 25) or good vanilla ice cream for the condensed milk ice cream.

Cocoa Tart Pastry

½ cup (4 ounces/113 grams) unsalted butter, at room temperature

1 cup (4 ounces/113 grams) confectioners' sugar

¼ teaspoon salt

¼ cup (⅞ ounce/23 grams) unsweetened cocoa powder, preferably Dutch-processed

¼ cup (⅞ ounce/23 grams) almond flour

1⅓ cups (7⅛ ounces/203 grams) all-purpose flour, plus more for rolling

1 large egg

Nonstick cooking spray

Chocolate–Vietnamese Coffee Ganache

12 ounces (340 grams) bittersweet chocolate, chopped

1¾ cups (13⅞ ounces/392 grams) heavy whipping cream

½ cup (4 ounces/113 grams) evaporated milk

⅓ cup (1 ounce/28 grams) Vietnamese, chicory, or French Roast coffee powder

½ teaspoon salt

2 large eggs

¼ cup (2⅓ ounces/65 grams) sweetened condensed milk

1. To make the tart shell: Put all the ingredients except the egg in the bowl of a food processor and pulse until the mixture resembles cornmeal, about 10 times. With the machine running, add the egg, and process just until the dough comes together; it will be

quite sticky. Form the dough into a ball, press into a 1-inch-thick disk, and wrap tightly in plastic wrap. Chill until firm, at least 4 hours.

2. Spray an 8-inch tart pan with a removable bottom or an 8-inch tart ring set on a parchment paper–lined baking sheet with nonstick cooking spray and set aside. Lightly flour a work surface and a rolling pin. Roll the dough to a ⅛-inch thickness, rotating the circle a quarter turn with each roll. Lightly flour the dough and loosely roll it around the rolling pin, then unroll the dough into the prepared tart pan and press it up against the sides. Trim off any excess, and freeze until hard, at least 30 minutes.

3. Preheat the oven to 325°F.

4. Line the tart shell with parchment paper and fill with pie weights or dried beans. Bake for 15 minutes. Remove the pie weights and parchment paper, and bake until the dough is dry to the touch, about 5 minutes more. Cool completely on a rack. Turn the oven down to 275°F.

5. Make the ganache: Put the chocolate in a large mixing bowl and set aside. Stir together the cream, evaporated milk, coffee powder, and salt in a small saucepan and set over low heat. As soon as it simmers, strain the mixture through a fine-mesh sieve over the chocolate. Immediately begin whisking the chocolate into the cream. Once the chocolate melts and the mixture becomes smooth and shiny, whisk in the eggs one at a time, then the sweetened condensed milk. Continue whisking until the mixture is smooth, then pour into the cooled tart shell.

6. Bake the tart for 10 minutes, then rotate the pan and bake for about 10 minutes more. When done, the middle should still jiggle slightly but not be wet. Remove from the oven, cool completely on a rack, and unmold before serving.

■

CARAMEL NUT TART

Like a sophisticated European nut tart or an American candy bar, this tart features the sticky goodness of nuts and caramel encased in a thin buttery pastry shell. But it's the coconut—both the chewy shreds mixed with the nuts and the coconut milk in the caramel—that sets it apart. As the tart bakes, your house will be filled with a nutty, sugary tropical fragrance.

Caramel Nut Filling

½ cup (2⅞ ounces/80 grams) cashews

½ cup (2⅛ ounces/60 grams) unsalted shelled pistachios

½ cup (2½ ounces/70 grams) pecan halves

½ cup (2⅛ ounces/60 grams) walnut halves

½ cup (2½ ounces/70 grams) hazelnuts

½ cup (1½ ounces/44 grams) finely shredded unsweetened dried coconut

¼ teaspoon salt

2 tablespoons cornstarch

1 cup (6⅔ ounces/190 grams) sugar

⅓ cup (4 ounces/114 grams) corn syrup

1 teaspoon fresh lemon juice

¼ cup (2 ounces/57 grams) unsweetened coconut milk

2 tablespoons evaporated milk or milk

½ cup (4 ounces/113 grams) unsalted butter, at room temperature

1 teaspoon vanilla extract

All-purpose flour for rolling

Gingered Tart Dough (page 132)

1. Preheat the oven to 350°F.

2. To make the filling: Spread all the nuts on a rimmed baking sheet and toast until golden and fragrant, about 5 minutes. Add the coconut, stir, and toast for 3 minutes more. Remove from the oven and cool slightly, then toss with the salt and cornstarch.

3. To make the shell: Lightly flour a work surface and a rolling pin. Roll the dough to a ⅛-inch thickness, rotating the circle a quarter turn with each roll. Lightly flour the dough and loosely roll it around the rolling pin, then unroll it into a 10-inch tart pan with a

removable bottom or a 10-inch tart ring set on a parchment paper–lined baking sheet and press it up against the sides. Trim off any excess.

4. Line the tart shell with parchment paper and fill with pie weights or dried beans. Bake for 10 minutes. Remove the pie weights and parchment paper, and bake until the dough is golden and dry to the touch, about 10 minutes more. Cool completely on a rack.

5. Put the sugar, corn syrup, and lemon juice in a large saucepan and set over high heat. Bring to a medium caramel, about 7 minutes.

6. Remove the caramel from the heat and add the coconut milk and evaporated milk in a slow, steady stream, whisking constantly, then add the butter. Set over high heat and whisk constantly for 3 minutes. (The mixture will attempt to boil over—just keep whisking vigorously.) Add the nut mixture and stir vigorously with a heatproof spatula or a wooden spoon for 3 minutes. Remove from the heat and stir in the vanilla extract.

7. Pour the filling into the cooled tart shell. Bake until bubbly in the center, about 10 minutes. Remove from the heat and cool completely before serving.

■

CHINESE PUFF PASTRY

If you are neither a professional pastry chef nor an accomplished home baker, the term "puff pastry" probably intimidates you. Picking up a package of frozen puff pastry from the market may be the closest you've ever come to the real thing at home. And it's true that this glorious French creation—layer upon layer of buttery and paper-thin pastry—is a delicate art. The temperature of the butter must be just right, as must be your working conditions. Although the results are often well worth the effort, you should try the quick and easy Chinese version of puff pastry here.

Puff pastry is an integral part of many Chinese dishes, both sweet and savory. The puff pastry found in northern Chinese dishes is actually more like bread, with fine, translucent layers. Depending on the proportion of flour to water, the result can range from crumbly to chewy. Delicate, flaky versions are used in little round pastries filled with sweet beans, stir-fried onions, or grated radish, while chewier versions are made into large rounds and served as a side dish or formed into rectangular "sandwich" breads and stuffed with meats and vegetables. The scallion pancakes popular in America are another variation, with green onions rolled between thin layers of crisp and chewy dough.

Hong Kong bakeries often feature a version of puff pastry that resembles the traditional French recipe, although it employs lard instead of butter for an even richer taste and texture. The most popular of these snacks is *gah laay go,* a half-moon of pastry stuffed with aromatic curry (not unlike an Indian samosa). Dim sum fans may also recognize *char siu so,* finely chopped barbecued pork encased in small puff pastry rectangles. The honeyed pork melts into the tender, rich interior of the pastry, while the pastry's surface remains flaky and light.

Although lard-based puff pastry is scrumptious, the version used in desserts is generally made with oil rather than lard or butter. For one thing, oil is not nearly as temperamental as these other fats—it doesn't need to be chilled or warmed before using. Also, Chinese puff pastry is most commonly fried. When this is done properly, the pastry actually absorbs very little oil, instead becoming crisp, delicate, and more impervious to liquid than ordinary puff pastry. As a result, it can be layered with any number of dry or moist toppings or fillings. Frying Chinese puff pastry also has an aesthetic appeal, as the layers of pastry tend to fan out into a decorative flower as the dough becomes a golden brown puff.

CHINESE PUFF PASTRY

Makes 32 small pastry rounds

This is the easiest puff pastry recipe you'll ever find. It requires no resting and can be used immediately after it's made. Although this dough is usually fried, so that it puffs up to reveal beautiful layers of flaky pastry, it is also delicious when baked, crisp on the outside with tender layers in between. Use the pastry the same day it is made, or it will dry out. It can be made quickly, especially once you get the hang of the technique.

CHEF'S TIP: Keeping your hands moist by touching a wet towel prevents your fingers from sticking to the dough and helps the layers stay together.

2 cups (10⅛ ounces/288 grams) cake or all-purpose flour

¾ teaspoon salt

½ cup plus 2 tablespoons (5 ounces/140 grams) canola, vegetable, or other neutral oil

1 tablespoon sugar

1. Put ⅔ cup of the flour and ¼ teaspoon of the salt in a mixing bowl and combine with your hands. Add 1 tablespoon of the oil and mix well with your hands. Continue adding oil 1 tablespoon at a time until the dough holds together and forms a ball when you squeeze it; you should need about ¼ cup. Roll the dough into a 16-inch-long log. Wrap in plastic wrap and set aside.

2. Put the sugar, the remaining 1⅓ cups flour, and the remaining ½ teaspoon salt in a mixing bowl and combine with your hands. Add the remaining oil and mix well with your hands. Add ice water 1 tablespoon at a time until the dough holds together and forms a ball when you squeeze it; you should need about 3 tablespoons total. Roll the dough into a thick 16-inch-long log.

3. Cut both logs into 1-inch pieces, so that you have 16 smaller pieces and 16 larger pieces. Roll a larger piece into a ball and flatten it into a ¼-inch-thick 3-inch disk. Put a smaller piece of dough in the center of the disk, fold the disk over to make a half-moon, and seal

the edges tightly. Flatten the half-moon until it is ¼ inch thick, then roll out into a ⅛-inch-thick 4 × 8-inch rectangle. Starting from a short end, roll up the rectangle as you would a jelly roll, squeezing the dough firmly with each turn and then sealing the seam; you should end up with a 4-inch-long log. Cut the log in half into 2 cylinders. Turn one cylinder cut side up and flatten it into a ½-inch-thick disk, then roll it into a ¼-inch-thick 3-inch round. Repeat with the remaining dough, keeping the completed rounds covered with plastic wrap.

4. Use immediately in Peanut Turnovers (page 146) or Passion Fruit Dahn Taht (page 148).

PEANUT TURNOVERS

Makes 32 small turnovers

Flaky peanut cookies are a popular Chinese dessert, and puff pastry turnovers filled with savory curry or shredded turnips are a popular Hong Kong snack, so I combine the two in these little peanut turnovers. When you fry them, the pastry puffs up and fans out like flower petals. The peanut filling warms nicely and takes on a sticky sweet chew inside the delicate crisp shell.

CHEF'S TIP: A candy or deep-fry thermometer is very helpful here. Maintaining the right oil temperature while cooking will ensure pastries that are evenly browned and completely cooked through. It also prevents the pastries from absorbing too much oil, resulting in an extra light and crisp turnover.

1⅓ cups (7 ounces/200 grams) peanuts, toasted

1¼ cups (3½ ounces/100 grams) crushed palm sugar

2 tablespoons honey

2 tablespoons unsalted butter, at room temperature

¼ teaspoon salt

Chinese Puff Pastry (page 144)

Canola, vegetable, or other neutral oil for deep-frying

1. Put the peanuts, palm sugar, honey, butter, and salt into the bowl of a food processor and pulse until the peanuts are finely chopped and the mixture is starting to come together, about 20 times. (You can also do this by hand: Pound all the ingredients together in a large mortar with a pestle or chop the peanuts and mix with the other ingredients.) Form the mixture into ½-inch balls and place on a baking sheet. Cover with plastic wrap and freeze until hard, about 5 minutes.

2. Put a peanut ball in the center of a puff pastry round. Fold the circle over the filling to form a half-moon and press the edges with the tines of a fork to seal. Repeat with the remaining peanut balls and puff pastry rounds.

3. Fill a medium saucepan with oil to a depth of 2 inches and heat to 350°F. When the oil is ready (a pinch of flour will sizzle), add a few of the turnovers, without crowding the pan,

and cook until golden brown, about 1 minute, then flip and cook the other side until golden brown, about 2 minutes more. Remove with a slotted spoon and drain on paper towels. Repeat with the remaining turnovers. Serve warm or at room temperature.

PASSION FRUIT DAHN TAHT

Makes 32 mini tarts

This classic dim sum item actually originated in Portugal, where it's called *pasties de nata,* roughly translated as "pastries of cream." The Portuguese version is a firm egg custard in a hard shell. The Chinese version, found in just about every Chinese bakery and dim sum restaurant, is baked a little less so that the pastry and custard remain soft. My version combines the two with crisp pastry and a supple custard. I also add sweet-tart passion fruit seeds for a more complex flavor and texture.

Nonstick cooking spray	3 large eggs
Chinese Puff Pastry (page 144)	¾ cup (6 ounces/168 grams) whole milk
6 passion fruits, seeds, pulp, and juice removed and reserved	⅔ cup (4½ ounces/126 grams) sugar

1. Spray three mini-muffin tins with nonstick spray. Press a puff pastry round into each cup, using your fingers to press the dough flat on the bottom and up the sides of the mold. Chill in the freezer, uncovered, while you preheat the oven.

2. Preheat the oven to 425°F.

3. Bake the tartlet shells until golden brown and dry to the touch, about 10 minutes. Remove from the oven and cool completely in the pans. Turn the heat down to 325°F.

4. Put the eggs, milk, and sugar in a mixing bowl and whisk until the sugar dissolves and the mixture is smooth. Stir in the passion fruit seeds, pulp, and juice.

5. Divide the passion fruit mixture among the cooled tart shells. Bake just until the custard is set, about 10 minutes; it should still jiggle a little in the center. Remove from the oven and cool slightly, then remove from the muffin tins and serve.

Key Lime Dahn Taht: Substitute ½ cup (4 ounces/113 grams) fresh key lime juice for the passion fruit seeds, pulp, and juice. (Or use ⅓ cup regular lime juice.)

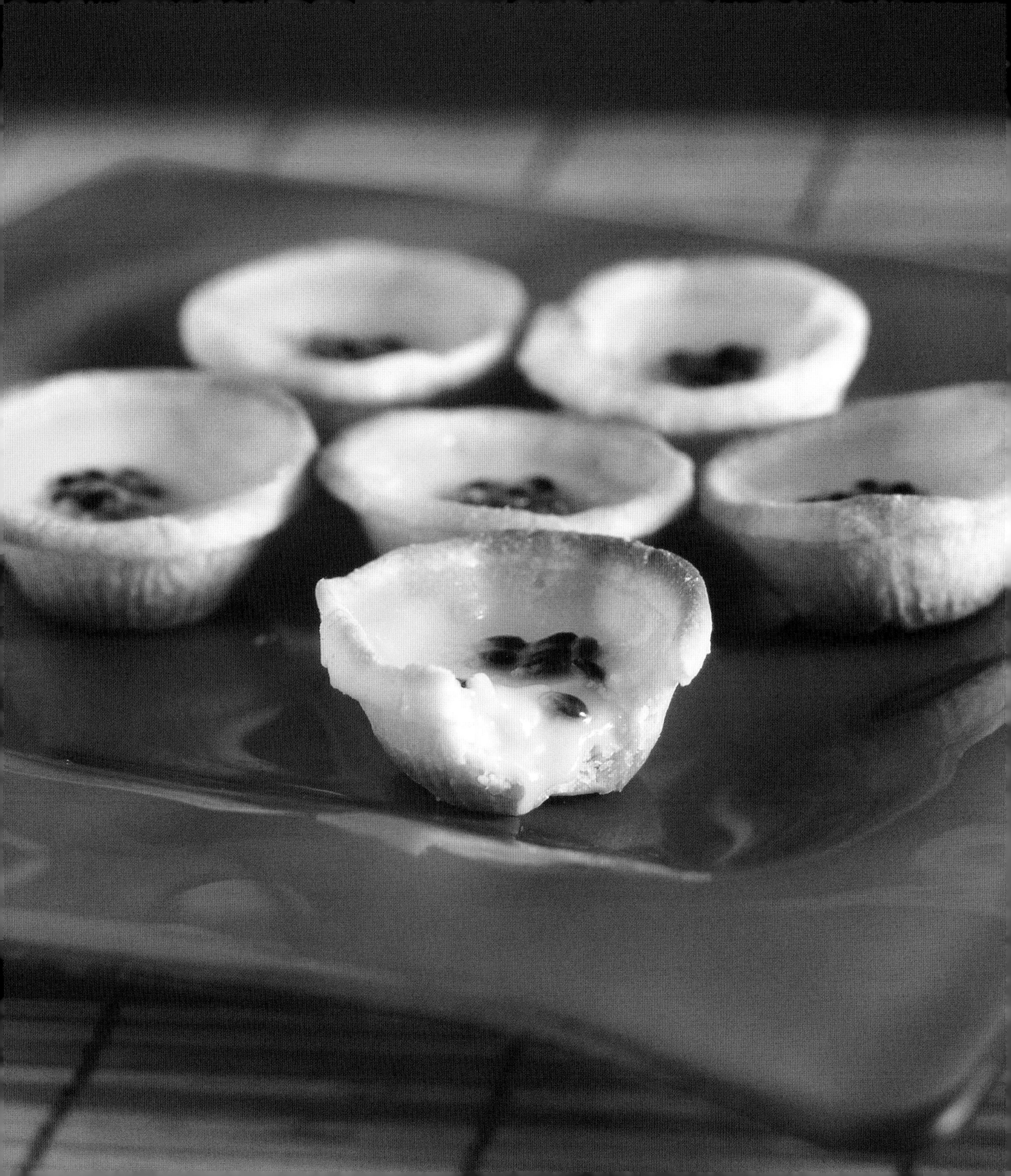

"TANGERINE PIE"—CARAMELIZED PINEAPPLE TURNOVERS

Makes 5½ dozen turnovers

Just to clarify—there are no tangerines in this recipe and it doesn't look like a pie. But it's still delicious. In Singapore, these turnovers, also known as kuey taht, are a highly prized gift for Chinese New Year. Traditionally, people give away fresh tangerines (*tangerine* is a homonym for "gold" in Chinese). When Western-style baked goods were introduced, this round turnover was created to resemble the real thing: thus its crackly orange egg yolk wash and clever little clove on top.

CHEF'S TIP: Don't eat the cloves. They are only a decorative touch, and biting into one will definitely be a shock to your palate.

Caramelized Pineapple Filling

2 small pineapples, peeled, cored, and finely diced (see page 213)

1 cup plus 2 tablespoons (6⅓ ounces/180 grams) crushed palm sugar

1 cinnamon stick

⅛ teaspoon salt

Pastry Dough

2 cups (10⅜ ounces/300 grams) all-purpose flour, plus more for rolling

⅓ cup plus 2 tablespoons (1¾ ounces/50 grams) custard powder

1 tablespoon dried milk powder

¾ cup plus 1½ teaspoons (6⅜ ounces/180 grams) unsalted butter, at room temperature

⅔ cup (2½ ounces/70 grams) confectioners' sugar

1 teaspoon salt

1 large egg

3 large egg yolks, beaten

66 whole cloves, optional

1. To make the pineapple filling: Put all of the ingredients into a medium saucepan, set over low heat, and cook, stirring occasionally, until the sugar has dissolved and all the liquid has evaporated, about 45 minutes. Transfer to a bowl, cover, and refrigerate for at least 2 hours, or as long as overnight.

2. To make the dough: Sift the flour, custard powder, and dried milk together and set aside.

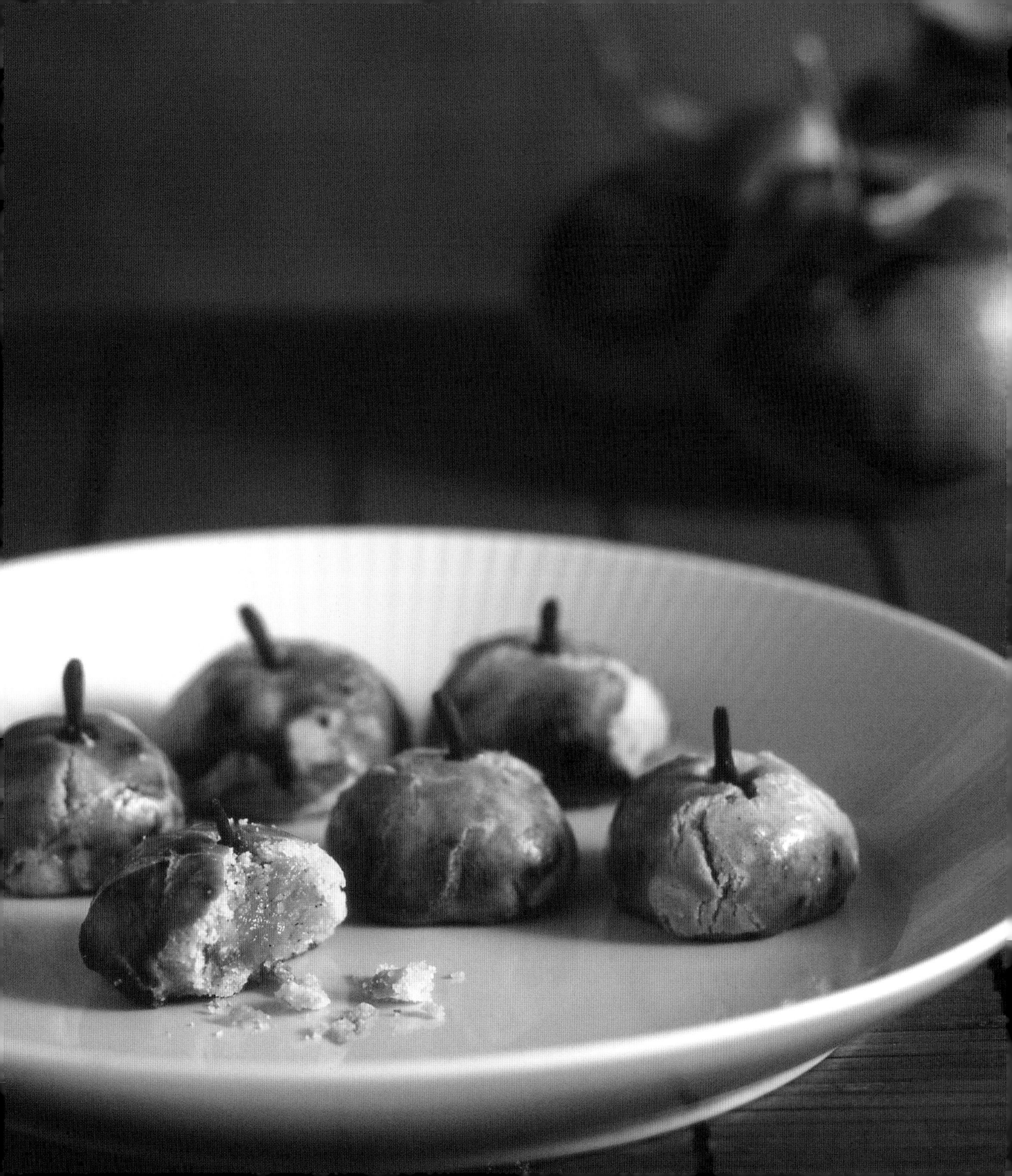

3. Put the butter, confectioners' sugar, and salt in the bowl of an electric mixer fitted with the paddle attachment and beat on medium speed until the mixture is light and creamy, about 4 minutes. Scrape down the sides and bottom of the bowl, add the flour mixture, and mix until incorporated. Add the egg and mix just until the dough comes together; it will be quite sticky. Form the mixture into a ball, press it into a 1-inch-thick disk, and wrap tightly in plastic wrap. Chill until firm, at least 2 hours, or as long as overnight.

4. Line two baking sheets with parchment paper. Unwrap the chilled dough and form it into 1-inch balls. Using your fingertips, press one ball into a thin 3-inch disk. Put 1 tablespoon of the pineapple filling in the center of the dough circle, fold over to make a half-moon, and pinch the edges together to seal. Twist off any excess dough, press and gently roll the half-moon shape into a ball. Repeat with the remaining dough and filling. Alternatively, roll the whole disk of dough out on a lightly floured surface to a 1/8-inch thickness, cut out 3-inch circles with a cookie or biscuit cutter, and fill and shape them. Put the filled balls 1 inch apart on the baking sheets, and chill until firm, about 15 minutes.

5. Meanwhile, preheat the oven to 350°F.

6. Brush the balls with the egg yolks and stick a clove, if desired, in the center of each. Bake until golden, about 12 minutes. Cool completely on a rack before serving.

PUDDINGS AND CUSTARDS

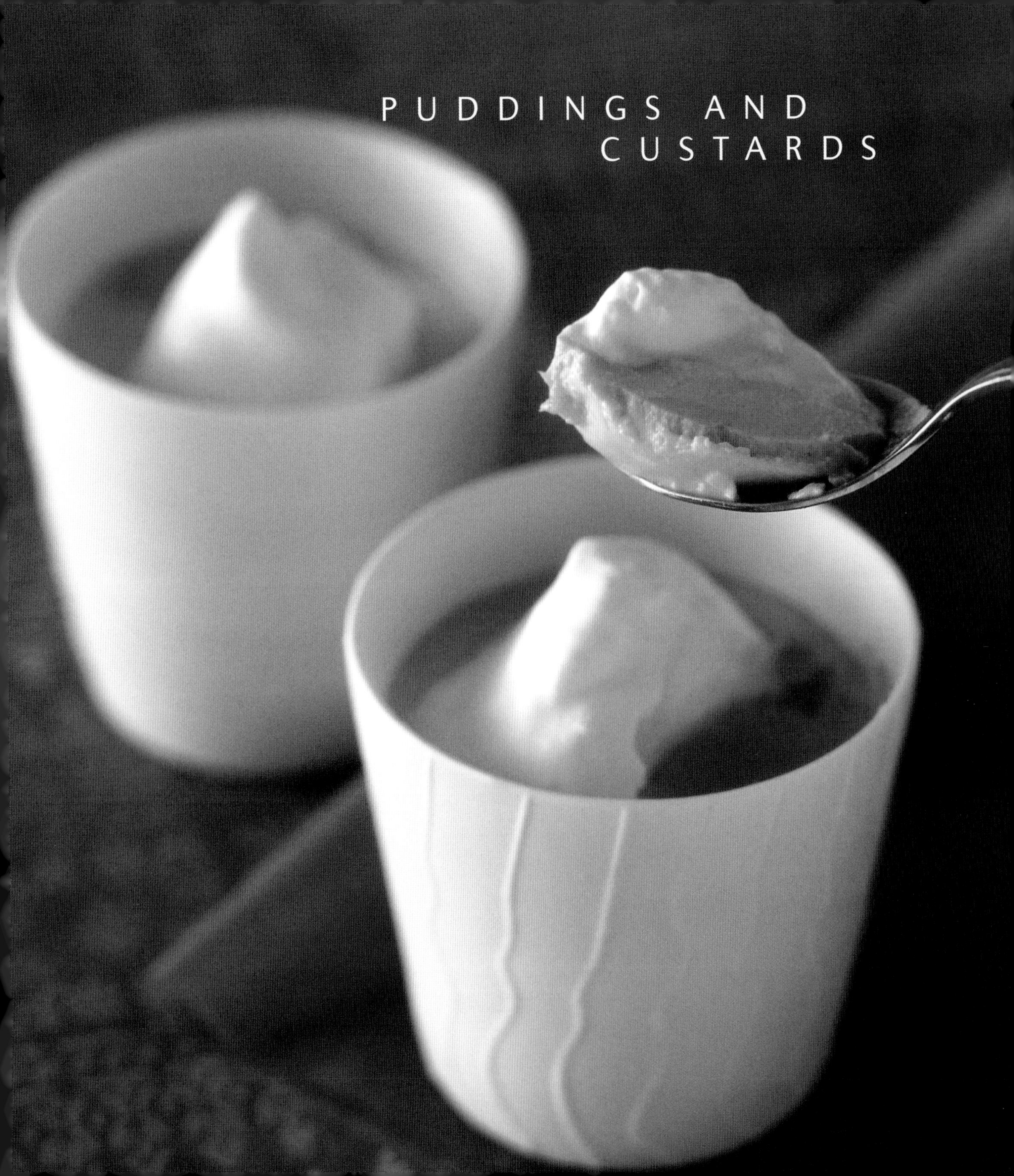

Traditional Western puddings are made on the stovetop and thickened with cornstarch. For a more delicate pudding, I turn to gelatin, which sets the pudding in a state that hovers between cream and solid. Because gelatin is made from animal by-products, many vegetarians, and many Asians in general, prefer to use agar-agar, a seaweed derivative that functions in much the same way. It is, in fact, a stronger gelling agent and can even set liquids at room temperature. Unfortunately, its strength is also its downfall, as it makes desserts too tough and slightly grainy.

Custards are similar to puddings except that the thickener of choice in custards is generally eggs or some form of starch, like rice or bread. I follow traditional techniques more closely with custards, but I often add coconut milk to the dairy mixture. Fresh, but still creamy, coconut milk is not itself sweet, but it can take on a succulent sweetness when combined with other ingredients.

CANTONESE DESSERTS

One of the most popular desserts at Cantonese dim sum and banquet palaces is something like a cross between pudding and Jell-O. Generations of Hong Kong chefs have adapted the flavors and textures of British puddings and related desserts to suit their diners' tastes. The result is an extraordinarily delicate dish that is firm enough to hold its shape but silken enough to melt in your mouth. My own pudding creations owe much to these unique Cantonese treats.

Perhaps the most common of these is the mango pudding often served as the ending to a haute cuisine Cantonese meal. The ideal mango pudding is soft and supple, fragrant but restrained. Tiny golden chunks of supremely fresh mango hang suspended in the ethereal cream. On special occasions at the best restaurants, the whole pudding is set in a decorative fish-shaped mold. Because the Cantonese word for fish is a homonym of the word for abundance, the chef closes the meal with a "fish" to affirm and celebrate the diners' surfeit of riches.

Most of the time, though, mango pudding is enjoyed in little plastic cups served from dim sum carts. On those same carts, you'll find a variety of cubed gelatin desserts. Flavored with coconut, taro, or red bean, these treats jiggle merrily as young and old alike (or young and old *especially*) wave their hands and shout for a plate.

MANGO PUDDING

Mango pudding is one of the most popular Hong Kong–style desserts, but its appeal has also been its downfall, as many dim sum palaces and banquet halls have turned to instant pudding mixes to meet the demand. I take this dessert back to its roots and make it with fresh mangoes and cream. Although sautéing the mangoes first is not a traditional technique, it makes this version even better than the original.

CHEF'S TIPS: Start with very ripe mangoes, preferably Alphonso or Champagne. If you cannot find them, you can use the Ratna brand of canned mangoes available at Indian markets.

This is a great dessert for parties because the recipe can be doubled and you can make the whole thing ahead of time and refrigerate it until ready to serve. It's best served the same day, but it can be refrigerated, covered, overnight if necessary.

6 mangoes, peeled, seeded, and chopped

2 tablespoons fresh lemon juice

½ teaspoon salt

1 cup plus 2 tablespoons (7½ ounces/212 grams) sugar

5 gelatin sheets, soaked in cold water until softened and drained, or 2½ teaspoons powdered gelatin, softened in 3 tablespoons cold water

4 cups (32 ounces/908 grams) heavy whipping cream

Sweetened Condensed Milk Chantilly (page 25), optional, or ½ cup (4 ounces/113 grams) evaporated milk

1. Put the mangoes, lemon juice, and salt in a large saucepan, set over medium heat, and cook, stirring occasionally, until the mangoes are very soft, about 5 minutes.

2. Add the sugar and continue cooking, stirring and scraping the bottom of the saucepan, until the mixture becomes thick and syrupy, with a few chunks of mango remaining, about 15 minutes. Do not let the sugar caramelize and brown. Remove from the heat and cool to lukewarm.

3. Stir the gelatin into the mango mixture until it dissolves, then stir in the cream until well incorporated.

4. Divide the mixture among eight 4-ounce ramekins or serving bowls. Chill in the refrigerator, uncovered, until set, about 3 hours. Serve cold, with chantilly on top, if desired.

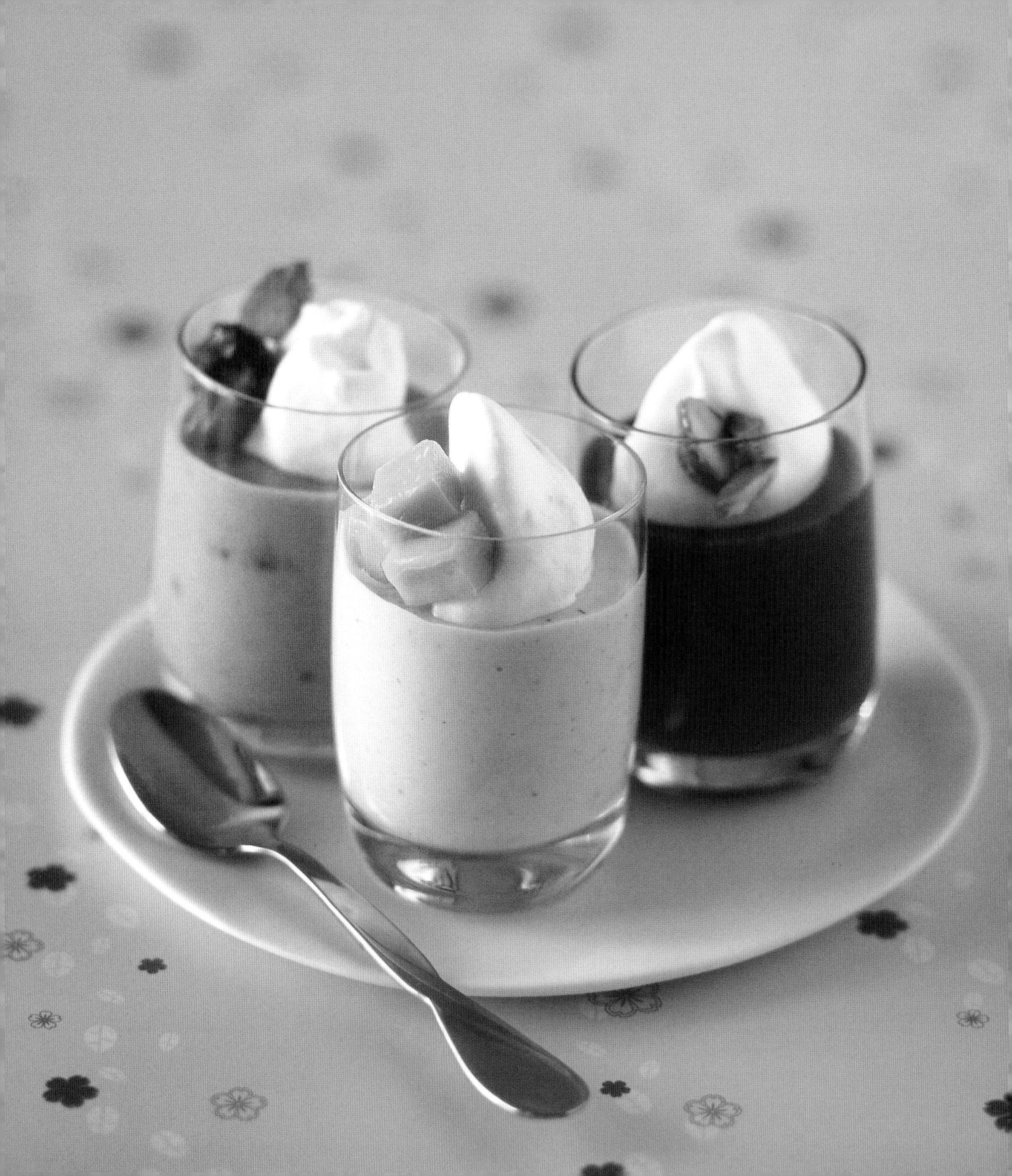

PUDDING TRIO: MALTED CHOCOLATE, GREEN TEA, AND RASPBERRY

Makes 8 servings

These puddings bring out the best in their main ingredients—rich malted chocolate, smoky green tea, and fresh raspberries—by suspending them in cream, without a hint of cornstarch. These pretty party desserts must be made ahead of time. Then they can just chill in the fridge while you entertain.

Malted Chocolate Pudding

1½ cups (12 ounces/340 grams) heavy whipping cream

½ vanilla bean, split lengthwise in half, seeds scraped out, and seeds and pod reserved, or 1 teaspoon vanilla extract

¼ teaspoon salt

¼ cup (1 ounce/28 grams) Horlicks powder

2 gelatin sheets, soaked in cold water until softened and drained, or 1½ teaspoons powdered gelatin, softened in 2 tablespoons cold water

5⅓ ounces (150 grams) bittersweet chocolate, finely chopped

½ cup (4 ounces/113 grams) whole milk

2 tablespoons sliced and roasted pistachios for garnish, optional

Green Tea Pudding

1½ cups (12 ounces/340 grams) whole milk

¼ cup plus 2 tablespoons (3¾ ounces/78 grams) sugar

⅛ teaspoon salt

2 gelatin sheets, soaked in cold water until softened and drained, or 1½ teaspoons powdered gelatin, softened in 2 tablespoons cold water

2 tablespoons matcha (green tea powder)

1 tablespoon fresh lemon juice

¼ cup diced mango for garnish, optional

Raspberry Pudding

1½ pints raspberries, plus more for garnish, optional

⅓ cup (2½ ounces/71 grams) sugar

¼ teaspoon salt

2 gelatin sheets, soaked in cold water until softened and drained, or 1½ teaspoons powdered gelatin, softened in 2 tablespoons cold water

1½ cups (12 ounces/340 grams) heavy whipping cream

2 tablespoons fresh lemon juice

Sweetened Condensed Milk Chantilly (page 25), for garnish, optional

1. To make the malted chocolate pudding: Put the cream, vanilla seeds and pod, if using, and salt in a small saucepan and bring to a simmer over medium heat. Add the Horlicks powder and whisk until completely dissolved, then bring the mixture to a boil. Immediately remove from the heat.

2. Add the softened gelatin and stir until dissolved, then add the chocolate. Stir until the chocolate melts completely and the mixture is smooth. Stir in the milk and the vanilla extract, if using, then strain the mixture through a fine-mesh sieve. Divide among eight small serving cups or bowls and refrigerate, uncovered, until set, about 3 hours.

3. To make the green tea pudding: Put the milk, sugar, and salt in a small saucepan and warm over medium heat just until bubbles begin to form around the edges. Add the gelatin and stir until dissolved. Remove from the heat and let the mixture sit until it cools to room temperature.

4. Whisk the green tea powder and lemon juice into the gelatin mixture and continue whisking until the green tea powder dissolves completely. Strain the mixture through a fine-mesh sieve. Divide among eight small serving cups or bowls and refrigerate, uncovered, until set, about 3 hours.

5. To make the raspberry pudding: Put the raspberries, sugar, and salt in a medium saucepan, set over medium heat, and cook, stirring, until thick and syrupy, 10 minutes. Remove from the heat, add the gelatin, and stir until dissolved. Stir in the cream and lemon juice.

6. Divide the raspberry pudding among eight small serving cups or bowls and refrigerate, uncovered, until set, about 3 hours.

7. To serve, place a cup of each pudding on each serving plate. You can chill the puddings for up to 1 day. Top the puddings with the chantilly and garnishes, if desired.

■

SPICED CHOCOLATE PUDDING WITH CARAMEL CRISPED RICE CEREAL

Makes 8 servings

Forget what you know about chocolate pudding. Instead, imagine a softer, creamier version of a richly spiced handmade truffle. Then top that with light, crispy bits of caramel. Yes, this is as good as it sounds. And no, it's not at all difficult to make.

Spiced Chocolate Pudding

3 cups (24 ounces/681 grams) heavy whipping cream

8 cardamom pods

4 whole star anise

1 vanilla bean, split lengthwise in half, seeds scraped out, and seeds and pod reserved, or 2 teaspoons vanilla extract

½ teaspoon salt

3½ gelatin sheets, soaked in cold water and drained, or 2½ teaspoons powdered gelatin, softened in 3 tablespoons cold water

9½ ounces (269 grams) bittersweet chocolate, roughly chopped

1 cup (8 ounces/227 grams) whole milk

Caramel Crisped Rice Cereal

½ cup (3⅛ ounces/90 grams) sugar

⅓ cup (3½ ounces/100 grams) corn syrup

6 tablespoons (3 ounces/85 grams) unsalted butter

3½ cups (3 ounces/85 grams) crisped rice cereal, preferably Rice Krispies

¼ teaspoon salt

Drunken Cherries (page 174), optional

Sweetened Condensed Milk Chantilly (page 25), optional

1. To make the chocolate pudding: Put the cream, cardamom, star anise, vanilla seeds and pod, if using, and salt in a small saucepan and bring to a simmer over medium heat. Remove from the heat and let the mixture sit, uncovered, for 30 minutes.

2. Set the pan over medium-low heat, add the gelatin, and stir until dissolved. Add the chocolate and stir until melted and smooth. Stir in the milk and vanilla extract, if using, then remove from the heat and strain through a fine-mesh sieve. Divide among eight serving cups or bowls and refrigerate until set, at least 3 hours.

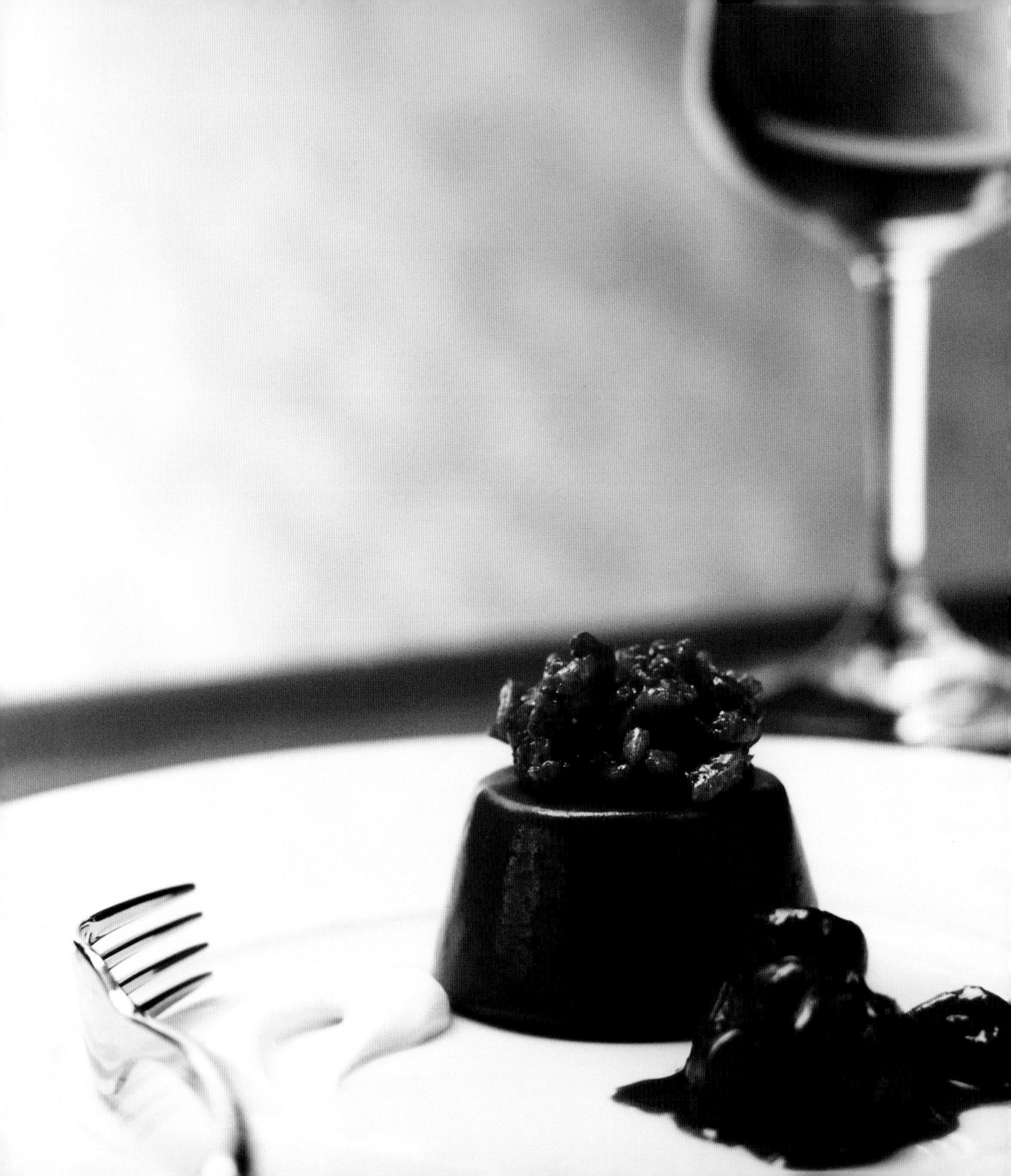

3. To make the caramel crisped rice cereal: Line a baking sheet with a nonstick baking mat or foil. Put the sugar, corn syrup, and butter in a medium saucepan and set over medium-high heat. Cook, swirling the pan occasionally to evenly dissolve the sugar, until the mixture becomes a medium-dark amber that registers 320°F on a candy thermometer, about 10 minutes.

4. Remove from the heat and stir the mixture well with a heatproof spatula, then add the cereal and salt and stir until all the cereal is well coated. Spread the caramelized cereal on the lined baking sheet, trying to separate the cereal into small clumps. Cool completely, until crisp. You can store the crisped cereal in an airtight container for up to 2 weeks.

5. To serve, unmold the puddings, if desired, and top with the caramel crisped cereal. If desired, garnish each with a spoonful of drunken cherries and a dollop of chantilly.

ALMOND TOFU AND FRESH FRUIT COCKTAIL

Makes 8 servings

This is my take on what is arguably the most popular dessert in Chinese restaurants around the world. From restaurants to potlucks to authentic home-cooked meals, almond tofu has been part of the Chinese dining scene since the 1960s. There isn't any tofu in the dessert—with its pristine white color and silky smooth texture it just closely resembles tofu. Although almond tofu is usually made with milk, I use soy and almond milk for a dairy-free delight. Most almond tofu is served with canned fruit cocktail, but I can't stand that muddled, mushy, overly sweet stuff. This fruit cocktail is fresh and complex with a medley of textures.

CHEF'S TIP: You can make both components ahead of time and assemble the dessert just before serving. For a more dramatic presentation, pour the almond tofu mixture into glasses and set the glasses on a rack or carton at an angle. Be sure to secure the glasses so that they do not tip over in the refrigerator.

Almond Tofu

1½ cups (12 ounces/336 grams) almond milk, preferably homemade (see page 20)

1 tablespoon powdered gelatin

1½ cups (12 ounces/336 grams) unsweetened, unflavored soy milk, preferably homemade (see page 20)

½ cup (3¾ ounces/106 grams) sugar

1 teaspoon almond oil or extract, optional

⅛ teaspoon salt

Fruit Cocktail

1 cup plus 2 tablespoons (7½ ounces/212 grams) sugar

¼ Asian pear, cut into ¼-inch dice

Eight 4-inch-long strips orange zest (removed with a vegetable peeler)

16 seedless red grapes, cut crosswise into ¼-inch slices

2 small peaches, pitted and cut into ¼-inch wedges

1. To make the almond tofu: Put the almond milk in a medium mixing bowl and sprinkle the gelatin over the milk. Set aside until softened, about 10 minutes.

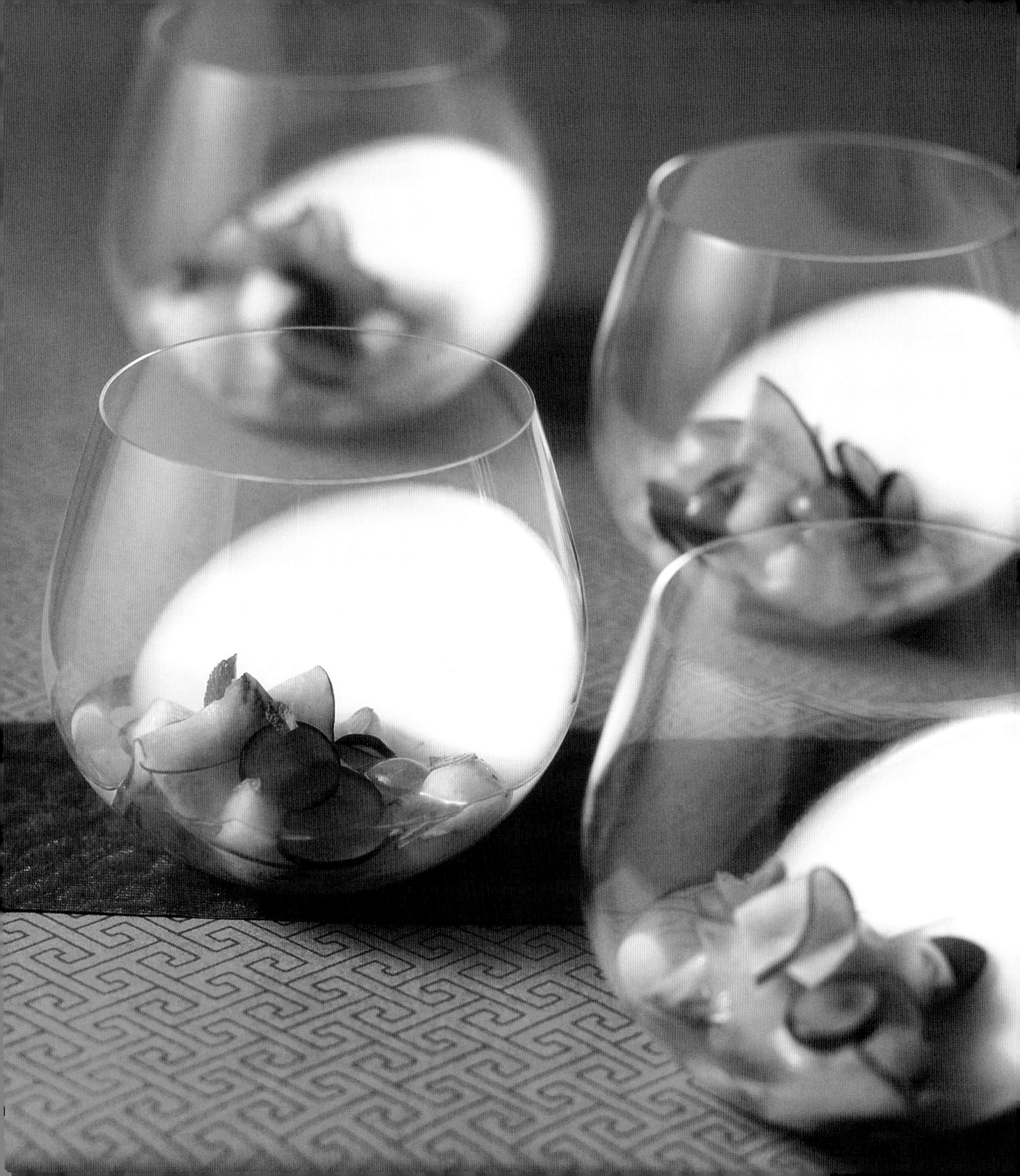

2. Meanwhile, put the soy milk and sugar into a large saucepan and warm over medium-high heat, stirring, just until the sugar is completely dissolved and bubbles begin to form around the edges of the pan. Remove from the heat and stir in the gelatin mixture until dissolved. Stir in the almond extract. Divide the mixture among eight serving bowls or glasses and refrigerate, uncovered, until set, about 3 hours.

3. Meanwhile, make the fruit cocktail: Put the sugar and 1 cup water in a small saucepan and bring to a boil over medium heat, stirring constantly. Boil, stirring, until the sugar dissolves and the syrup looks clear, about 2 minutes. Remove from the heat and add the pear and orange zest. Cool to room temperature.

4. Add the grapes and peaches to the fruit syrup. Refrigerate until ready to serve.

5. To serve, remove the orange zest from the fruit cocktail, and divide the fruit and syrup among the serving bowls.

■

THE FRUIT OF LIFE: COCONUTS

Some fruits symbolize life—coconuts sustain it. In many parts of South and Southeast Asia, coconut trees have helped generations survive. Every part of the coconut palm is useful. In Malaysia, in fact, coconut trees are called *pokok seribu guna*, "the tree of a thousand uses," while in the Philippines they are simply deemed "the tree of life." Thankfully, the usefulness of the coconut is more than matched by its luxurious flavor and texture. I find that Asian dishes bring out the best in this fruit.

Coconut meat, juice, and milk play an integral role in many Asian savory dishes, but they achieve their fullest expression in desserts. The simplest of these is a young green coconut with a hole drilled in it for a straw. The coconut juice sloshing around inside is floral and sweet, with light woody overtones, and the stiff straw is used to scrape the inside of the fruit so that chewy bits of fresh coconut meat are included in each refreshing gulp.

The creamy white coconut "milk" so popular in Asian desserts is actually made from the meat of the coconut. When coconuts are young and green, their flesh is tender, sweet, and juicy. As they age, their shells become harder and brown and their meat becomes firm and dry (and the minimal amount of juice remaining inside becomes quite bitter). The mature meat is grated and used as is, dried for the sake of those of us far away, or used to make coconut milk.

Coconut milk is made by soaking finely grated coconut meat in hot water and then straining it well. If the milk is then allowed to sit, the thick, rich solids rise to the top and become coconut cream. Of course, despite its creamy flavor and texture, there isn't actually any dairy in coconut milk or cream. The richness comes from the combination of the coconut oil and natural sugar.

Perhaps my favorite thing about coconut milk is its subtle floral, nutty flavor, which both pairs with and enhances nearly every other sweet. In this way, coconut milk is a kind of culinary chameleon, blending into its surroundings. But as generations of grateful Asians know, it's much more than that as well. I hope you enjoy a few of its thousand uses here.

COCONUT SQUARES

This recipe is for those who loved the fun, springy texture of Jell-O as a kid but left the generic flavors behind long ago. Here the coconut milk mixture strikes just the right balance between fruit and cream. A popular treat in Asian bakeries and dim sum houses, these coconut squares are often layered with other flavors of gelatin or served with fresh fruit and sponge cake.

¼ cup (2 ounces/58 grams) evaporated milk

½ cup (4⅜ ounces/125 grams) unsweetened coconut milk

¾ cup (4⅞ ounces/138 grams) sugar

⅛ teaspoon salt

2 gelatin sheets, soaked in cold water until softened and drained, or 1⅓ teaspoons powdered gelatin, softened in 1 tablespoon cold water

1 teaspoon coconut-flavored rum, preferably Malibu

2 large egg whites

1. Put the evaporated milk, coconut milk, ⅓ cup of the sugar, and the salt in a medium saucepan and bring to a boil over medium-high heat, whisking constantly. Boil, whisking, for 5 minutes.

2. Remove the mixture from the heat, add the softened gelatin, and stir until dissolved. Stir in the rum. Cool completely at room temperature.

3. Put the egg whites in the bowl of an electric mixer fitted with the whisk attachment. Whisk until frothy, then slowly add the remaining sugar with the machine running. Continue whisking until soft peaks form, about 5 minutes. (When you lift the whisk from the whites, a peak will form and fall back into the mixture.) Gently fold the whites into the cooled coconut mixture until fully incorporated.

4. Pour the mixture into a 9-inch square pan. Refrigerate, uncovered, until set, about 2 hours.

5. Cut the coconut dessert into 1½-inch cubes and serve chilled.

JASMINE RICE PUDDING

Makes 6 servings

The combination of jasmine rice and coconut milk is a classic one in both sweet and savory Asian dishes. With a refreshing scoop of Passion Fruit Sherbet to cut through the sweetness, this dessert became a favorite of many diners at Spice Market.

CHEF'S TIP: If you like the crunchy texture of burnt sugar as I do, sprinkle some sugar on top of the pudding and caramalize with a blow torch.

1 cup (8 ounces/227 grams) whole milk

1 cup (8 ounces/227 grams) skim milk

1 cup (9 ounces/255 grams) coconut milk

1 cinnamon stick

1 vanilla bean, split lengthwise in half, seeds scraped out, and seeds and pod reserved, or 2 teaspoons vanilla extract

1 teaspoon salt

1¼ cups (8⅞ ounces/250 grams) raw jasmine rice, rinsed well and drained

¾ cup (5 ounces/141 grams) sugar

¼ cup (1¼ ounces/34 grams) raisins, soaked in rum or water and drained

1¼ cups (10 ounces/283 grams) heavy whipping cream

1 teaspoon grated lime zest

Passion Fruit Sherbet (page 248), optional

1 tablespoon fresh passion fruit seeds for garnish, optional

1. Put the three milks, the cinnamon stick, and vanilla seeds and pod, if using, and salt in a large saucepan, stir well, and bring to a boil over medium-high heat. Add the rice and bring back to a boil, stirring and scraping the pan to make sure none of the rice sticks to the bottom. Turn the heat to low and simmer uncovered, stirring occasionally, until all the liquid has been absorbed by the rice and the rice is tender, about 30 minutes. Do not let the mixture brown at all.

2. Remove the rice from the heat and immediately add the sugar, stirring until it dissolves. Stir in the raisins. Set aside to cool completely.

3. Put the cream into the bowl of an electric mixer fitted with the whisk attachment. Whisk the cream at medium speed until soft peaks form. (When you lift the whisk from the cream, a peak will form and fall back into the mixture.)

4. When the rice mixture has completely cooled, fold in the whipped cream and lime zest. The pudding should be loose, with the rice kernels separated. Divide the pudding among serving bowls, top each with a scoop of Passion Fruit Sherbet and a few passion fruit seeds, if desired, and serve.

■

COCONUT BREAD PUDDING

Bread pudding is one of the easiest desserts to make and is ideal for using up stale bread. Adding a little coconut milk to the mixture makes this old standby more exciting. I don't like heavy, bready puddings, so I use only a thin slice of bread per serving here and let the light and flavorful custard dominate. It's still as substantial as the cafeteria version, but far more sublime.

¾ cup (4½ ounces/126 grams) crushed palm sugar

1 cup (9 ounces/255 grams) unsweetened coconut milk

⅛ teaspoon salt

1 cup (8 ounces/227 grams) half-and-half or ½ cup (4 ounces/113 grams) whole milk plus ½ cup (4 ounces/113 grams) heavy whipping cream

3 tablespoons dark rum

2 tablespoons unsalted butter, for greasing the ramekins

3 large eggs

8 slices stale white sandwich bread

1. Put the palm sugar and coconut milk in a medium saucepan and warm over medium heat, stirring occasionally, until the sugar has completely dissolved. Remove from the heat and stir in the salt. Pour the mixture into a large mixing bowl and stir in the half-and-half and rum. Set the mixing bowl in a larger bowl filled with ice and water and cool, stirring occasionally, until the mixture is cold to the touch.

2. Preheat the oven to 350°F. Generously butter eight 4-ounce ramekins and set aside.

3. Remove the coconut milk mixture from the ice water bath and whisk in the eggs until well combined. Divide the mixture among the ramekins, leaving ½ inch of room for the bread.

4. Use a 3-inch round cookie or biscuit cutter or a glass to cut circles out of the bread slices. Submerge a bread round in each ramekin, making sure it is completely soaked through, and let soften for 10 minutes.

5. Transfer the ramekins to a deep baking dish or roasting pan and fill with hot water up to the top of the pudding. Bake until a tester comes out clean, about 35 minutes. Remove from the oven and let cool before serving.

COCONUT PALM SUGAR FLAN

Makes 12 servings

Flan, a dessert frequently associated with Spain, is perhaps the one dessert found in every Asian country. Also known as crème caramel or custard, flan originated in Spain, was reinterpreted by the French and English, moved east, and took off. In Asia, the standard spiced cream version is far less popular than the coconut variety. This is for a good reason—the fruity aroma of coconut makes the custard tastier, richer, and more interesting.

CHEF'S TIPS: If you can't find palm sugar for the caramel, substitute white sugar. Simply bring it to a dark caramel before dividing it among the ramekins.

This flan is best when cooled completely at room temperature, then refrigerated for at least 4 hours and brought back to room temperature before serving. This allows the flavors to develop more fully and causes the custard to become so delicate it just melts in your mouth. Rest assured, though, that the flan is also delicious when served right away.

1⅔ cups (9 ounces/257 grams) crushed palm sugar

1 tablespoon fresh lemon juice

¾ teaspoon salt

2 cups (16 ounces/454 grams) whole milk

¾ cup (7 ounces/200 grams) unsweetened coconut milk

1 cup plus 2 tablespoons (3½ ounces/98 grams) finely shredded unsweetened dried coconut

¾ cup (5⅓ ounces/150 grams) sugar

¼ cup (2 ounces/58 grams) evaporated milk

4 large eggs

3 large egg yolks

1 tablespoon fleur de sel or Maldon salt, optional

1. Put the palm sugar, lemon juice, and ¼ cup water into a small saucepan, set over medium-high heat, and cook, stirring, to dissolve the sugar if necessary until the mixture becomes dark brown and registers 350°F on a candy thermometer, about 12 minutes. Remove from the heat and stir in ¼ teaspoon of the salt. Carefully divide the caramel among twelve 4-ounce ramekins.

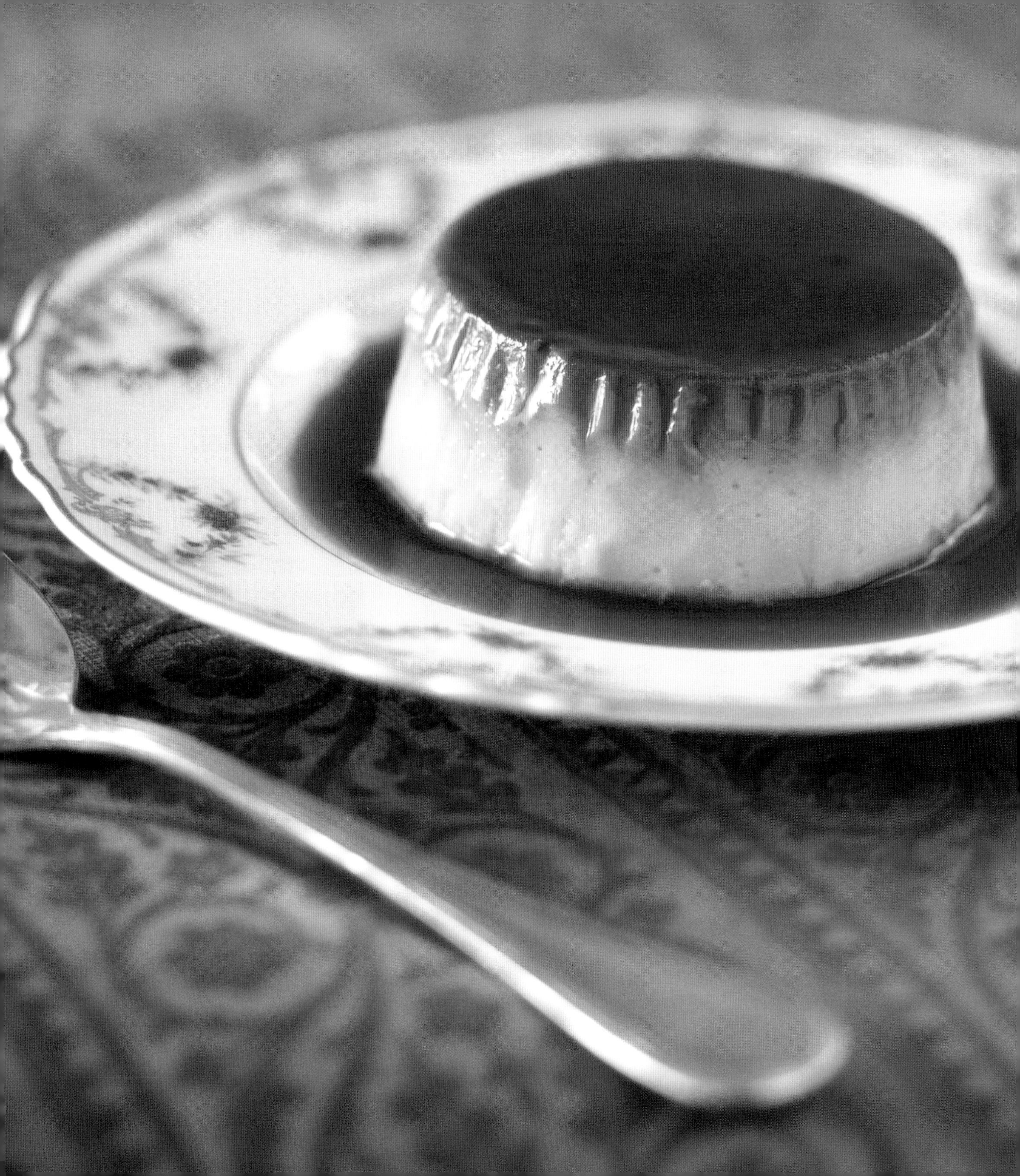

2. Put the milk, coconut milk, coconut, sugar, and the remaining ½ teaspoon salt into a medium saucepan, set over medium heat, and warm, stirring occasionally, until bubbles begin to form around the edges. Remove from the heat and let steep for 30 minutes.

3. Preheat the oven to 350°F.

4. Add the evaporated milk to the coconut mixture.

5. Whisk the eggs and egg yolks in a large mixing bowl until the yolks are broken, then add the milk mixture in a slow, steady stream, whisking constantly. Strain the mixture through a fine-mesh sieve into a bowl, pressing on the coconut to extract as much liquid as possible. Set the mixture in a larger bowl filled with ice and water and chill completely until cold.

6. Divide the coconut mixture among the prepared ramekins and put in a deep baking dish or roasting pan. Carefully pour enough hot water into the pan, without spilling any into the ramekins, to reach halfway up the ramekins. Bake until the flan is just set, about 45 minutes—the sides should be firm but the center still quite jiggly. Cool completely in the pan.

7. Serve the flan once it has cooled or, for even better results, cover and refrigerate for at least 4 hours. Invert the flans onto serving plates. If the flan seems stuck, run a thin-bladed knife around the edges of each ramekin, and then invert. Sprinkle each flan with fleur de sel, if desired.

■

A GIFT FROM INDIA: FRESH CHEESE

In India, a large proportion of the population practice religions that encourage and sometimes require vegetarianism. Milk and its products—butter, yogurt, and cheese—are the primary protein source for many, and cow's milk is one of the most sacred food items in Hinduism.

Indian cheese—a fresh, soft cheese similar to Italian ricotta—is called *paneer* when in cake form and *chenna* when in curd form. Since neither form is readily available in your neighborhood markets here, it is best to make your own. This is one instance in which cheese making is remarkably easy. Simply curdle milk with buttermilk or with lemon juice (which produces the softest curds) and let drain until the desired consistency.

The dry curds that constitute chenna are both chewy and delicate. Because no salt is added in the cheese-making process, chenna also has a faint sweetness that works beautifully in desserts. The distinct flavor and subtle creaminess of the cheese enhance sweets without overpowering them.

Chenna is often cooked to increase its flavor and delicacy, as it is in rasmalai, where the cooked cheese is known as ras. I also enjoy it fresh, paired with other vibrant flavors, which I do here. Indeed, I consider fresh cheese for dessert a divine gift from India.

DRUNKEN CHERRIES WITH ORANGE BLOSSOM CHENNA

Makes 8 servings

This simple dessert is based on the pairing of fresh milk cheese with three of my favorite flavors: cherries, orange blossom, and sake. Chances are you've never had a dessert made with both sake and balsamic vinegar. The convergence of three great culinary traditions—Indian, Italian, and Japanese—in one mouthful is fusion at its best.

CHEF'S TIPS: You can buy chenna in Indian markets, or make it yourself by following through step 2 the ras recipe in Rasmalai with Rose Water and Pistachios (page 177). Or strain all the liquid out of fresh ricotta cheese, through a fine-mesh sievel as a substitute.

You can make both the chenna and cherries ahead of time and assemble the dessert just before serving.

Orange Blossom Chenna

1⅓ cups (15 ounces/425 grams) chenna

¼ cup plus 2 tablespoons (3½ ounces/100 grams) sour cream

⅓ cup (2½ ounces/70 grams) sugar

2 tablespoons grated orange zest, plus more for garnish

2 teaspoons orange blossom water

½ teaspoon salt

Drunken Cherries

2 pounds (907 grams) cherries, stemmed and pitted

2 tablespoons sugar

1 tablespoon balsamic vinegar

½ vanilla bean, split lengthwise in half, seeds scraped out, and seeds and pod reserved, or 1 teaspoon vanilla extract

¼ cup (2 ounces/56 grams) sake

¼ cup (1⅛ ounces/31 grams) shelled pistachios, toasted and salted, for garnish

1. To make the chenna: Lightly mix all the ingredients together in a bowl until combined. Cover and refrigerate.

2. To make the drunken cherries: Put all the ingredients into a large mixing bowl and stir well. Cover and refrigerate for 4 to 6 hours; do not let sit overnight.

3. To serve, remove the vanilla bean, and divide the cherries and the juices among 8 glasses. Top with the chenna, garnish with the pistachios and orange zest, and serve.

■

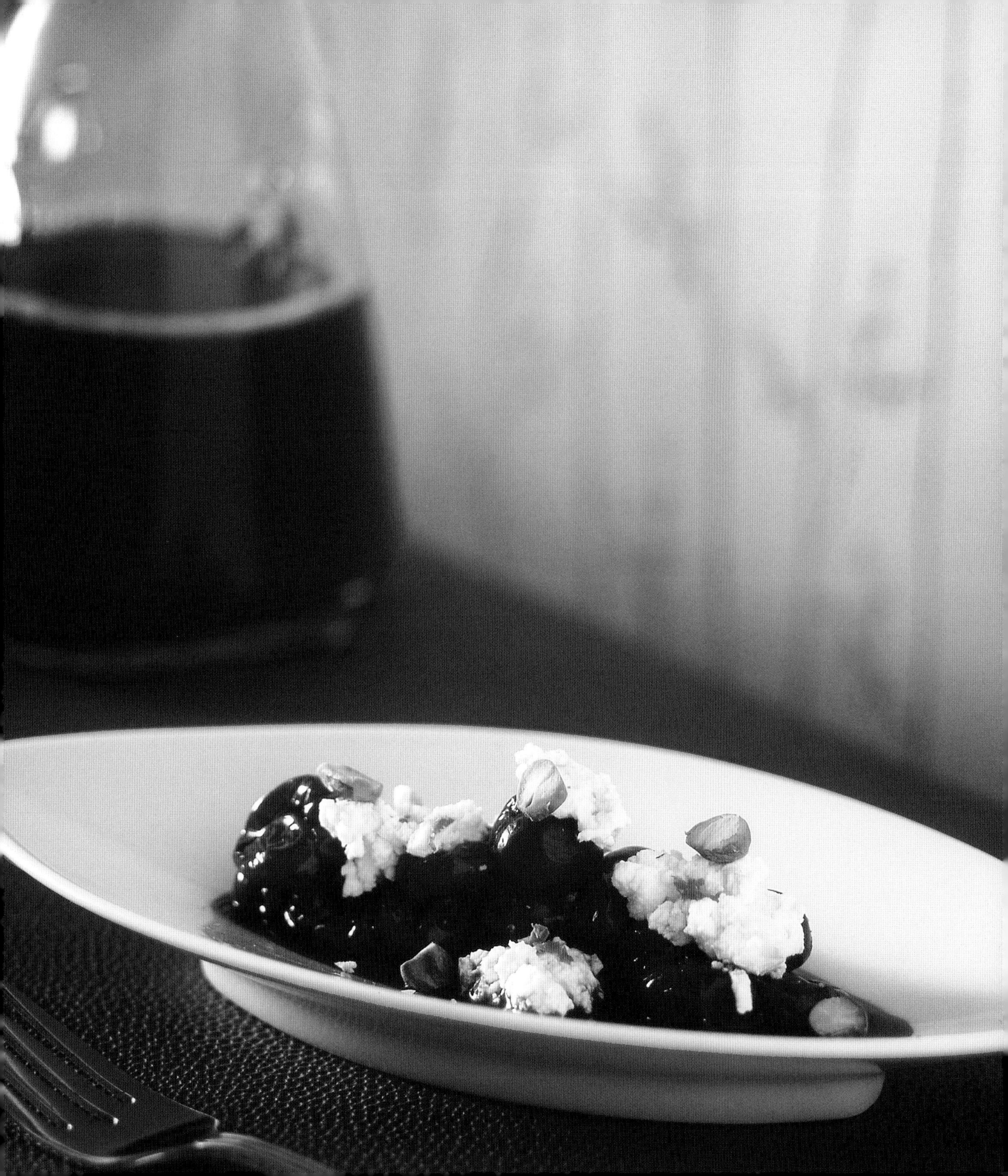

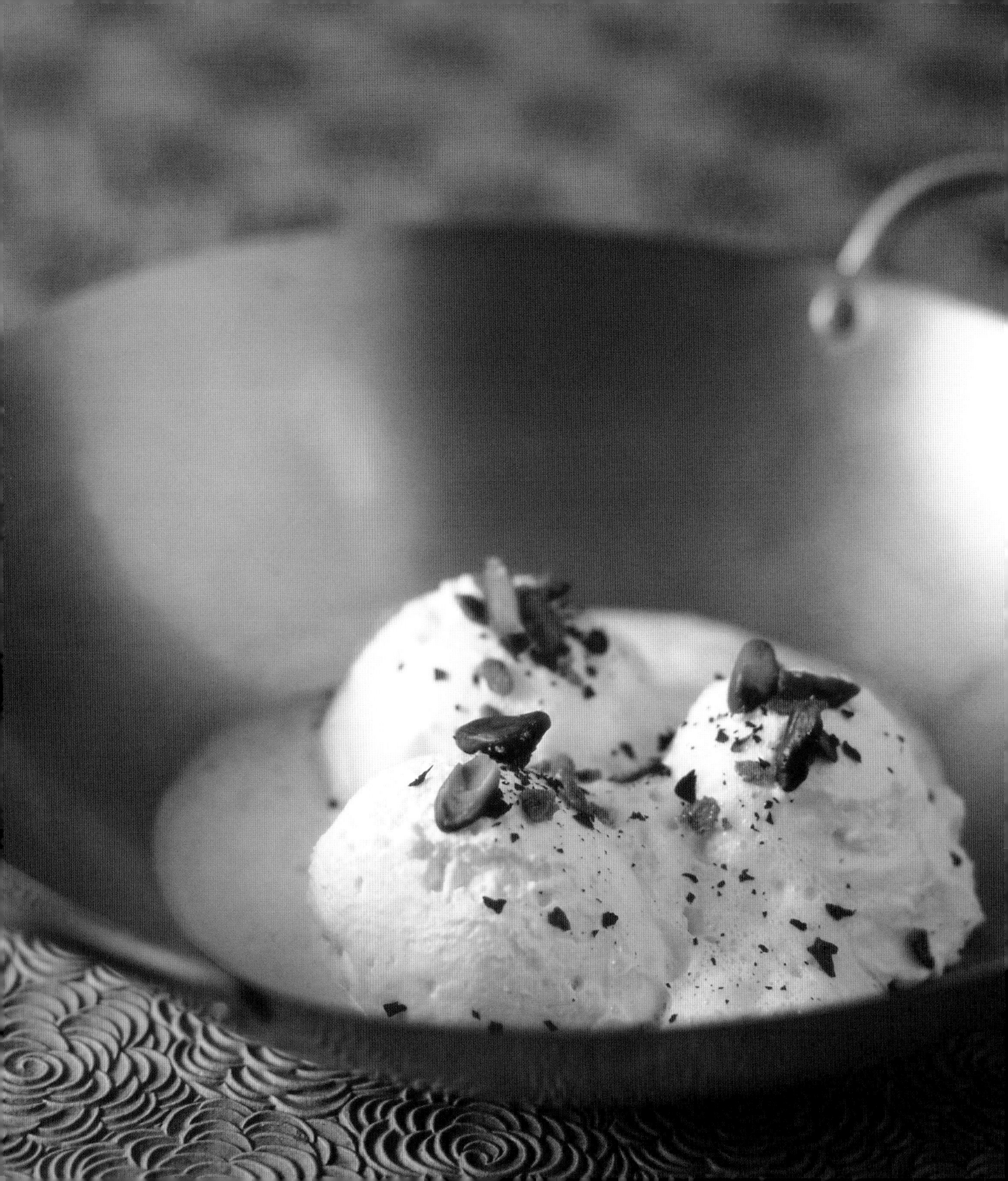

RASMALAI WITH ROSE WATER AND PISTACHIOS

Makes 8 servings

This Punjabi specialty is a creamy dessert that manages to be both richly scrumptious and ethereally light. The key is the fresh cheese, which is very easy to make. The resulting velvety cheese dumplings are swathed in a reduced milk sauce scented with rose water. The pistachios add a salty edge and satisfying crunch.

CHEF'S TIP: Use a high-quality organic milk for the best-tasting dessert.

Ras

3 quarts (96 ounces/2,683 grams) milk

⅓ cup (2⅔ ounces/75 grams) fresh lemon juice

1 tablespoon sugar

3 tablespoons all-purpose flour

¼ teaspoon salt

Rose-Scented Malai

1 cup (8 ounces/227 grams) whole milk

1 cup (8 ounces/227 grams) heavy whipping cream

2 tablespoons plus 1 teaspoon sugar

1 cinnamon stick

1 teaspoon dried rose petals, plus more for garnish

4 cardamom pods

⅛ teaspoon salt

¾ teaspoon rose water

¼ cup (1⅛ ounces/31 grams) shelled pistachios, toasted and salted, plus more for garnish

1. To make the ras: Put the milk in a large saucepan and bring to a boil over medium-high heat. As soon as it boils, remove from the heat and stir in the lemon juice. The mixture should curdle within 10 seconds. If it doesn't, set the pan over low heat and stir slowly until most of the milk has curdled, then remove from the heat.

2. Set a fine-mesh sieve lined with cheesecloth over a large mixing bowl, with at least 2 inches between the bottom of the sieve and the bottom of the bowl. Strain the milk

mixture through the sieve, and let sit for at least 20 minutes. (If you plan to let this sit for more than 30 minutes, cover the bowl with plastic wrap and refrigerate.)

3. When all the liquid has been drained, transfer the cheese remaining in the cheesecloth to the bowl of an electric mixer fitted with the paddle attachment. Add the sugar, flour, and salt and mix on medium speed until well incorporated, about 5 minutes.

4. Scoop the cheese into 1½-inch balls with your hands, press into little patties about 2 inches in diameter and 1 inch thick, and set on a plate. Set aside.

5. To make the malai: Put all of the ingredients into a large saucepan, stir well, and set over medium heat. Bring to a steady simmer and cook, stirring, until reduced by half and thickened, about 10 minutes.

6. Add the cheese dumplings to the malai and cook, stirring gently, for 2 minutes, then turn the dumplings over and cook for 2 minutes more. Divide the cheese dumplings and sauce among eight serving bowls, discarding the cinnamon stick and cardamom pods. Garnish with the pistachios and rose petals and serve warm.

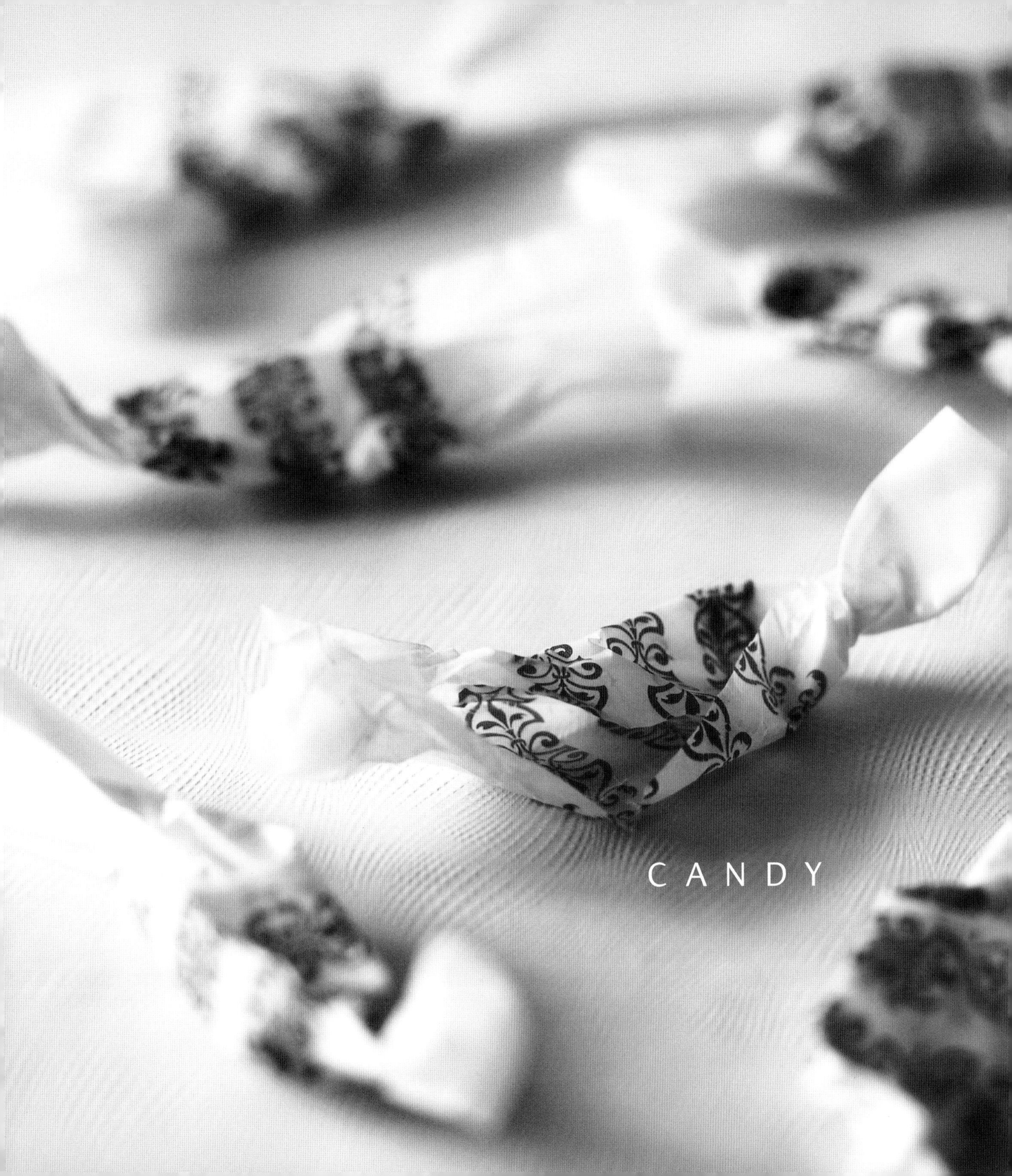

CANDY

With row upon row of packaged candies in the supermarket, why make your own? Isn't it a lot of work for something not any better than what you could get at the store? Truth is, homemade candy is surprisingly easy to make and significantly better than store-bought versions.

Chances are you have all the equipment you need to make candy except a candy thermometer, which is very handy for making caramels. I set my candies in standard baking pans and then cut them to the shapes and sizes I want. Most candies are made on the stovetop and set at room temperature, meaning you don't have to fuss with a hot oven.

The best candy-making tip is this: To clean the hardened caramel off a saucepan, put water in the pan, cover, and bring to a boil. The boiling water will dissolve the sugar right off.

Once you make chocolates or caramels, you'll realize just how easy it is. The Asian-inspired rice-based candies here are even easier. Although rice may not sound like a candy flavor you crave, it produces a chewiness not unlike that of gumdrops. Think how good *fresh* gumdrops made with natural ingredients would taste and you'll have some idea of what's in store for you in these recipes.

MILK CHOCOLATE AND PEANUT BARS

Makes 8 servings

Peanuts, long popular in traditional Asian desserts, have become even more so with the introduction of Western-style candy bars to Asia. This is my interpretation of Reese's Peanut Butter Cups.

CHEF'S TIP: If you love peanut butter, you can spread a final layer of creamy peanut butter over the top of the whole frozen candy bar. Bring to room temperature before serving for the best flavor and texture.

Peanut Chocolate Base

1 tablespoon plus 1 teaspoon canola, vegetable, or other neutral oil, plus more for greasing the pan

4 ounces (113 grams) milk chocolate, chopped

½ cup (4¼ ounces/120 grams) peanuts, toasted and chopped

¼ teaspoon salt

Peanut Butter Chocolate Filling

3½ ounces (99 grams) milk chocolate, chopped

½ cup plus 2 tablespoons (5 ounces/140 grams) heavy whipping cream

3 tablespoons cream cheese, at room temperature

3 tablespoons creamy peanut butter, preferably all-natural, plus ½ cup (4½ ounces/128 grams) for garnish, optional

¼ teaspoon vanilla extract

¼ teaspoon fleur de sel or other mild sea salt, such as Maldon, optional

1. To make the chocolate base: Lightly grease a 9 × 4-inch loaf pan and set aside. Bring a small saucepan of water to a boil and remove from the heat. Put the chocolate in a heat-proof bowl and set over the saucepan. Stir the chocolate just until melted, then add the peanuts, salt, and oil and stir well.

2. Pour the chocolate mixture into the prepared loaf pan and spread into an even layer. Freeze, uncovered, until hard.

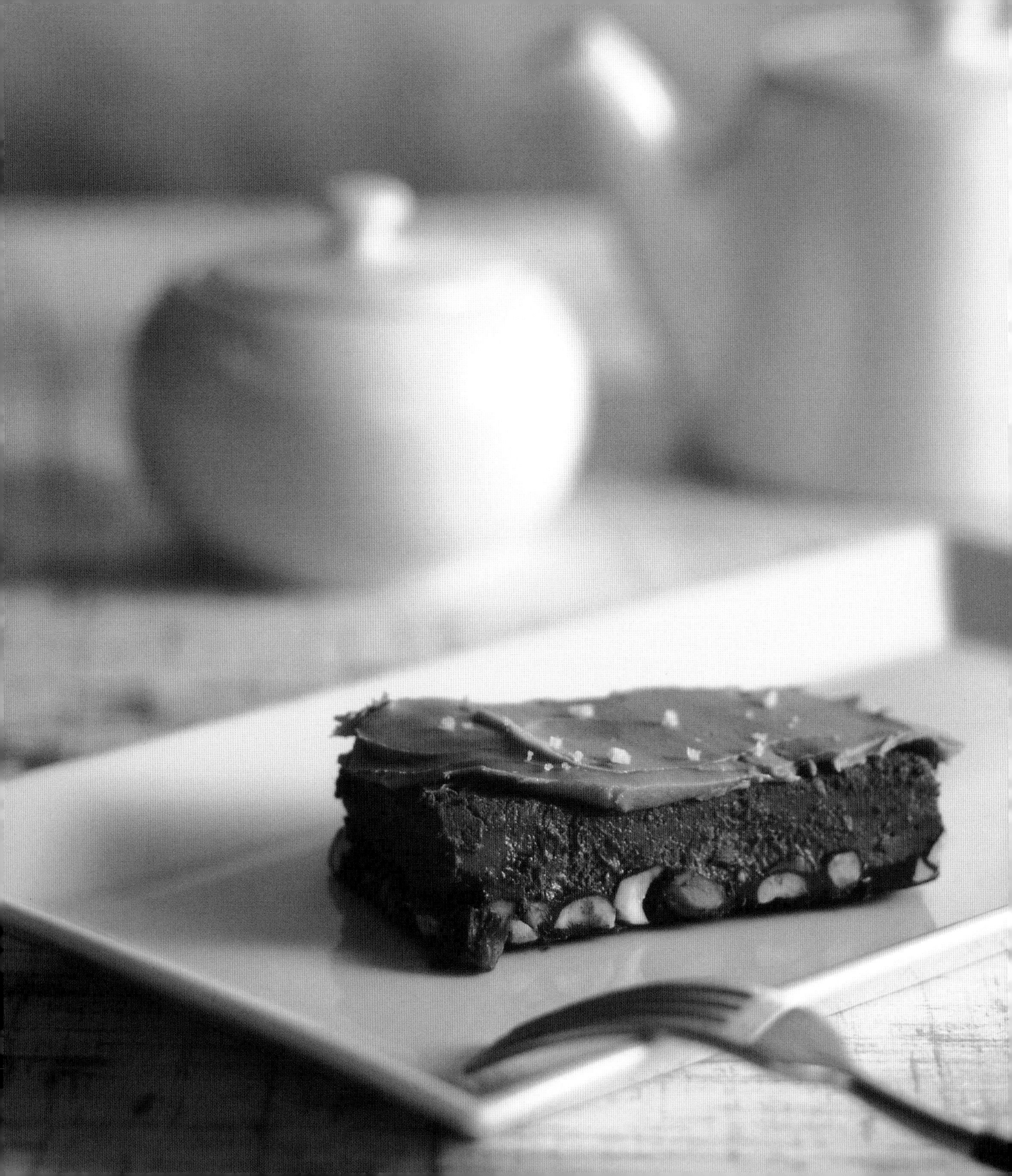

3. Meanwhile, make the filling: Bring a small saucepan of water to a boil and remove from the heat. Put the chocolate in a heatproof bowl and set over the saucepan. Stir the chocolate just until melted, then remove the bowl, and set aside.

4. Whisk the cream in an electric mixer fitted with the whisk attachment until medium peaks form. (When you lift the whisk from the cream, a peak will form and the very tip of the peak will fall back down.) Transfer to another bowl and set aside.

5. Put the cream cheese, peanut butter, and vanilla extract into the bowl of the electric mixer fitted with the paddle attachment. Beat on medium speed until light, fluffy, and doubled in volume, about 7 minutes. Scrape down the sides and bottom of the bowl, turn the mixer speed to low, and add the melted chocolate in a slow, steady stream. Once all the chocolate has been incorporated, gently fold in the whipped cream.

6. Spread the filling on the frozen peanut chocolate base in an even layer and freeze until hard, at least 2 hours.

7. To unmold, invert the loaf pan onto a cutting board and gently tap the bottom to release the chocolate bar. Spread the peanut butter on top and sprinkle on the fleur de sel, if desired. Use a sharp serrated knife to cut the loaf crosswise into 1-inch-wide bars. Let come to room temperature before serving, or store in the refrigerator, covered, for up to 1 week.

STICKY, CHEWY, SAVORY, SWEET:
CARAMELS

Caramel is a universal treat, and every cuisine has its own way of coaxing the best out of the sticky, sugary sweetness. Techniques and flavors vary, of course, and so do the sugars from which the caramel originates.

In China, rock sugar is the most common sweetener. Less sweet than white sugar, it comes in amber or cloudy crystals and dissolves readily when cooked in water. Dessert makers in India and Southeast Asia often rely on sugars derived from palm trees and coconut. Palm sugar ranges in color from tan to dark brown and in texture from thick and honey-like to hard and crumbly. Although palm sugar is actually sweeter than white sugar, it also has complex aromatics that make it perfect for both sweet and savory dishes. Coconut sugar, known as jaggery in India, comes in dark brown blocks and is used primarily for confections.

I often experiment with different types of sugars, but I also have found that granulated white sugar can be manipulated easily to achieve different caramel flavors. While the American version of caramel is supersweet, soft, and sticky, Asian caramels take a gentler approach.

Chinese caramels tend to be only slightly sweet. One of the most popular desserts in China is fruit dipped into a hot caramel and then immediately transferred to a bowl of ice water so that the caramel quickly hardens into a brittle candy coating. Caramel-coated nuts—hard, crunchy, and sweet-savory—are another Chinese favorite. Chewy Chinese caramels are often made from maltose, a soft malt sugar that's like honey in texture when warmed, but much less sweet.

In Vietnam, sugar is often cooked to a dark caramel with a bitter edge that lends an intense complexity to both savory and sweet dishes. Indian caramels also feature complex flavors, although these usually originate in the spices added to heighten the already fragrant palm or coconut sugar. Other Southeast Asian countries make caramels from the sugar derived from the sap of coconut trees. Chewy and fruity, these candies have a rich tropical flavor.

Cooked in the right way, caramels can take on some fantastic characteristics. The following caramels work both as sweet endings to a meal or as midafternoon treats. Be warned—these are addictive snacks.

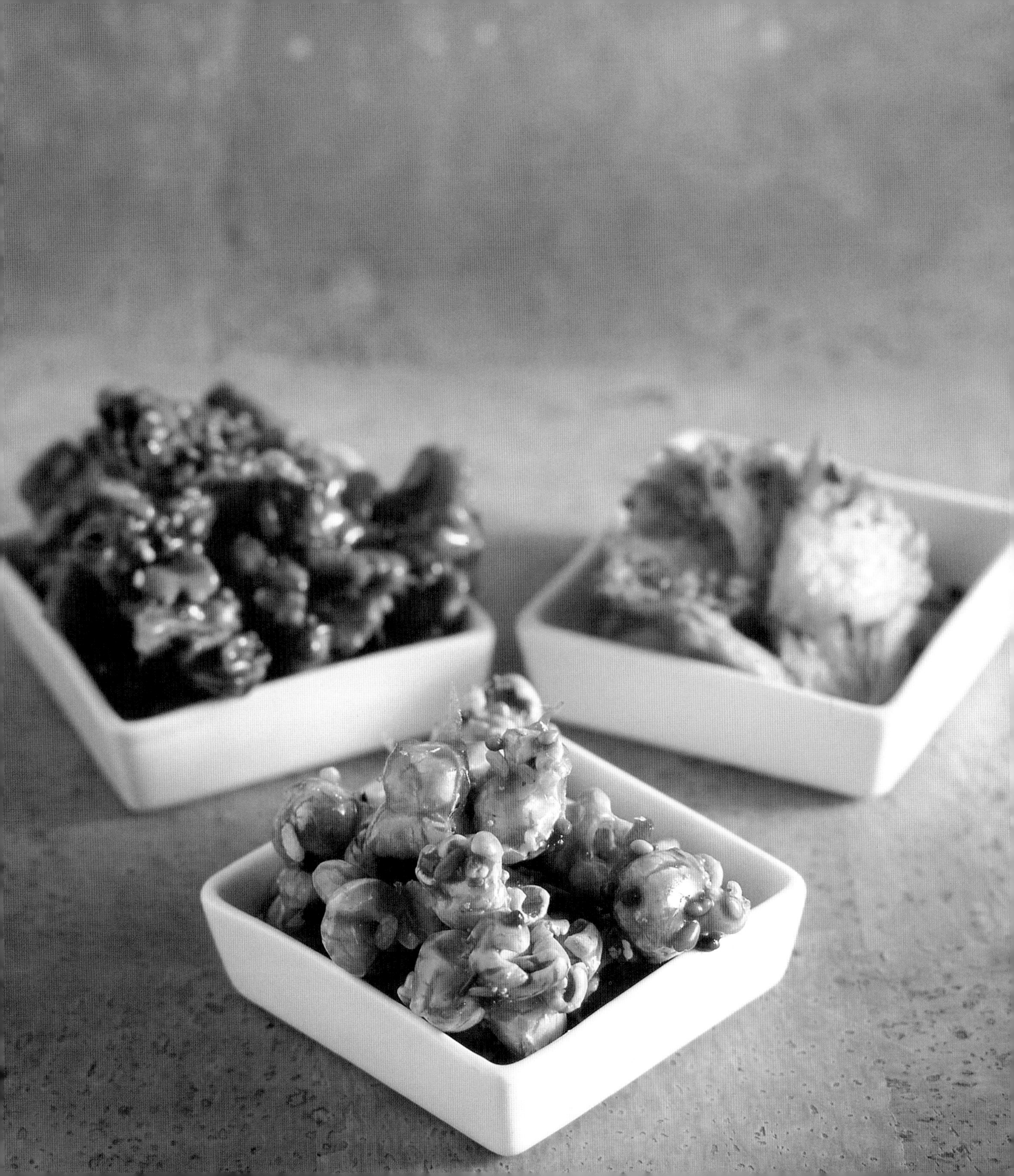

SALT AND PEPPER
CASHEW DRAGÉES

Makes 3½ cups

Nicole Plue, the pastry chef whose desserts have awed diners in highly acclaimed restaurants from New York to California, created these Asian-inspired sweet, salty, and spicy cashew dragées. Dragées are typically decorative almond candies with a hard sugar coating. Nicole usually coats her cashew version in chocolate, but with or without the chocolate, these candies pack a fantastic crunch. A touch of sesame oil accentuates the nuttiness of these mouthwatering sweet and savory treats. They are perfect with cocktails or as a snack any time of day.

3½ cups (18⅔ ounces/530 grams) unsalted cashews

¾ cup (5⅔ ounces/160 grams) sugar

1½ tablespoons fresh lemon juice

1 teaspoon unsalted butter

½ teaspoon Asian (dark) sesame oil

½ teaspoon salt

¼ teaspoon freshly ground black pepper

1. Preheat the oven to 325°F.

2. Spread the cashews in a single layer on a rimmed baking sheet and toast in the oven until fragrant and lightly browned, about 10 minutes. Remove from the oven and cool completely.

3. Line a baking sheet with a nonstick baking mat or aluminum foil and set aside. Put the sugar, lemon juice, and ¼ cup water in a medium saucepan, set over medium-high heat, and cook, shaking the pan occasionally to evenly dissolve the sugar, until the mixture becomes a dark amber and registers 350°F on a candy thermometer, about 5 minutes. Remove from the heat, add the butter, sesame oil, salt, and pepper, and immediately stir rapidly and carefully until fully incorporated. Add the cashews and stir until they are evenly coated with the caramel.

4. Transfer the coated nuts to the lined baking sheet and carefully separate them with a heatproof spatula. Cool completely. Store these candies in an airtight container for up to 2 weeks.

HONEY-GLAZED WALNUTS

Makes 2½ cups

These walnuts are my father's favorite snack. He likes to start his meals with them—even breakfast. These light, crunchy, candied, and sesame-coated walnuts can be found in almost every Cantonese restaurant, most commonly in the popular shrimp stir-fry with walnuts. I also use them as a topping for ice cream sundaes.

CHEF'S TIP: Boiling the walnuts in salted water first results in the lightest candied walnuts. They become so crisp and crumbly they seen almost hollow.

2½ cups (9⅞ ounces/280 grams) walnut halves

1 teaspoon salt

¾ cup (5 ounces/140 grams) sugar

Canola, vegetable, or other neutral oil for deep-frying

1 tablespoon honey

1 tablespoon maltose or additional honey

¼ cup white sesame seeds

1. Bring 4 cups water to a boil in a medium saucepan over high heat. Add the walnuts and salt and boil for 5 minutes. Drain, rinse under cold running water, and drain again.

2. Line a rimmed baking sheet with a nonstick baking mat or foil. Put the sugar and drained walnuts in the same saucepan and bring to a boil over medium heat. Cook, stirring constantly, until the walnuts have a thick, shiny, sticky coating of melted sugar, about 2 minutes. The melted sugar should still be clear, not caramelized or browned. Spread the walnuts out on the baking sheet in a single layer and let cool and dry for 10 minutes.

3. Fill a saucepan with oil to a depth of 2 inches and heat the oil to 300°F. When the oil is ready, add the walnuts and fry, carefully stirring constantly, until crisp and golden brown, about 4 minutes. Transfer the walnuts to a fine-mesh sieve set over a bowl and blot dry with paper towels. Let dry completely in the sieve. Set the baking sheet aside.

4. Put 2 tablespoons water in a medium saucepan and bring to a boil over high heat, then stir in the honey and maltose until well blended. Add the walnuts and sesame seeds and stir well to coat. Transfer to the lined baking sheet and cool completely. The nuts can be stored in an airtight container for up to 2 weeks.

■

CHINESE DELIGHT

Makes 36 pieces

These candies are *very* chewy. The combination of dates and nuts is classically Middle Eastern, as in Turkish delight, but Chinese confectioners have adopted the combination as their own. You will often see versions of this easy-to-make candy around the Chinese New Year. A celebratory gift, they are traditionally wrapped in thin rice paper, but plastic wrap works just as well.

CHEF'S TIP: Maltose gives this candy its distinctive subtle sweetness and chewy texture. It can be found in most Asian or natural food markets.

2 tablespoons canola, vegetable, or other neutral oil, plus more for greasing the pan

3 cups (11⅛ ounces/314 grams) walnut halves

9 (7 ounces/200 grams) dried dates, preferably Medjool or Barhi, pitted

¾ teaspoon salt

2 cups (22¼ ounces/632 grams) maltose

1 teaspoon ground cinnamon

1. Preheat the oven to 300°F. Lightly grease a 9 × 4-inch loaf pan, line with plastic wrap, and grease the plastic wrap. Set aside.

2. Put the walnuts on a rimmed baking sheet and toast in the oven until golden brown and fragrant, about 10 minutes. Remove from the oven and cool completely.

3. Bring 4 cups water to a boil in a medium saucepan. Add the dates and ½ teaspoon of the salt and cook for 10 minutes. Drain and spread the dates in a single layer on a cooling rack to dry.

4. Microwave the maltose on high heat until softened, about 40 seconds. Put the maltose, walnuts, dates, cinnamon, oil, and the remaining ¼ teaspoon salt in a medium sauce-pan and set over medium heat. Cook, stirring vigorously, until the mixture is thick, about 15 minutes. Remove from the heat and cool slightly in the pan, then transfer to

the cake pan. Spread in an even layer and let cool completely and harden at room temperature.

5. To unmold, invert the candy onto a cutting board and peel off the plastic wrap. Cut into 1-inch cubes with a greased knife. The candies can be individually wrapped in plastic wrap and stored at room temperature for up to 1 week.

■

COCONUT CARAMEL SQUARES

Makes 64 caramels

Throughout South and Southeast Asia, coconut candies are often made with coconut sugar, known in India as jaggery. The intense, complex flavors of coconut sugar can be an acquired taste, so I've created my own version using white sugar and coconut milk. The result is a soft and chewy creamy caramel that everyone will love.

CHEF'S TIP: Caramel is hot, so add the liquids at an arm's length, preferably using a ladle. Stir gently, and if the mixture bubbles up too much, remove from the heat and wait until it subsides a little before stirring again.

2 teaspoons canola, vegetable, or other neutral oil, plus more for greasing the pan

1½ cups (10⅜ ounces/294 grams) sugar

1 tablespoon fresh lemon juice

¼ cup (2⅞ ounces/80 grams) corn syrup

¼ cup (2 ounces/57 grams) heavy whipping cream

¾ cup plus 2 tablespoons (8 ounces/226 grams) unsweetened coconut milk

¼ cup (2 ounces/57 grams) unsalted butter

¼ cup (2 ounces/57 grams) coconut-flavored rum, preferably Malibu

⅛ teaspoon salt

1 teaspoon fleur de sel or other mild sea salt, such as Maldon, optional

1. Lightly grease an 8-inch square cake pan and set aside. Put the sugar in a large saucepan and moisten with the lemon juice and corn syrup. Set over high heat and cook to a medium caramel, constantly swirling the saucepan over the flame to evenly cook the sugar. The caramel should be a golden brown amber and register 325°F on a candy thermometer.

2. Remove the caramel from the heat and add the cream, coconut milk, butter, rum, and salt, whisking vigorously. The mixture will bubble up—be careful not to burn yourself. Set the pan over high heat, with the candy thermometer set in the pan, and continue whisking until the mixture reaches 245°F. (This is known as the "firm ball" stage—if you drop a bit of the mixture into ice water, it will make a firm ball.)

3. Transfer the mixture to the greased cake pan. While still hot, sprinkle with the fleur de sel, and let cool completely at room temperature.

4. When the caramel has completely cooled and set, cut it into ½-inch squares with a lightly greased knife. The caramels can be individually wrapped in plastic wrap and stored at room temperature for up to 2 weeks.

SPICED CARAMEL POPCORN

As a kid, I loved Cracker Jacks. A prize hidden among sticky sweet pieces of popcorn? Ingenious. But as an adult, I've discovered that, unfortunately, the prize is the best part of Cracker Jacks. Homemade caramel corn is infinitely better and not at all difficult to make.

To give the popcorn a little kick, I add mukwa, Indian candied fennel seeds. These look like neon sprinkles but have an anise aroma under their candy crunch.

CHEF'S TIPS: Mukwa is available at Indian markets or ask your neighborhood Indian restaurant if you can buy some.

½ cup (4 ounces/113 grams) unsalted butter, at room temperature

1 teaspoon salt

1 teaspoon baking soda

2⅓ cups (16 ounces/450 grams) sugar

2 tablespoons corn syrup

1½ tablespoons fresh lemon juice

11 cups (4⅛ ounces/117 grams) plain unsalted popcorn

½ cup mukwa (candied fennel seeds)

¼ cup poppy seeds

1. Preheat the oven to 275°F. Line two baking sheets with nonstick baking mats or parchment paper and set aside.

2. Mix together the butter, salt, and baking soda and set aside.

3. Put the sugar and corn syrup in a large deep skillet and moisten with the lemon juice and 2 tablespoons water. Set over high heat and stir until well combined. Cook, undisturbed, until the caramel begins to color, about 3 minutes. Continue to cook, stirring occasionally, until it becomes a deep golden brown, about 7 minutes. Remove from the heat and add the butter mixture, stirring very carefully. Once the butter is completely incorporated, add the popcorn and stir well to coat the kernels evenly.

4. Transfer the caramel popcorn to the lined deep baking dish or roasting pans and spread into an even layer. Bake until dry, about 10 minutes. Remove from the oven and carefully stir again to coat the popcorn evenly with the caramel. Bake for another 10 minutes. Stir in mukwa and poppyseeds and bake for 1 more minute.

5. Remove from oven and invert dish onto a work surface. Working very quickly with your hands, separate popcorn into small bite-size clusters in an even layer, and let cool completely. It can be stored in an airtight container at room temperature for up to 1 week.

Spiced Caramel Popcorn Crust: To use the popcorn as a topping, transfer the cooled caramelized popcorn to gallon-size resealable plastic bags, filling each bag halfway. Seal the bags, squeezing out all of the air, then use a heavy skillet or rolling pin to crush the mixture into tiny pieces. Store in an airtight container at room temperature for up to 1 week.

■

STICKY RICE TREATS

As a basic starch, rice seems an unlikely basis for candy. Who would ever think of eating, say, potatoes for dessert? But, as much of Asia knows, short sweet rice grains have a unique chewiness and subtle sweetness perfect for confections. More important, sticky rice treats have become integral to Lunar New Year celebrations, the most important holiday throughout Asia. Rounds of sticky rice, symbolizing unity, are served at family gatherings and offered to ancestors on altars.

There are countless varieties of rice, each with its own distinctive flavor and texture. The types used for desserts tend to have a large amount of starch, which makes them sticky and chewy. Glutinous rice, often called sweet or sticky rice, itself comes in several varieties. Japanese *mochigome* rice has grains that are very short, almost round. Chinese sticky rice grains, called *louw maiy,* are similar but slightly firmer. Thai sticky rice is actually a variety of long-grained jasmine rice with a lovely floral aroma and a rich chew. Unlike Japanese and Chinese desserts, in which the rice is pounded into a uniform mass, Thai dessert recipes tend to use the sticky rice as is.

Japanese mochi is probably the most popular sticky rice dessert. Traditionally, soaked and steamed mochi rice is pounded in a wide *usu,* or mortar, with a *kine,* a large pestle that more closely resembles a giant hammer. To ensure consistency, the rice is pounded by one person, while another person turns the warm rice in the bowl between each strike of the *kine.* In America, it's not difficult to find mochi rice powder—the most widely available brand is Mochiko—which is virtually foolproof and yields good results.

Mochi cakes are grilled, broiled, used in soups, wrapped in seaweed, or served as a dessert or sweet snack. They are often filled with a sweet red adzuki bean or sesame paste, but the mochi itself may also be flavored. With coffee and chocolate mochi now nearly as common as the traditional green tea and red bean varieties, both the flavors and fillings commonly used reflect the prevalence of Western cuisine throughout Japan.

YUZU MOCHI

Plain mochi is little more than chewy rice. To give it flavor, it's put into soups, topped with sweet soy sauce, or filled with sweet pastes and ice cream. But even these gussied-up mochi dishes are generally still a little bland, so I flavor the mochi itself. Yuzu, a distinctively tart citrus juice from Japan, gives mochi a great tang. Enjoy these as a dessert or a snack any time of day.

CHEF'S TIP: Mochiko flour is a good brand which is available in most Asian and specialty markets. Potato starch is available in most Asian markets.

2 teaspoons canola, vegetable, or other neutral oil for greasing the pan

1 cup (5 ounces/142 grams) mochi rice flour

¾ cup (4¾ ounces/136 grams) sugar

2 teaspoons yuzu juice or 1 tablespoon fresh lemon juice

3 tablespoons potato starch

1 tablespoon confectioners' sugar

⅛ teaspoon salt

1 teaspoon grated lemon zest

1. Lightly grease an 8-inch square cake pan with the oil. Set aside.

2. Put the rice flour, sugar, yuzu juice, and ⅔ cup cold water in a large microwave-safe bowl and whisk together until the sugar dissolves. Microwave on the high setting for 4 minutes. The mixture should be sticky and a little wet. Stir vigorously with a rubber spatula, then microwave for another 2 minutes. Stir again and continue microwaving in 2-minute increments until the mixture is stretchy, soft, and dry and no longer smells like raw rice flour; it is overcooked if it bubbles or hardens. Since microwaves heat at different rates, start checking carefully after 8 minutes; it should take a total of about 10 minutes.

3. Transfer the mixture to the greased cake pan and spread evenly. Cool completely.

4. Lightly dust the mochi, a serving plate, and a sharp serrated knife with the potato starch. Cut the mochi into 1-inch squares and transfer to the serving plate. Sift the confectioners' sugar and salt over the mochi, sprinkle with the lemon zest, and serve immediately.

SESAME BALLS WITH DRUNKEN FIG FILLING

Sesame balls are classic dim sum. In the *yum cha* (dim-sum dining) culture, these sticky-sweet treats are eaten between savory bites throughout the meal. Traditionally, the dough is made only with glutinous rice flour, which is quite sticky and will leave you searching for a toothpick. I add taro to make the dough more tender, more tasty, and a lovely shade of lavender. I substitute flavorful figs for the traditional lotus seed and red bean fillings.

CHEF'S TIPS: In Chinese cooking, sesame seeds are never deeply browned—their white color symbolizes purity. Be sure to start with untoasted white sesame seeds for a light golden color when the balls are done.

Most fried desserts are best eaten right away, but these stay delicious and crisp even at room temperature.

Drunken Fig Filling

2¼ cups (15¾ ounces/448 grams) dried figs, preferably Black Mission, stemmed and quartered

½ cup (3½ ounces/98 grams) sugar

1 teaspoon salt

¼ cup (2 ounces/56 grams) cognac or dark rum

Sesame Balls

1 cup (7 ounces/200 grams) sugar

1 tablespoon salt

1½ teaspoons baking soda

5⅓ ounces (150 grams) taro, deeply peeled and cut crosswise into ½-inch slices

3½ cups (16⅛ ounces/462 grams) glutinous rice flour

Canola, vegetable, or other neutral oil for deep-frying

1 cup (3⅜ ounces/96 grams) white sesame seeds

1. To make the drunken fig filling: Put all the ingredients into a large mixing bowl and stir well to coat the figs with the sugar. Cover and set aside at room temperature for at least 30 minutes, or as long as overnight.

2. Transfer the figs and liquid to the bowl of a food processor or an electric mixer fitted with the paddle attachment. Process or beat the mixture until mashed to a paste. (You can also

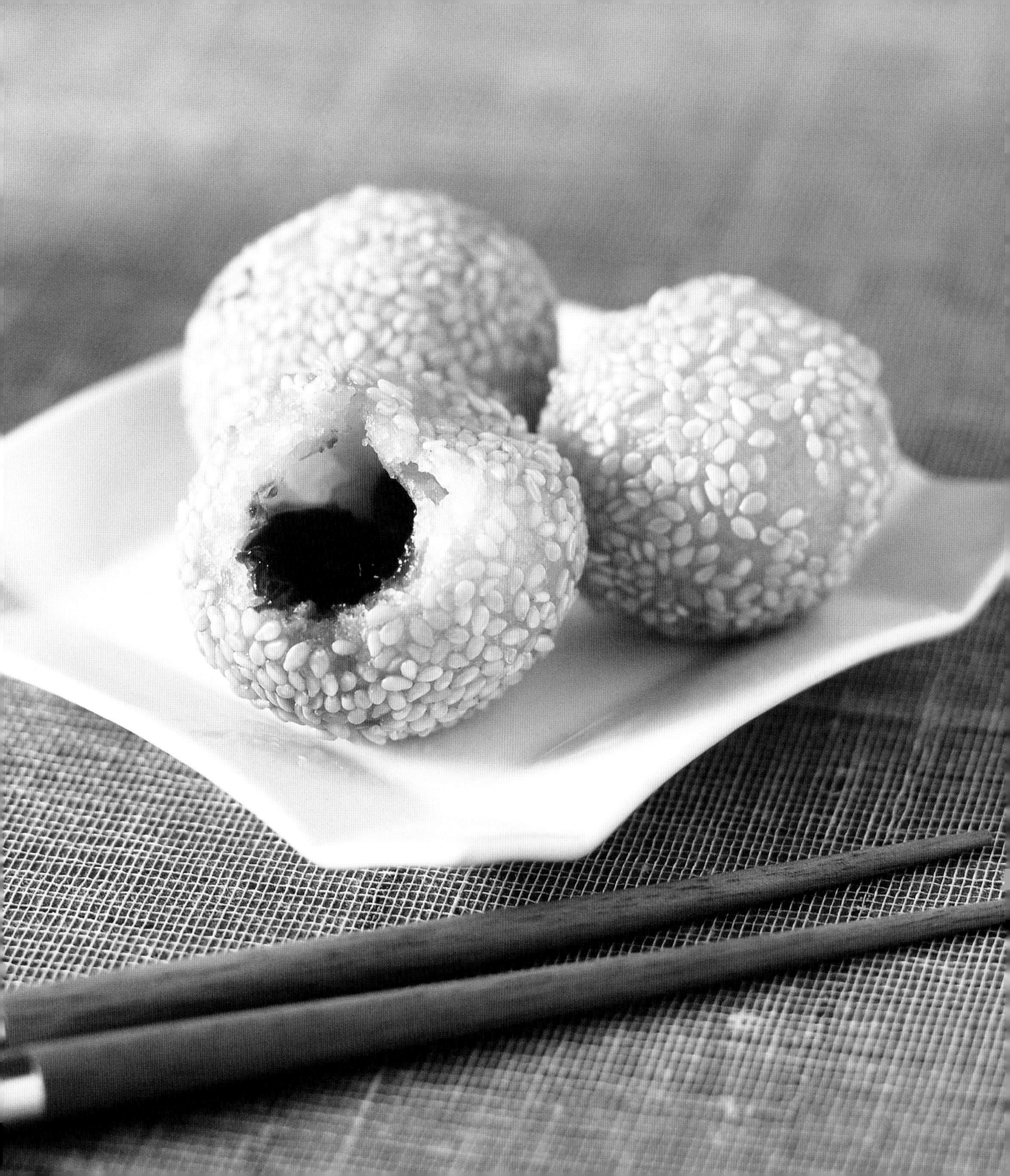

mash the mixture by hand with a fork.) Cover and refrigerate until ready to use; the filling can be kept for up to 2 weeks.

3. To make the sesame balls: Put the sugar, salt, and baking soda into the bowl of an electric mixer fitted with the paddle attachment and mix well; set aside.

4. Fill a large saucepan fitted with a steamer basket or rack with water to a depth of 2 inches and bring to a rolling boil. Put the taro in the basket and steam until very soft, about 10 minutes; it should fall apart if poked with a knife. Immediately add the taro to the sugar mixture, and beat on medium speed until smooth and pasty, about 5 minutes.

4. Meanwhile, bring 1 cup plus 2 tablespoons water to a boil.

5. Turn the mixer speed to low and add the glutinous rice flour. When the mixture is crumbly, add the boiling water all at once. (The water must be boiling when added.) Continue beating until the dough is soft and only slightly sticky. Squeeze the dough into a ball, wrap in plastic wrap, and set aside until it cools to room temperature.

6. Shape the dough into a log 1 inch in diameter, and cut the log into 2-inch lengths. One at a time, flatten each piece of dough with your palm into a circle 4 inches in diameter and ¼ inch thick. Put 1 tablespoon of the chilled fig filling into the center of the circle, then bring the edges together to form a half-moon and pinch to seal. Pinch off the excess dough at the two ends and roll the filled dumpling into a ball. Set aside.

7. Fill a deep, heavy saucepan with oil to a depth of at least 3 inches and heat to 300°F. Fill a shallow dish with ⅛ inch of water and another shallow dish with the sesame seeds. Roll a sesame ball in the water, just enough to moisten, then roll in the sesame seeds until well coated. Press the seeds so they stick to the balls, if necessary. Carefully lower the coated ball into the oil and cook, without stirring, until it floats and is crisp and light golden brown, about 5 minutes. You can cook about 8 balls at a time, but do not overcrowd the pan. Carefully remove from the oil and drain on paper towels. Repeat with the remaining balls. Serve hot or at room temperature.

■

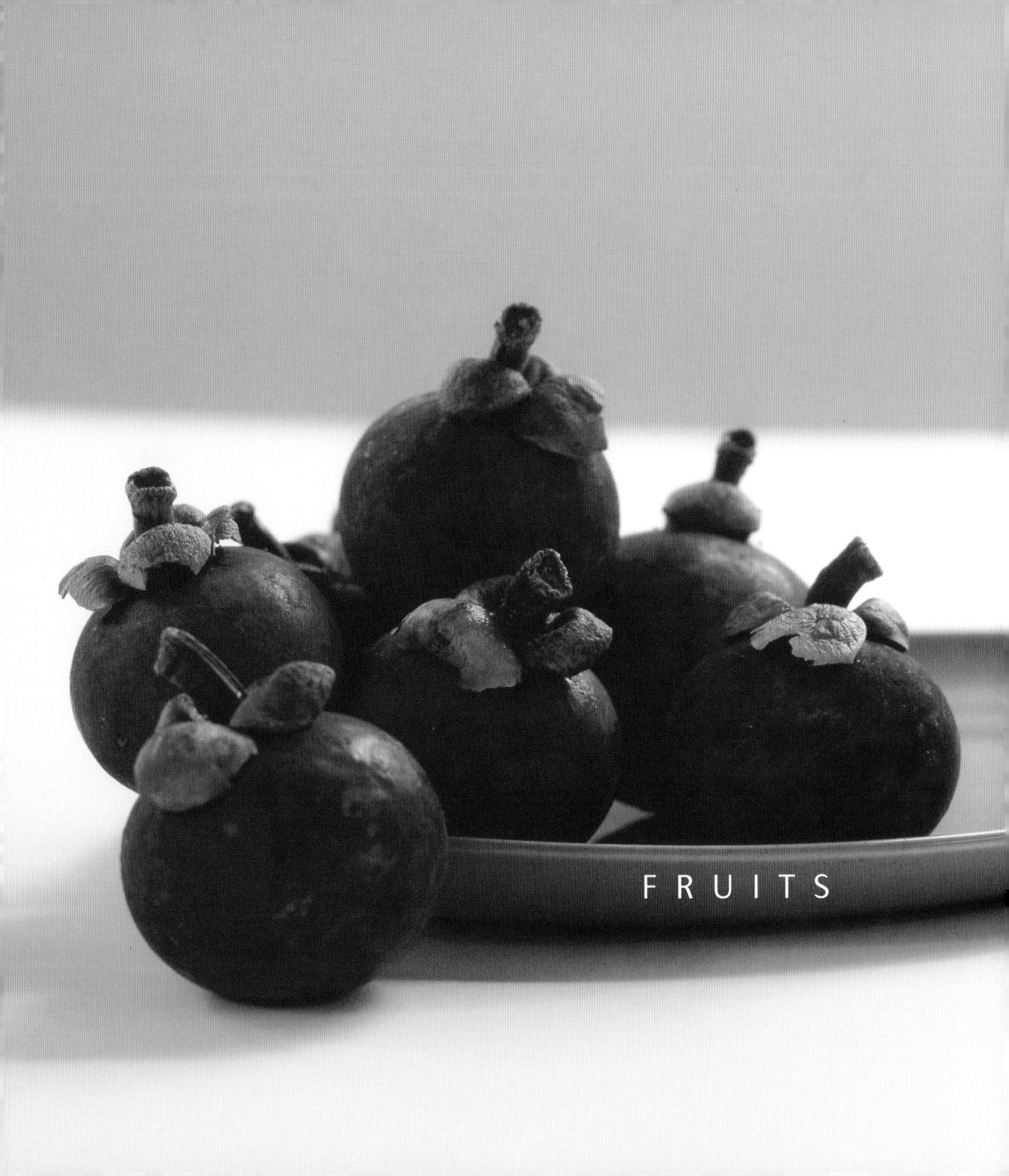

FRUITS

If you were to ask the average Asian, he would probably tell you that the quintessential Asian dessert is a plate of cut-up fresh fruit. Sweets are not usually served at the end of a meal. And even if there is an actual "dessert"—say, at a formal banquet—it will be preceded by a plate of fresh fruit and a pot of tea. Sweet treats are enjoyed during the day as snacks; fruit is for dessert.

This preference has its health benefits, of course, but it's also true that Asian palates seem to prefer natural sweetness over processed sugar. Perhaps this is because of the enormous range and quality of Asian fruits. Oranges, the most popular (and auspicious) of all Asian fruits, are just one of a vast number that are easily grown in the temperate and tropical climates that predominate through-out East and Southeast Asia. Watermelons, peaches, plums, dates, pears, strawberries, cherries, quinces, persimmons, pineapples, coconuts, and mangoes are just some of the Asian-grown fruits that are also common in the West.

My favorite Asian fruits are those that aren't easily found elsewhere. Some of these are unique varieties of more common fruits, like the tender and silken Champagne mango, while others are unique to Asia—lychee, longan, mangosteen, jackfruit, rambutan, durian, starfruit, passion fruit, and pawpaw.

In all of my desserts, I do my best to restore the integrity of the flavors I love. I hope the desserts that follow open your eyes (and your mouth) to a whole new kind of Asian dessert.

JICAMA WITH LIME-SPICED SUGAR-SALT

Makes 6 servings

Fruit is by far the most popular way to finish a meal in Asia—just a nice, big plate of fresh fruit. There are variations, of course. In Thailand, for instance, walking street vendors, loaded with fragrant tropical fruits, offer an accompanying bag of sugar spiced with dried shrimp and chiles. This recipe is a nod to them. I add fleur de sel for a savory note, as its delicate saltiness brings out the juiciness of the fruit.

This spiced dipping salt is best with watery and crunchy fruits, like medium-ripe papayas, mangoes, water chestnuts, or jicama, but it works well with pineapple, watermelon, apple, or most any fruit in season. When I crave something a little more creamy, I enjoy this with just-ripe avocado.

CHEF'S TIP: The lime-spiced sugar-salt will keep in an airtight container for 2 days, but will lose its aroma over time, so use it sooner rather than later.

½ cup (4 ounces/112 grams) muscovado sugar or other raw sugar, such as "Sugar in the Raw"

½ long red finger chile or 2 small Thai red chiles, seeded, deveined, and minced

2 teaspoons grated lime zest

1 tablespoon fleur de sel or other mild sea salt, such as Maldon

¼ cup (1⅔ ounces/48 grams) sugar

1 pound (454 grams) jicama, trimmed, peeled, and soaked in cold water

1. Put the muscovado sugar, chile, and lime zest in a small mixing bowl and stir well to mix. Add the fleur de sel and sugar and mix well.

2. Drain the jicama and pat dry, then cut crosswise into ½-inch slices. Cut the slices into ½-inch-thick batons, which will vary in length.

3. Arrange the jicama decoratively on a serving plate and serve with the spiced sugar-salt in a small dipping bowl.

■

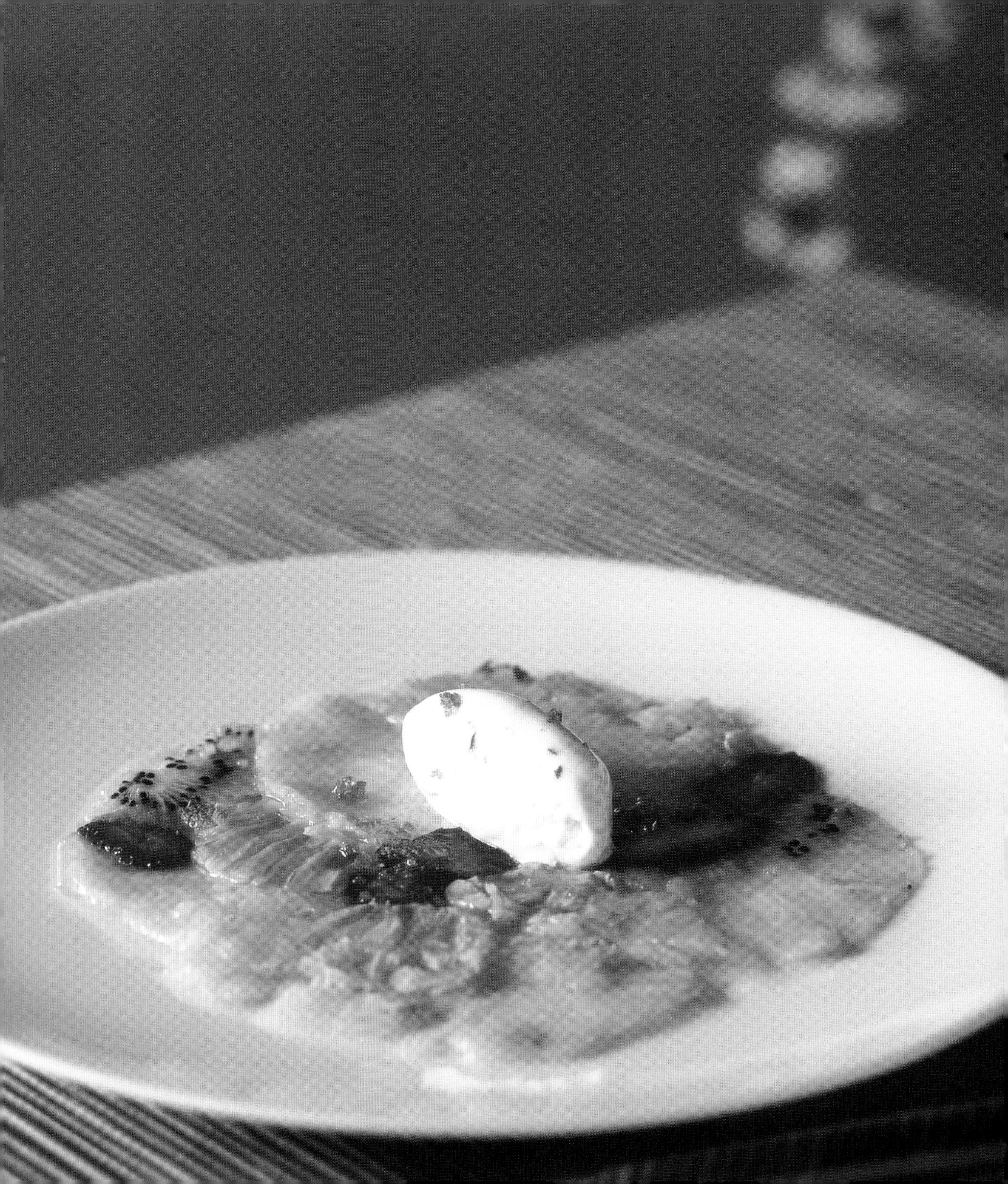

PINEAPPLE, LYCHEE, AND KIWI CARPACCIO WITH JALAPEÑO CREAM

Makes 8 servings

This fresh fruit dessert is quick and easy but looks incredibly impressive. It's formal enough for a sit-down dinner and casually elegant enough for an outdoor barbecue. The contrasts in color, texture, and taste of the pineapple, lychee, and kiwi work well, but use whatever is in season. The lemongrass glaze and jalapeño cream, which is captivatingly spiced but not spicy, pair well with any fruit. Such subtle refinements to fresh fruit make this the perfect exotic finish to any meal.

CHEF'S TIP: Everything can be prepared ahead of time and chilled until ready to assemble and serve. In fact, the fruit tastes better and more refreshing when served cold on a chilled plate.

Lemongrass Glaze

One 3-inch piece lemongrass, split in half lengthwise

½ cup (3½ ounces/100 grams) sugar

1 teaspoon fresh lemon juice

12 lychees, preferably fresh, peeled if fresh, seeded, and halved

1 small pineapple, peeled, cored, halved crosswise, and thinly sliced (see page 213)

3 kiwis, peeled and thinly sliced

4 strawberries, hulled and thinly sliced

Jalapeño Cream

½ cup (4 ounces/113 grams) heavy whipping cream

3 tablespoons sugar

½ cup (4¼ ounces/120 grams) crème fraîche

½ teaspoon chopped seeded jalapeño

1 teaspoon grated lime zest

¼ teaspoon salt

1. To make the glaze: Put the lemongrass, sugar, lemon juice, and ½ cup water in a small saucepan and bring to a simmer over medium heat. Simmer gently, stirring occasionally, until the mixture is thick and syrupy, about 20 minutes. Set aside to cool.

2. Arrange the fruit decoratively on eight individual flat serving plates or on one large flat

serving plate. Cover with plastic wrap and use a large offset spatula to gently pound the fruit into an even layer, shaping the arrangement until beautiful. Refrigerate until ready to serve.

3. To make the jalapeño cream: Put the cream in the bowl of an electric mixer fitted with the whisk attachment and whisk on medium speed until frothy. With the machine running, add 2 tablespoons of the sugar, and continue whisking until soft peaks form. (When you lift the whisk from the mixture, a peak will form and then fall back down.)

4. Put the crème fraîche, jalapeño, lime zest, salt, and the remaining tablespoon of sugar in a large mixing bowl and mix well. Add one-third of the whipped cream and mix well, then gently fold in the remaining whipped cream. Refrigerate until just set, at least 1 hour.

5. To serve, brush or spoon the lemongrass glaze over the fruit. Top with a scoop (or scoops) of jalapeño cream and serve.

ORANGES WITH ORANGE BLOSSOM SABAYON

Makes 8 servings

When I developed this aromatic sabayon recipe, the restaurant I was working in did not yet have its gas lines turned on, so the stove was inoperative. Left to my own devices, I turned to the microwave—and it worked beautifully. I often make this easy sabayon to pair with different fruit desserts, including this one when fresh oranges are in season.

CHEF'S TIP: Use an assortment of oranges, like Valencia, navel, blood, or Cara Cara, for the most interesting flavor and a striking presentation.

4 large egg yolks

1 tablespoon sugar

2 tablespoons sake

1 tablespoon orange blossom water

2 teaspoons corn syrup

½ cup (4 ounces/113 grams) heavy whipping cream

8 small oranges, preferably a variety

½ cup (2⅛ ounces/60 grams) slivered almonds, toasted and salted

2 mint leaves, torn, optional

1. Fill a large bowl with ice and water and set aside. Put the yolks, sugar, sake, orange blossom water, and corn syrup in a microwave-safe bowl and whisk until well combined. Microwave on the high setting, uncovered, for 10 seconds. Remove from the microwave, whisk well, and microwave for another 10 seconds. Repeat this procedure until the mixture is as thick as custard and almost like soft scrambled eggs in consistency, about 80 seconds total. The time will vary depending on the strength of your microwave, so start watching the consistency closely after 1 minute.

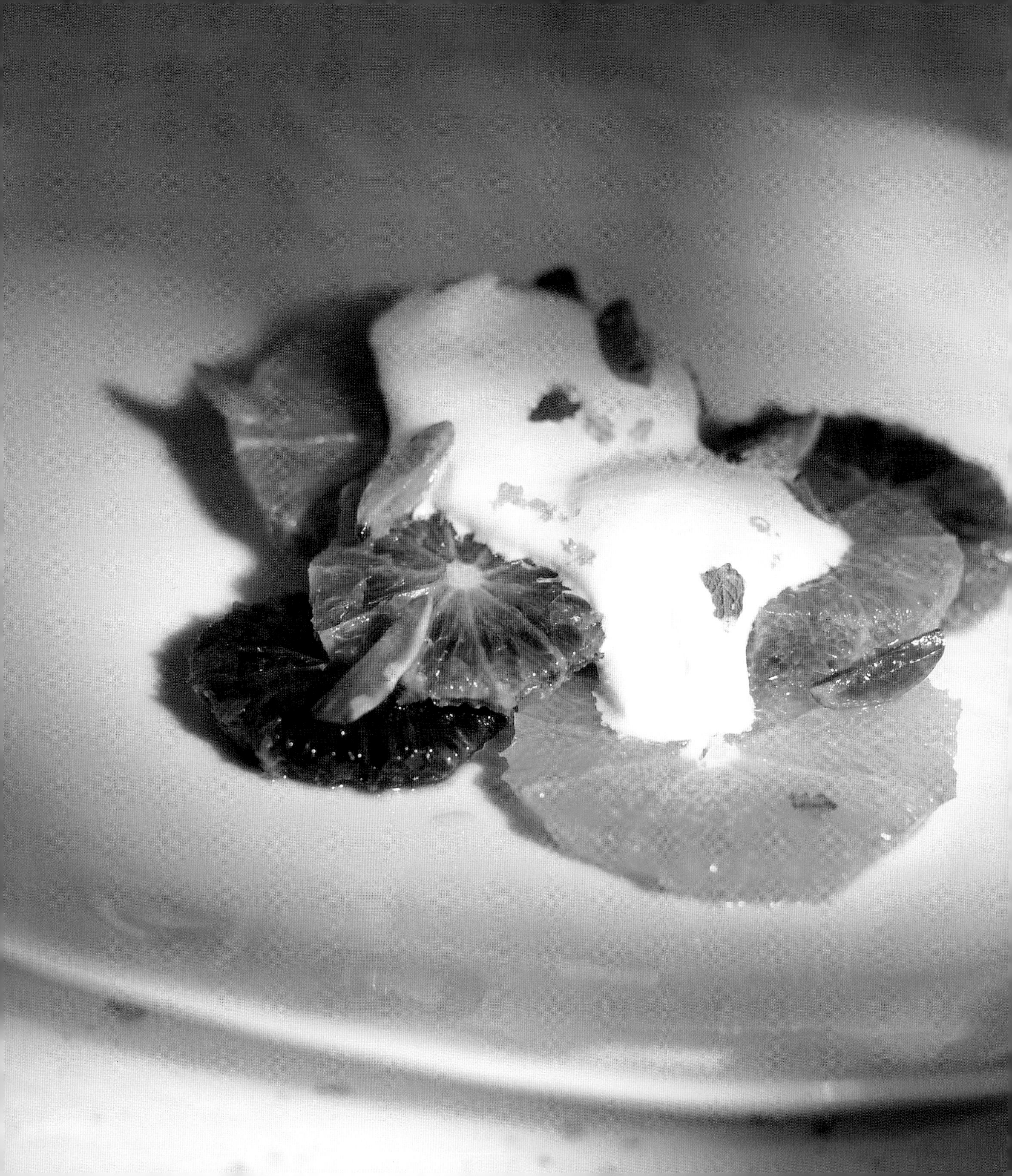

2. Continue whisking as you remove the bowl from the microwave and set it on top of the ice water bath. Whisk constantly until the mixture is cool to the touch.

3. Put the cream in the bowl of an electric mixer fitted with the whisk attachment and whisk until soft peaks form. (When you lift the whisk from the mixture, a peak will form and then fall back down.) Gently fold the whipped cream into the yolk mixture until well incorporated. Cover and refrigerate for at least 1 hour.

4. Trim off the ends of each orange. Stand an orange on one end and use a sharp knife to peel off the skin from top to bottom in strips, leaving no white pith. Repeat with the remaining oranges. Cut the oranges into ¼-inch-thick slices crosswise, and set aside.

5. Arrange the orange slices decoratively on individual dessert plates. Top with the sabayon and garnish with the toasted almonds and mint, if desired. Serve immediately.

■

WATERMELON SHAVED ICE WITH SALT AND PEPPER

Makes 8 servings

On the warmest days of summer, the one thing I crave most is watermelon. When we worked together, pastry chef Melissa Sacco fulfilled this craving with a watermelon sorbet spiked with salt and pepper. I loved the combination so much I interpreted it as a shaved ice dessert. Frozen watermelon juice, shaved into a granita-like confection and seasoned with a dash of salt and pepper, heightens the pleasures of this summer fruit even more.

CHEF'S TIP: This simple, light treat can be prepared ahead of time and kept frozen until ready to be eaten. Simply fluff the shaved ice with a fork before serving or scrape again if it has solidified.

¼ cup (1⅔ ounces/48 grams) sugar

One 3-pound (1,361 grams) watermelon, preferably seedless, rind removed, seeded if necessary, and cut into chunks

1 tablespoon grated lime zest

1 teaspoon fleur de sel or other mild sea salt, such as Maldon

½ teaspoon freshly ground black pepper

1. Put the sugar into a small saucepan with ¼ cup water and bring to a boil over medium-high heat, stirring occasionally. Continue cooking until the sugar is completely dissolved and the mixture is clear, about 2 minutes. Remove from the heat and cool completely.

2. Put the watermelon chunks and the cooled sugar syrup into a blender and puree until smooth. Strain the mixture through a fine-mesh sieve and pour into a large wide plastic or glass container, such as a baking pan.

3. Sprinkle the lime zest on top of the mixture, cover with plastic wrap, and place in the freezer. Stir and break up the ice crystals with a fork every 45 minutes to keep the mixture light and fluffy.

4. When the mixture is a completely frozen mountain of shaved ice, stir in the salt and pepper. Divide among eight serving bowls and serve immediately.

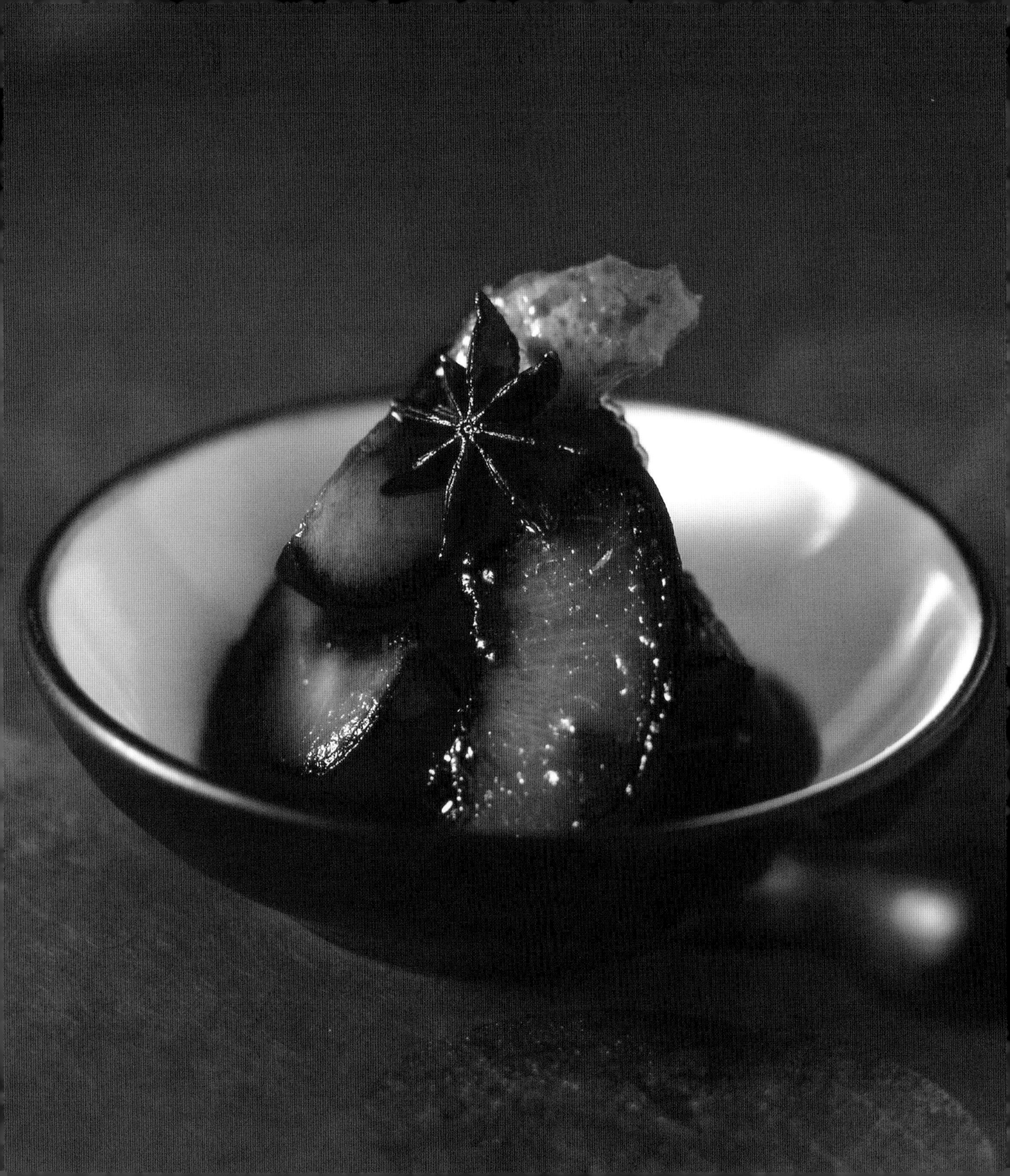

SAKE-SAUTÉED PLUMS WITH GINGER AND STAR ANISE

Makes 8 servings

When plums are abundant, juicy, and ripe in the summer, this light dessert brings out the best in their tart sweetness. Easy to prepare but complex in flavor, it's ideal after simple grilled dishes, particularly those with Asian accents. Because it is not too sweet, it can even serve as a sauce or garnish for gamy meats, like duck. For show, I flambé the plums, but that can be a risky experiment unless you've tried it before. It tastes just as good quickly sautéed in a pan, as in this recipe.

1½ pounds (680 grams) plums, preferably Black Mission, quartered and pitted

1⅓ cups (7 ounces/200 grams) packed light brown sugar

One 1½-inch piece fresh ginger, cut into ¼-inch slices

3 whole star anise

⅔ cup (5⅓ ounces/150 grams) sake

2 tablespoons fresh lemon juice

Two 4-inch-long strips lemon zest (removed with a vegetable peeler)

½ teaspoon salt

Ginger–Rum Raisin Ice Cream (page 222) or ½ cup crème fraîche, optional

1. Put all of the ingredients, except for the optional ice cream, into a large mixing bowl and stir well. Cover and refrigerate for 4 to 6 hours; do not let the mixture sit overnight.

2. Set a large deep skillet over high heat and heat for 3 minutes. Add the plum mixture all at once and cook, stirring, until the alcohol burns off and the plums are just softened, about 4 minutes. Remove from the heat and remove the ginger slices, star anise, and lemon zest. You can also reserve the star anise and lemon zest for garnish, if desired.

3. Divide the plums among serving bowls, top with the ice cream, if desired, and serve.

■

POACHED ASIAN PEARS IN OOLONG TEA

Makes 8 servings

Tea-poached pears are often served at high-end Chinese restaurants throughout Asia. Be sure to use a high-quality black tea here—as Asian pears readily absorb the poaching liquid, an excellent tea will yield an excellent dessert.

CHEF'S TIP: Prepare the whole dish ahead of time and keep it in its cooking liquid, covered and refrigerated, for up to 2 days. You can then either serve it cold or reheat it with its poaching liquid in a saucepan.

4 cups (27½ ounces/780 grams) sugar

2⅔ cups (21⅛ ounces/600 grams) dry white wine

One ½-inch piece fresh ginger, cut into 2 slices

4 cinnamon sticks

2 tablespoons allspice berries

2 tablespoons loose oolong or other black tea leaves

Four 4-inch-long strips orange zest (removed with a vegetable peeler)

4 large Asian pears, peeled, halved, and cored

1. Preheat the oven to 275°F.

2. Put the sugar in a large ovenproof saucepan and cover with 4 cups water. Bring to a boil over medium heat, stirring constantly, and boil, stirring, until the sugar is completely dissolved and the mixture is clear, about 5 minutes. Add the wine, ginger, cinnamon, allspice, tea leaves, and orange zest and bring to a boil again. Remove from the heat and add the pears. The pear halves should be submerged under the liquid.

3. Carefully cover the saucepan with a lid or foil and transfer to the oven. Bake, turning the pear pieces every 30 minutes, until tender but still crisp, about 1½ hours. A knife should pierce through a pear with just a little effort. Serve warm, or let cool and refrigerate, covered, in the cooking liquid for up to 2 days.

■

A TROPICAL TREAT—PINEAPPLES

Pineapples are one of the defining fruits of Southeast Asian desserts. Eaten fresh or cooked into jams, cakes, cookies, and candies, they are incredibly versatile and are enjoyed year-round.

Pineapples aren't very difficult to handle. A sharp knife easily lops off the top crown of leaves and the thick base. Use the same knife to cut off the skin from top to bottom. If little brown "eyes" remain, cut them out with the point of the knife—or simply take off a thicker layer of skin. The center, or core, of the pineapple is tough and fibrous, but it is also sweeter than the surrounding flesh. Cut the pineapple crosswise in half, then cut each half lengthwise into quarters. Each piece will have a strip of the core on the interior cut side. Look for the core (it will be a paler shade of yellow) and remove by cutting lengthwise along the edge of the core. From there, you can keep those pieces whole or cut them into slices, wedges, or dice. That's it—a fresh pineapple ready to eat.

You know a pineapple is ripe if it smells sweet, floral, and fruity, especially at the base. The fruit should be firm but not too hard, and you should be able to easily pluck a leaf from the top.

Once you taste a perfect pineapple, you'll never settle for the canned stuff again. And you'll understand why pineapples are so popular in Southeast Asia, where farmers grow many more interesting varieties than the low-acid hybrids that dominate the American market.

I've spent years experimenting with the unique textures and tastes of pineapple—tender and chewy, sweet and savory—and combining it with surprising ingredients in inventive new desserts. Pineapple pairs so well with so many things that I use Palm Sugar–Roasted Pineapple in everything from tarts to cookies to sweet drinks.

OVEN-DRIED PINEAPPLE SNACKS

These tangy, chewy treats are almost like candy, as the sugar coating provides not only sweetness but also a nice crunch. Don't be intimidated by the fleur de sel, chile, and lime zest—this common Southeast Asian combination of sweet, salty, spicy, and tart is subtle and makes these a great bar snack with cocktails.

CHEF'S TIP: If you have a gas oven, you can simply leave the pineapple in the oven overnight. The heat from the pilot light will dry out the pineapple very nicely.

1 small pineapple

2 tablespoons raw sugar, such as Demerara or "Sugar in the Raw"

1 teaspoon fleur de sel or other mild sea salt, such as Maldon

1 fresh Thai chile, seeded, deveined, and minced

1 teaspoon grated lime zest

1. Preheat the oven to 225°F.

2. Use a sharp knife to trim the ends off the pineapple and to deeply cut away the skin. Cut the pineapple crosswise in half, then cut each half lengthwise into quarters. Each piece will have a strip of the core on the interior cut side. Look for the core (it will be a paler shade of yellow) and remove by cutting lengthwise along the edge of the core. Discard the core and cut each remaining pineapple piece crosswise into ½-inch-thick slices.

3. Put the pineapple slices on a rimmed baking sheet in one layer. Bake, turning occasionally, until completely dried and light golden brown, about 4 hours. Let cool to room temperature.

4. Mix the remaining ingredients together in a large mixing bowl. Add pineapple, toss well, and serve. You should eat this snack within a few hours.

■

PALM SUGAR–ROASTED PINEAPPLE

I have always wondered why canned diced pineapple is used as an ice cream topping. The bright yellow pieces of generic sweetness just don't do anything for me. I decided to create a pineapple topping that actually complements, rather than diminishes, ice cream. Slowly roasted, the pineapple takes on a smoky, exotic flavor from the palm sugar and a lovely aroma from the vanilla and lime zest. This fruit "confit" is the ideal filling for Asian-style pastries, like Pineapple Wontons (page 216), or for a succulent and creamy lime mascarpone tart (page 134).

1 small pineapple

⅓ cup (2 ounces/56 grams) crushed palm sugar

¼ teaspoon salt

1 vanilla bean, split lengthwise in half, seeds scraped out, and seeds and pod reserved

½ teaspoon grated lime zest

1. Use a sharp knife to trim the ends off the pineapple and to deeply cut away the skin. Cut the pineapple crosswise in half, then cut each half lengthwise into quarters. Each piece will have a strip of the core on the interior cut side. Look for the core (it will be a paler shade of yellow) and remove by cutting lengthwise along the edge of the core. Discard the core and cut each remaining pineapple piece into a ¼-inch dice.

2. Put the diced pineapple in a large skillet with the palm sugar, salt, and vanilla seeds and pod. Set over high heat and cook, stirring occasionally, until the sugar dissolves, about 5 minutes. Turn the heat down to low and simmer gently, stirring every 10 minutes, until the mixture is dry, about 1 hour total. The mixture should simmer continuously but not burn; when done, the pineapple should be a light golden brown. Remove from the heat and cool.

3. Stir the lime zest into the pineapple. It can be refrigerated, covered, for up to 2 weeks.

PINEAPPLE WONTONS

Wontons, a Cantonese specialty, are traditionally never sweet and never deep-fried. But some rules are just made to be broken. These bite-sized sweets are a cross between an ultra-crisp turnover and a creamy fruit cheesecake. Assemble the wontons ahead of time for a party; once fried, they should be eaten right away.

CHEF'S TIP: Buy wonton wrappers, which you can find in Asian and some specialty stores, not other dumpling wrappers, which tend to be thicker. Made with eggs, wonton wrappers are very thin and straw-colored.

Palm Sugar–Roasted Pineapple
(page 215)

12 ounces (336 grams) cream cheese,
at room temperature

2 large eggs, lightly beaten

2¾ cups (8⅞ ounces/250 grams) finely
shredded unsweetened dried coconut

Forty-eight 4-inch square wonton
wrappers

Canola, vegetable, or other neutral oil for
deep-frying

¼ cup (1 ounce/28 grams)
confectioners' sugar

1. Mix the roasted pineapple and cream cheese together in a small bowl just until combined. Refrigerate until ready to use.

2. Line a baking sheet with parchment or wax paper and set aside. Mix the eggs with 1 tablespoon water and set aside. Put the coconut in a shallow bowl; set aside. Trim off a 1-inch strip from each of two adjoining sides of a wonton wrapper to make a 2-inch square. Repeat with the remaining wrappers—you can cut stacks of 10 at a time with a sharp knife.

3. Put 1 tablespoon of the pineapple filling in the center of a wonton wrapper. Brush 2 adjoining edges with the beaten egg, then fold the wrapper in half diagonally and press the edges together gently. The wonton will be fat and the edges should be stuck tightly. Repeat with the remaining wrappers and filling. Brush the outside of both sides of a wonton with the egg, then dredge in the coconut. Transfer to the lined baking sheet. Repeat with the remaining wontons. Cover the baking sheet with plastic wrap and refrigerate for at least 4 hours.

4. Fill a medium saucepan with oil to a depth of 2 inches and heat the oil to 325°F. When the oil is ready (a tiny pinch of flour will sizzle), add several wontons and cook, turning once, until floating and golden brown, about 3 minutes. You can cook about 6 at a time, but do not crowd the pan. Drain on paper towels and repeat with the remaining wontons. Dust the hot wontons with the confectioners' sugar and serve immediately.

■

MANGO STICKY RICE

Throughout Southeast Asia, glutinous rice, also called "sticky rice," is often mixed with coconut milk as a dessert base. The toppings, however, change according to season and chef. Bananas, durians, or kaya, a traditional custard found in many southeast Asian countries, may be decoratively set atop the sticky rice for a simple and deeply satisfying dessert. Mango remains my fruit of choice, since, when fully ripe, it combines a fresh fruitiness with a custard-like texture.

CHEF'S TIPS: Champagne mangoes are in season in early spring and can be found in most Asian markets. They have yellow skin and flesh and a small pit and should be used for this dish when very ripe, shriveled, and spotted.

2 cups (15 ounces/428 grams) glutinous (sticky) rice, rinsed well and drained

3 cups plus 2 tablespoons (28¼ ounces/800 grams) coconut milk

1⅓ cups (7½ ounces/212 grams) crushed palm sugar

1 vanilla bean, split lengthwise in half, seeds scraped out, and seeds and pod reserved, or 2 teaspoons vanilla extract

2 teaspoons salt

1 frozen pandan leaf, optional

4 ripe mangoes, preferably Champagne, peeled, seeded, and sliced

2 teaspoons white and black sesame seeds, toasted, optional

1. Put the rice in a large bowl, cover with 8 cups cold water, and soak for at least 2 hours.

2. Line a steamer insert or basket with a large piece of cheesecloth and bring the water in the steamer to a steady simmer. Drain the rice well, transfer to the steamer, wrap with the cheesecloth, and steam, covered, until tender, about 20 minutes.

3. Meanwhile, put the coconut milk, palm sugar, vanilla seeds and pod, if using, the salt, and pandan leaf, if desired, in a large saucepan and set over medium heat. Bring to a steady simmer, stirring occasionally, and cook, stirring, until the sugar dissolves and the mixture has reduced, about 15 minutes. Remove from the heat.

4. Transfer the rice to a large mixing bowl and stir in half the warmed coconut milk. Set the remaining coconut milk aside. Divide the rice among eight serving bowls and let sit until slightly cooled. The rice will absorb the liquid and the mixture will become thick.

5. Top each bowl with mango slices and spoon the remaining coconut milk on top of the mangoes. Sprinkle with sesame seeds, if desired, and serve immediately.

■

FRIED BANANAS

Fried bananas are one of the most popular sweet street snacks in Thailand and often turn up on menus at American Thai restaurants as well. This batter is made in a traditional style with glutinous rice flour. This takes longer to fry than one made with all-purpose flour, but it makes for a crisper exterior and causes the banana inside to become as soft as pudding. To top it off, coconut gives this dish a sweet fragrance and flavor. You can enjoy these on their own or with ice cream.

CHEF'S TIP: Baby bananas have a custardy sweetness and are ideal for frying. They can be found in Asian, Latino, and specialty markets. If you can't find them, substitute eight ripe regular bananas.

1⅔ cups (7 ounces/200 grams) glutinous rice flour

1⅓ cups (4¼ ounces/120 grams) finely shredded unsweetened dried coconut

½ cup (3½ ounces/100 grams) sugar

2 teaspoons salt

1¾ cups (16¼ ounces/460 grams) coconut milk

¼ cup (⅞ ounce/24 grams) white sesame seeds

Canola, vegetable, or other neutral oil for deep-frying

16 baby bananas

Condensed Milk Ice Cream (page 266) or vanilla ice cream

1. Put the flour, coconut, sugar, salt, coconut milk, and half the sesame seeds in a mixing bowl and whisk until smooth. Set aside to rest for 1 hour.

2. When ready to fry, fill a medium saucepan with oil to a depth of 3 inches and heat the oil to 350°F. When the oil is ready (a small drop of batter will sizzle), peel a few of the bananas, generously coat with the batter, lower gently into the oil, and fry, turning once, until golden brown, about 4 minutes total. Drain on paper towels and sprinkle with some of the remaining sesame seeds. Cook the remaining bananas in batches; do not crowd the pan. Serve warm, with the ice cream, if desired.

■

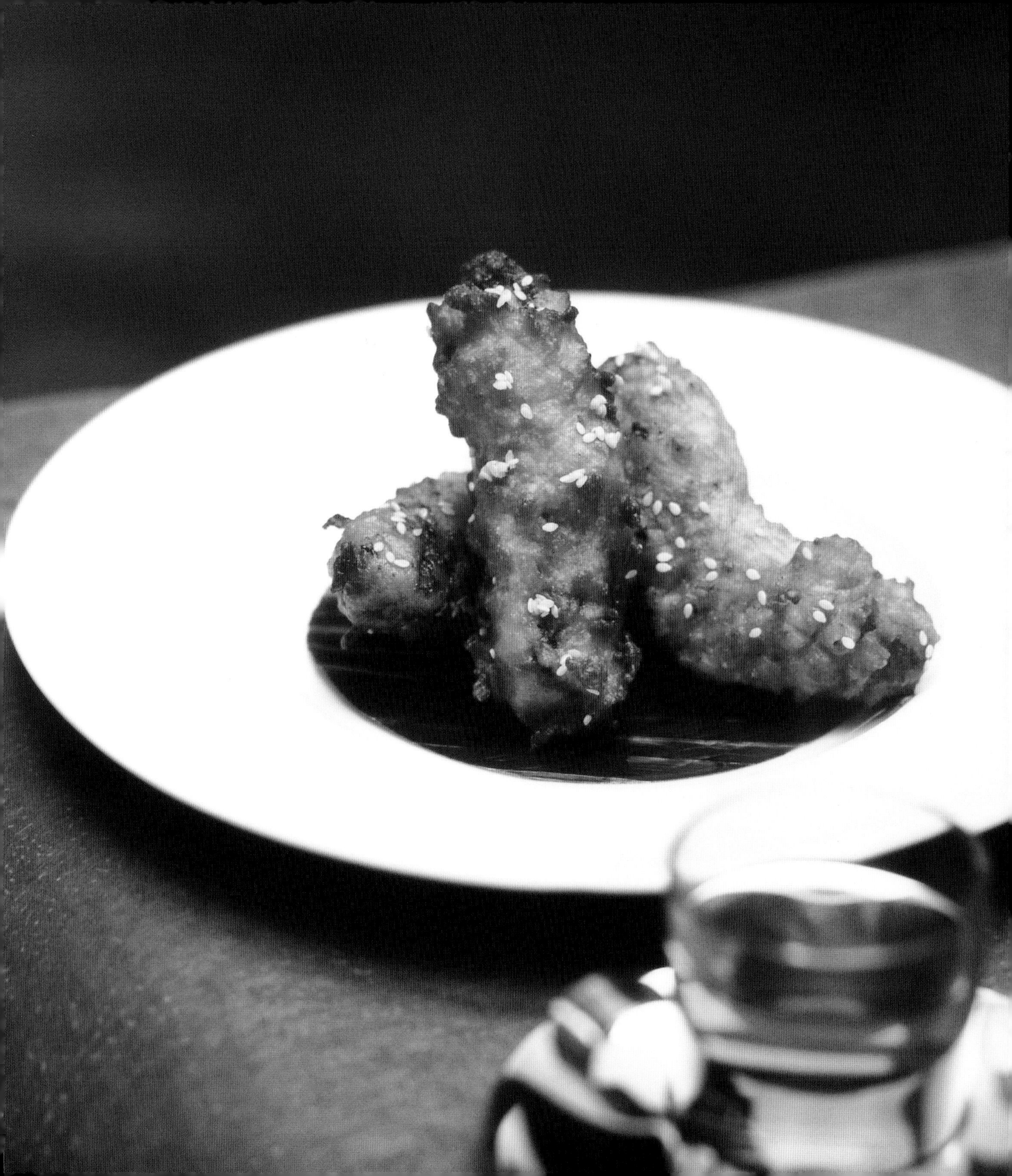

APPLE AND CRANBERRY SESAME CRISP WITH GINGER–RUM RAISIN ICE CREAM

Makes 8 servings

This is one of my favorite ways to cook apples in the fall. The sesame seeds in the topping make the crisp, well, crisper than most, with a distinct smoky nuttiness. This dish is even better when baked ahead, cooled, and then warmed again before serving. The apples then settle into a full-bodied filling and the topping takes on a delicate crunch. The ice cream complements the crisp perfectly, but the crisp is also delicious on its own.

CHEF'S TIP: Be sure to use firm, tart apples, such as Granny Smiths, which are available year-round. During apple season, you can also try other tart varieties, like Macoun or Sierra Beauty.

Ginger–Rum Raisin Ice Cream

One 2-inch piece fresh ginger, peeled and chopped

2 tablespoons sugar

¼ teaspoon salt

4 large egg yolks

½ cup (4 ounces/113 grams) whole milk

1½ cups (12 ounces/339 grams) heavy whipping cream

2 tablespoons unsalted butter

3 tablespoons dark rum

½ cup (2⅜ ounces/68 grams) golden raisins soaked overnight in 3 tablespoons rum

Apple and Cranberry Sesame Crisp

8 tart apples, such as Granny Smith, peeled, cored, and each cut into eighths

1 tablespoon cornstarch

3 tablespoons fresh lemon juice

1¾ cups (11⅞ ounces/336 grams) sugar

¼ teaspoon salt

1½ cups (12 ounces/339 grams) unsalted butter, cut into ½-inch cubes and chilled

1 cup (3⅛ ounces/88 grams) fresh or frozen cranberries

1⅔ cups (9¼ ounces/261 grams) all-purpose flour

1 cup (5⅓ ounces/150 grams) packed light brown sugar

2 teaspoons ground cinnamon

1 teaspoon ground ginger

⅓ cup (1 ounce/28 grams) black sesame seeds

⅓ cup (1 ounce/28 grams) white sesame seeds

2 teaspoons fleur de sel or other mild sea salt, such as Maldon

1. To make the ice cream: Put the ginger, sugar, salt, and 1 cup water in a small saucepan, stir well, and bring to a boil over medium-high heat. Turn the heat to low and simmer, stirring occasionally, until the mixture becomes syrupy and very thick, about 5 minutes. Set aside to cool.

2. Whisk the egg yolks in a medium mixing bowl until broken; set aside. Put the milk and 1 cup of the cream in a medium saucepan and warm over medium heat, stirring occasionally, until bubbles begin to form around the edges. Remove from the heat and pour ½ cup of the warm milk mixture onto the yolks in a slow, steady stream, whisking constantly. Transfer the yolk mixture back to the saucepan. Set over low heat and cook, stirring constantly, until the mixture is thick enough to coat the back of a wooden spoon and registers 165°F, about 5 minutes. Remove from the heat and stir in the butter until the butter melts.

3. Strain the cream mixture through a fine-mesh sieve into a large mixing bowl and stir in the remaining ½ cup cream and rum. Strain the ginger syrup into the same bowl, pressing on the ginger to extract as much liquid as possible. Set over a larger bowl of ice and water and stir occasionally until cold to the touch, about 40°F. Alternatively, cover and refrigerate until cold.

4. Transfer the mixture to your ice cream maker and freeze following the manufacturer's instructions. After churning, stir in the raisins and transfer to a freezer container. The ice cream will be soft when just churned but will firm up in the freezer. It is best fresh, but it will keep in an airtight container in the freezer for up to 3 days.

5. To make the crisp: Preheat the oven to 350°F.

6. Toss the apple wedges with the cornstarch and 2 tablespoons of the lemon juice, and set aside.

7. Put 1 cup of the sugar and the remaining tablespoon of lemon juice into a medium saucepan and set over medium-high heat. Cook, stirring occasionally to evenly dissolve the sugar, until the mixture becomes a medium amber that registers 320°F on a candy thermometer, about 10 minutes. Add the apples, plain salt, and 2 tablespoons of the butter and stir well. Remove from the heat, stir in the cranberries, and set aside to cool.

8. Put the flour, brown sugar, cinnamon, ginger, sesame seeds, and the remaining ½ cup sugar into a large mixing bowl and mix well. Add the remaining 1¼ cups plus 2 tablespoons butter and the fleur de sel, and cut in the butter with a pastry cutter or your fingers until the mixture resembles small peas.

9. Divide the apple-cranberry mixture among eight 4-ounce ramekins, or put it all in a shallow 4-quart baking dish. Top with the sesame crisp mixture. Bake until the topping is golden brown and the apples bubbling, about 45 minutes for the individual ramekins, 55 minutes for the baking dish.

10. Cool the crisp slightly and serve warm with the ice cream. (You can also cool the crisp completely, cover, and refrigerate for up to 2 days. Reheat in the oven for 20 minutes at 350°F before serving.)

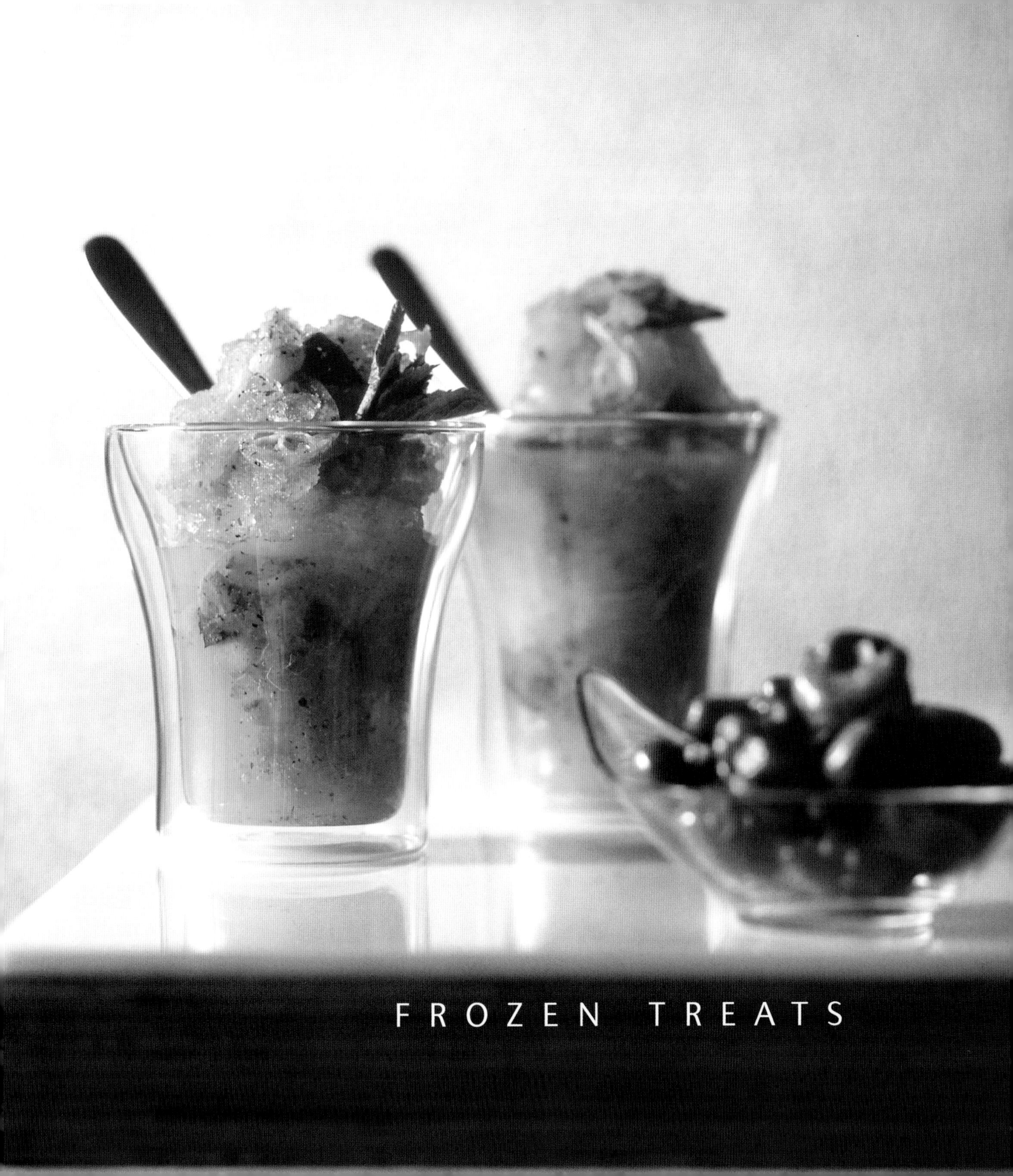

FROZEN TREATS

Although it takes a little effort, homemade ice cream is fresher and smoother than the commercial stuff. The churning process fills the custard with invisible air bubbles that remain intact for a short time thereafter, imparting a fullness of flavor and silky richness to the ice cream. I steal a bite or two right then and there and freeze the rest to enjoy later.

If you love good ice cream, an ice cream maker is one of the best kitchen investments you can make. Good machines are available for less than fifty dollars, and you'll be able to make delectable ice cream within an hour. For those who like ice cream, but not quite enough to buy an ice cream maker, I include some delectable frozen treats that require nothing more than your freezer. The kulfi and Popsicle creations are both easy to make and better than anything you can buy at the store.

There's more to this chapter, however, than ice cream and Popsicles. I grew up eating a variety of cold treats that are unfamiliar to most Americans. Desserts like shaved ice with fresh fruit and tapioca both captured the essence of my summers in Asia and provided some sweet relief from their oppressive heat and humidity. I've transformed some of those treats here into sophisticated desserts that are meant to be enjoyed year-round.

ICE CREAM FROM INDIA: KULFI AND POPSICLES

Most Asian countries neither produce nor consume many dairy products, but India is the world's leading milk producer. Yogurt, of course, is common in Indian food, as is *ghee,* a type of clarified butter that gives many Indian dishes their characteristic light lusciousness. But my favorite Indian dairy product is *kulfi,* or Indian ice cream.

Kulfi was first enjoyed in India in the sixteenth century. It has since become a street food favorite—not only in India, but also in Singapore and Malaysia—and is usually shaped into dense cones akin to Popsicles.

Kulfi's rich flavor and unique texture stem not so much from any exotic ingredient as from the first step in the kulfi-making process—cooking the milk down until it is reduced to a thick cream. This concentrated cream is then sweetened, flavored, and frozen. You don't even need an ice cream maker. The resulting kulfi tastes as though it has a rich custard base when, in fact, it contains no eggs at all.

The most popular kulfi flavors are those found in other Indian desserts—cardamom, saffron, pistachio, mango, and coconut. I decided to make kulfi with Ovaltine, the malted chocolate drink mix, which is very popular in South and Southeast Asia. The addition of Ovaltine, which is essentially flavored milk powder, makes the final product as rich and fudgy as traditional kulfis. Think of the result as a supremely high-quality Fudgsicle.

I also have included recipes for other frozen treats common in Asia, such as a parfait based on bread and milk. And most of my Popsicles are fruit-flavored, like the ones sold by street vendors throughout Asia on hot, steamy days. These are not as rich as kulfi but they are refreshing and easy to make, and they pack a whole lot of flavor.

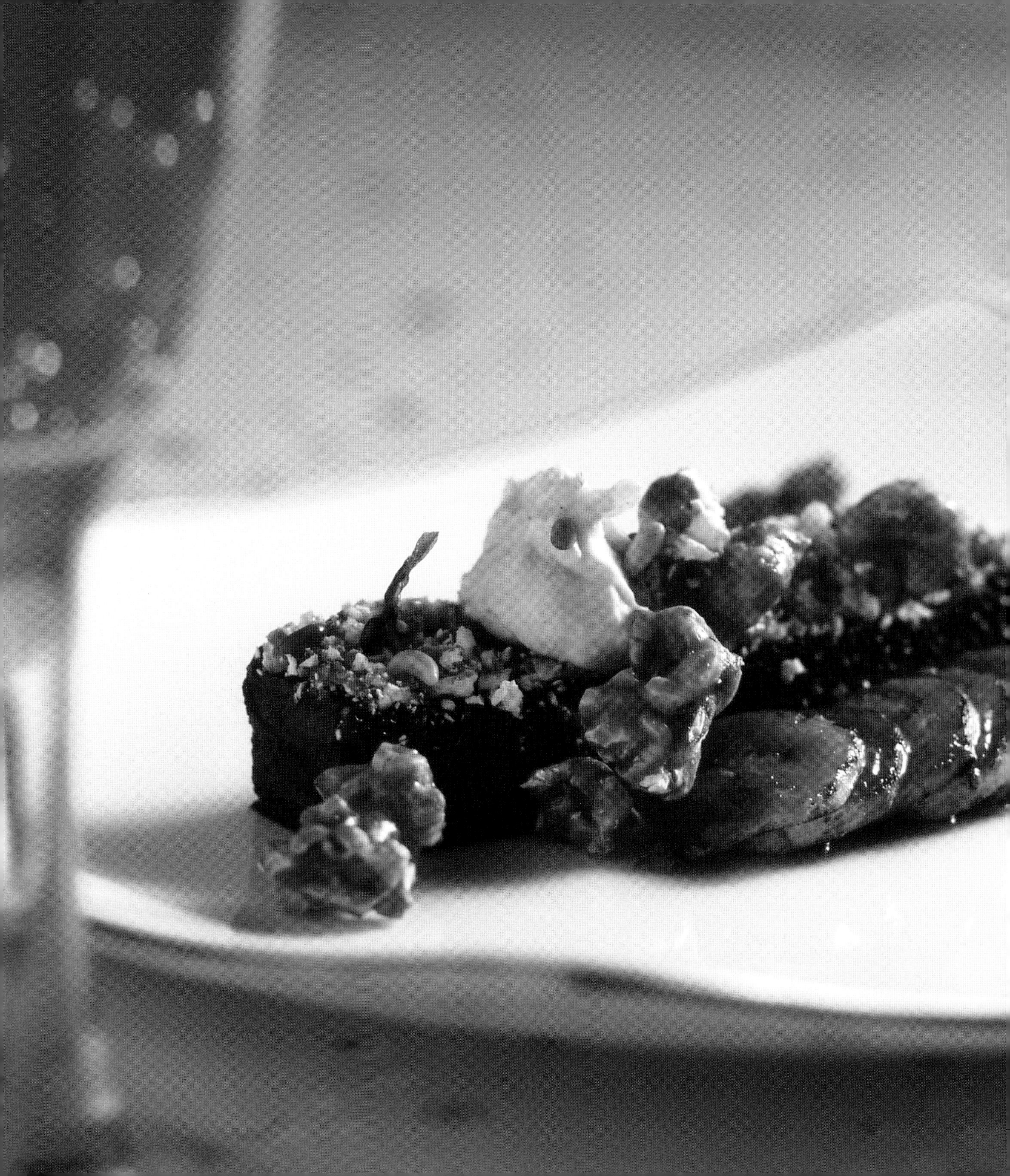

OVALTINE AND MILK CHOCOLATE KULFI WITH CARAMELIZED BANANA

Makes 12 servings

Many variations of kulfi made their way on and off the Spice Market menu, but the one flavored with Ovaltine, commonly enjoyed all over Asia, is by far the most popular. In fact, this rich, chocolate-malt confection is one of the bestselling dishes in the restaurant, sweet or savory! And some people order it twice because they can't get enough of it.

CHEF'S TIP: You can use 3-ounce wax-lined paper cups to shape the kulfi. Simply peel off the cups when ready to serve. For a more portable snack, insert a Popsicle stick into the center of each kulfi after the mixture is set but before it has completely hardened.

4 cups (32 ounces/907 grams) heavy whipping cream

1 teaspoon salt

1 vanilla bean, split lengthwise in half, seeds scraped out, seeds and pod reserved

1 cup (4⅛ ounces/116 grams) Ovaltine powder

14 ounces (397 grams) milk chocolate, roughly chopped

Spiced Caramel Popcorn Crust (page 192), optional

4 baby bananas or 2 regular bananas, optional

3 tablespoons sugar, optional

Sweetened Condensed Milk Chantilly (page 25), optional

1. Put the heavy cream, salt, and vanilla seeds and pod in a large saucepan and bring to a steady simmer over medium-low heat. Cook until the cream has thickened and reduced by about a third, about 35 minutes.

2. Vigorously whisk in the Ovaltine until smooth, and the mixture comes to a boil, then remove from the heat, add the chocolate, and stir until it melts. The mixture should be totally smooth and have a fudgelike consistency. Strain through a fine-mesh sieve and pour the mixture onto a 12 x 8½ sheet pan lined with plastic wrap. Sprinkle the top with spiced caramel popcorn crust, if desired, and pat gently to secure. It should be filled

almost to the brim. Wrap the sheet pan completely with plastic wrap and place on a flat surface in the freezer.

3. When the kulfi is frozen, invert the pan onto a piece of parchment on a flat work surface. Cut the kulfi into 2 x 6-inch pieces. Place the kulfi pieces back onto the tray and freeze until ready to serve.

4. If garnishing with the bananas, peel the bananas and cut into ¼-inch slices and put in a single layer on a baking sheet. Sprinkle with the sugar and caramelize the sugar with a blowtorch. If you do not have a kitchen torch, you can put the bananas under a hot broiler for about 1 minute. Arrange the bananas, kulfis, and chantilly, if desired, on serving plates and serve immediately.

■

PISTACHIO KULFI WITH POMEGRANATE SOUP

This is a popular Indian technique for making a quick and easy ice cream that requires neither a custard base nor an ice cream machine. In lieu of eggs, slices of bread create a substantial, smooth texture, and the resulting mixture freezes very nicely in Popsicle molds, which closely resemble the traditional kulfi shape, as shown in the photo on page 232. If you don't have the time or ingredients to make the pomegranate soup, the kulfi is delicious on its own.

CHEF'S TIP: Honey can be substituted for the pomegranate molasses, which can be found in most Middle Eastern markets. See page 22 for how to make fresh pomegranate juice.

Pistachio Kulfi

1 cup (8 ounces/227 grams) heavy whipping cream

½ cup plus 2 tablespoons (5¾ ounces/164 grams) evaporated milk

¼ cup (1⅛ ounces/31 grams) shelled unsalted pistachios, plus more for garnish

2 cardamom pods

⅛ teaspoon salt

3 slices (2 ounces/56 grams) soft white sandwich bread, crusts trimmed

½ cup (5½ ounces/156 grams) sweetened condensed milk

Pomegranate Soup

1 cup (8 ounces/227 grams) pomegranate juice

½ cup (4 ounces/113 grams) apple juice

2 tablespoons pomegranate molasses

½ cup (3¾ ounces/106 grams) sugar

¼ cup (2 ounces/56 grams) Riesling or other sweet white wine

¼ cup pomegranate seeds for garnish, optional

1 small orange, peeled, white pith removed, and segments cut from the membranes, for garnish, optional

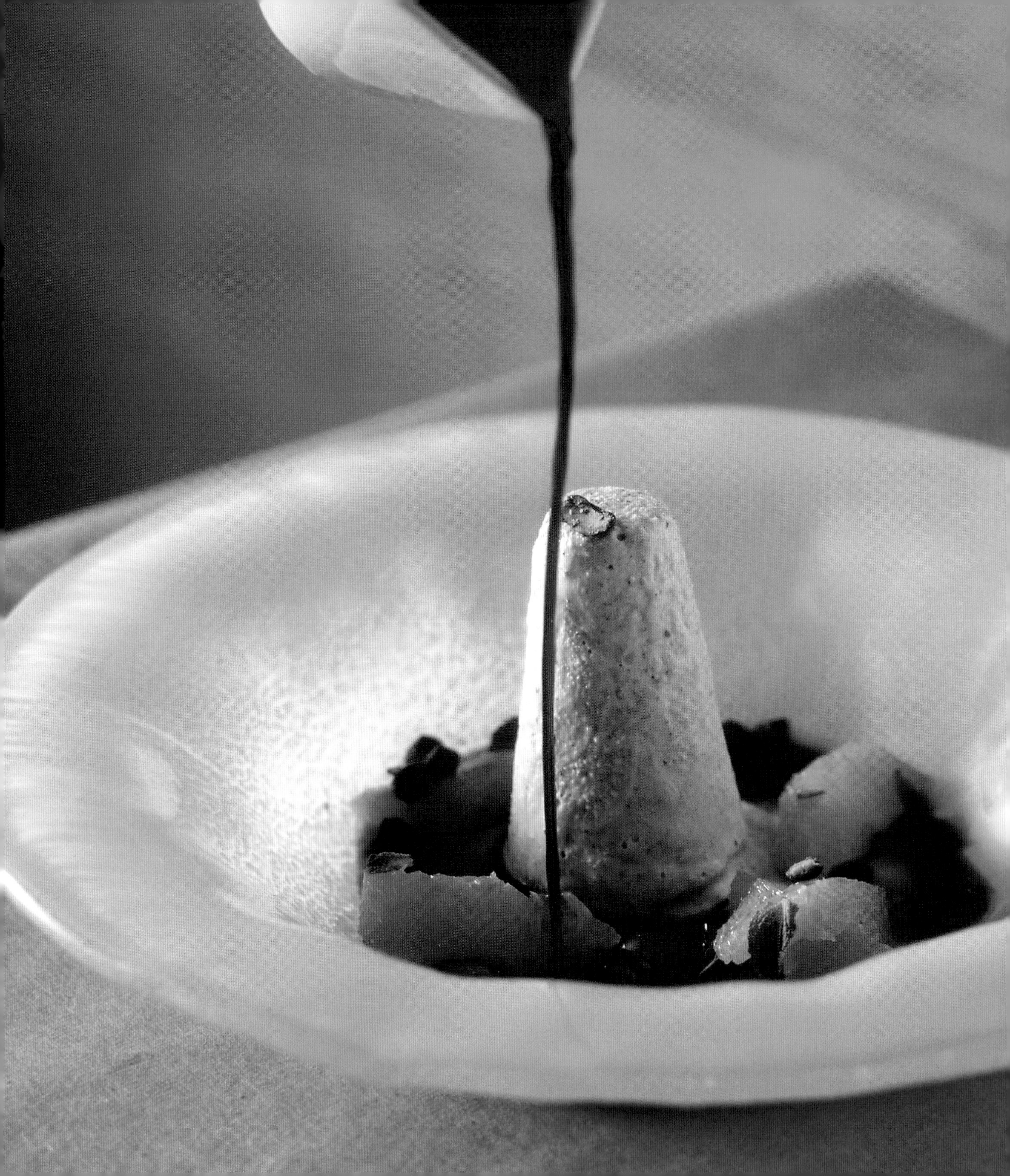

1. To make the kulfi: Put the cream, evaporated milk, pistachios, cardamom pods, and salt into a medium saucepan and bring to a boil over medium heat. Remove from the heat and let stand for 1 hour.

2. Remove the cardamom pods. Add the bread to the cream mixture and submerge until completely soaked, then stir in the sweetened condensed milk. Transfer the mixture to a blender and blend until smooth. Divide among eight 3-ounce Popsicle molds or paper cups and freeze until frozen hard.

3. Meanwhile, make the pomegranate soup: Put the pomegranate juice, apple juice, pomegranate molasses, sugar, and wine into a medium saucepan, set over medium heat, and warm, stirring, until the sugar is completely dissolved. Transfer to a mixing bowl. Set the bowl in a larger bowl of ice and water and cool completely, stirring occasionally. Refrigerate until ready to serve.

4. Unmold the kulfis; if you have trouble getting the kulfis out, dip the molds in hot water for 10 seconds to release them. Put a kulfi in the center of each serving bowl. Scatter the pomegranate seeds, orange wedges, and pistachios, if desired, decoratively all around, pour in the chilled soup, and serve.

FRUIT "CREAMSICLE" POPS

Frozen fruit pops are a sidewalk treat in many of the world's bustling cities during the unbearable summer months. Most of them are nothing but frozen fruit juice on a stick, but I've chosen to add a touch of creaminess with yogurt, coconut milk, and cream.

CHEF'S TIP: Cooling the Creamsicle base until slightly chilled but not set before filling the molds will help the fruit bits suspend as they freeze. Transfer the base to a bowl and set it in another bowl of ice water, stirring the mixture constantly, until the gelatin thickens. Then quickly pour the liquid into the molds.

Blueberry Yogurt Pops

3 cups (14⅛ ounces/400 grams) fresh blueberries, picked over and rinsed well

3 tablespoons fresh lemon juice

½ cup plus 2 tablespoons (4⅔ ounces/130 grams) sugar

¼ teaspoon salt

½ cup (3½ ounces/100 grams) whole milk

1¾ cup (14⅛ ounces/400 grams) plain whole-milk yogurt

Coconut Pops

2½ cups (22 ounces/625 grams) unsweetened coconut milk

½ cup (3¾ ounces/106 grams) sugar

¼ teaspoon salt

2 teaspoons vanilla extract

¼ cup (2 ounces/56 grams) heavy whipping cream

¼ cup (¾ ounce/22 grams) finely shredded unsweetened dried coconut, toasted

Lemon Cream Pops

1 cup (8 ounces/227 grams) heavy whipping cream

1 cup (8 ounces/227 grams) whole milk

⅔ cup (4⅜ ounces/125 grams) sugar

¼ teaspoon salt

4 large lemons

1. To make the blueberry pops: Put the blueberries, lemon juice, sugar, and salt in a medium saucepan, set over medium-high heat, and cook, stirring occasionally to dissolve the sugar, until the mixture is thick enough to coat the back of a spoon, about 20 minutes. It should be deep violet and saucy with a few whole berries remaining. Remove from the heat and cool for 10 minutes.

2. Stir the milk and yogurt into the blueberry mixture until well blended. Once cooled, divide among eight 3-ounce Popsicle molds or paper cups, insert Popsicle sticks, and freeze until hard.

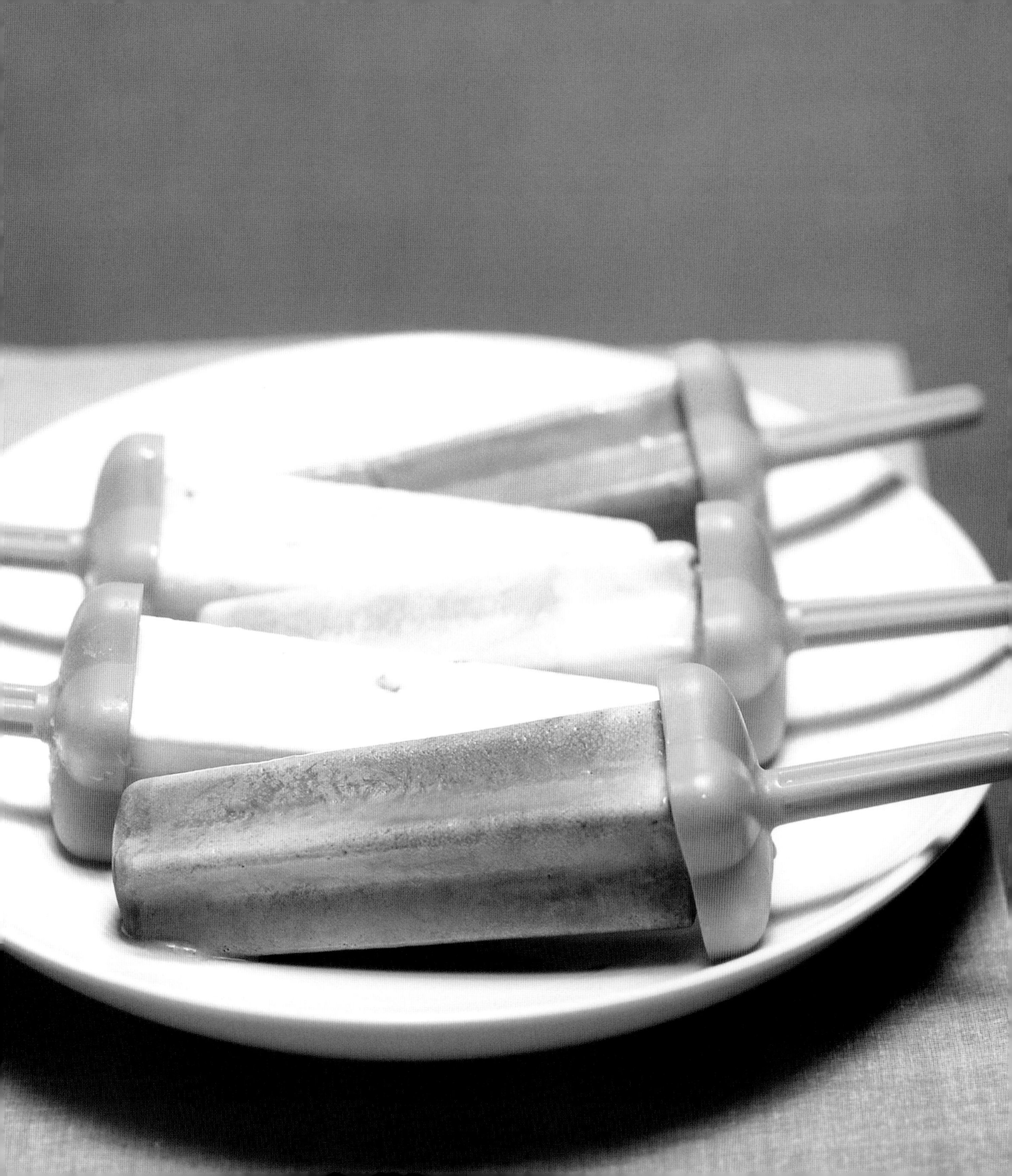

3. To make the coconut pops: Put the coconut milk, sugar, and salt in a medium saucepan and warm over medium heat, stirring, just until the sugar dissolves. Remove from the heat and cool completely.

4. Put the cream in the bowl of an electric mixer fitted with the whisk attachment and whisk until stiff peaks form. (When you lift the whisk from the mixture, a peak will form and stay upright.) Add half the whipped cream to the coconut milk mixture and stir until well blended. Gently fold in the remaining whipped cream and the shredded coconut. Divide the mixture among eight 3-ounce Popsicle molds or paper cups. Insert Popsicle sticks, and freeze until hard.

5. To make the lemon cream pops: Put the cream, milk, sugar, and salt in a medium saucepan and bring to just a simmer, stirring occasionally, over medium heat. As soon as bubbles form around the edges of the pan, remove from the heat and set aside to cool for 10 minutes.

6. Zest the lemons directly into the milk mixture. Cut the lemons in half and juice them into a small bowl, straining out the seeds. Add the lemon juice into the milk mixture, and stir to combine.

7. Divide the lemon mixture among eight 3-ounce Popsicle molds or paper cups. Insert Popsicle sticks, and freeze until hard.

8. For large servings, unmold the pops and place one of each flavor on each serving plate. Or unmold one pops at a time to enjoy at your leisure. The pops will keep, well covered, for up to 1 week in the freezer.

■

TEA AND COFFEE POPS

Creamy iced teas and coffees are well-known Asian sweet drinks. So why not enjoy them frozen? Serve these as an alternative to the traditional tea and coffee at the end of a meal on hot summer days.

CHEF'S TIP: Freeze the empty molds until you are ready to fill them, so the cold bases set as they are being poured in. Before adding the green tea powder to the milk base, make sure the liquid has cooled or the mixture will lose its vibrant green color.

Green Tea Pops

1 cup (8 ounces/227 grams) heavy whipping cream

1⅓ cups (11 ounces/313 grams) whole milk

½ cup (3¾ ounces/106 grams) sugar

¼ teaspoon salt

2 tablespoons matcha (green tea powder)

1 tablespoon fresh lemon juice

1 tablespoon vanilla extract

Thai Coffee Pops

2 cups (16 ounces/454 grams) whole milk

¼ teaspoon salt

⅔ cup (3⅛ ounces/88 grams) finely ground Thai coffee or other finely ground dark-roast coffee

⅔ cup (7 ounces/200 grams) sweetened condensed milk

1. To make the tea pops: Put the cream, milk, sugar, and salt in a medium saucepan and warm over medium heat, stirring, just until the sugar dissolves. Set aside to cool for 10 minutes.

2. Whisk the green tea powder, lemon juice, and vanilla extract into the cream mixture until well blended. Strain through a fine-mesh sieve, and divide among eight 3-ounce Popsicle molds or paper cups, and insert Popsicle sticks. Freeze until frozen hard.

3. To make the coffee pops: Put the milk and salt in a medium saucepan and bring just to a simmer over medium heat. As soon as bubbles form around the edges, stir in the coffee.

Remove from the heat and strain through a fine-mesh sieve into a bowl. Stir in the sweetened condensed milk and cool to room temperature.

4. Divide the coffee mixture among eight 3-ounce Popsicle molds, insert Popsicle sticks, and freeze until frozen hard.

5. For large servings, unmold the pops and place one of each flavor on each serving plate. Or unmold one pops at a time to enjoy at your leisure. The pops will keep, well covered, for up to 1 week in the freezer.

■

The Chinese invented ice. Okay, not ice itself, but how to collect and store it. This nature-defying discovery changed the world in a lot of ways, but as far as I'm concerned, the one that matters most is the one that follows dinner and precedes coffee. In fact, in addition to "inventing" ice, the Chinese were the first to create iced drinks and desserts. There are no exact records of any of this, mind you, but a poem in the *Shih Ching* (the *Food Canons*), written around 1100 B.C., records ice harvesting and storage, and we can safely assume that iced sweets weren't far behind.

To date, of course, the Chinese have had little to do with ice cream as we know it. Fresh dairy products have only recently become readily available in East and Southeast Asia, with ice cream becoming a big hit. Red bean and green tea are the most popular flavors, but mango, lychee, and other local fruit varieties are not far behind. In Japan, mochi ice cream—a thin layer of sticky rice mochi wrapped around a ball of ice cream—is the rage. But while countless Asian ice cream makers are creating flavors to suit Asian tastes, I use Asian flavors to suit a universal palate.

I may add an ingredient to make a standard more complex—thus, sweetened condensed milk creates a richer vanilla. Other times, I simply create something new altogether, like Mangosteen Sherbet. I always try to create flavors that are complex without being shocking and tasty without being too predictable.

RED BEAN ICE CREAM

Makes 1 quart

If you've had red bean ice cream for dessert after sushi, trust me when I say that this quintessential Asian ice cream is infinitely better homemade. Red bean ice cream is best when there are a lot of beans in the mixture. The unique earthy nuttiness of the beans adds a richness to the ice cream that even the custard base cannot rival.

CHEF'S TIP: You can find dried sweet red beans, known as *adzuki* beans in Japanese, in most Asian and some specialty markets. Do not use the red kidney beans from the local supermarket—they are very different in flavor and texture. You can substitute 1⅓ cups canned sweet red beans, also found in Asian and some specialty markets, for the cooked dried beans. Simply drain the beans, rinse well, and drain again before adding to the ice cream.

Red Beans

½ cup (3¾ ounces/107 grams) dried adzuki beans, picked over and rinsed

1 teaspoon fresh lemon juice

2 tablespoons sugar

⅛ teaspoon salt

Custard

3 large egg yolks

1 cup (8 ounces/227 grams) whole milk

¾ cup (5 ounces/141 grams) sugar

¼ teaspoon salt

1 cup (8 ounces/227 grams) heavy whipping cream

2 teaspoons vanilla extract

1. To cook the red beans: Put the red beans, lemon juice, sugar, and salt into a small saucepan and cover with 1¾ cups water. Bring to a boil over high heat and boil vigorously for 3 minutes. Turn the heat to low and simmer, uncovered, stirring occasionally, until the beans are tender, about 2 hours. If the mixture starts to look dry at any point, add ½ cup water. Set aside to cool completely.

2. To make the custard: Whisk the egg yolks in a medium mixing bowl until broken; set aside. Put the milk, sugar, salt, and ½ cup of the cream in a medium saucepan and warm over medium heat, stirring occasionally, until bubbles begin to form around the edges.

Remove from the heat and pour ½ cup of the warm milk mixture onto the yolks in a slow, steady stream, whisking constantly. Transfer the yolk mixture back to the saucepan, set over low heat, and cook, stirring constantly, until the mixture is thick enough to coat the back of a wooden spoon and registers 165°F, about 5 minutes. Remove from the heat and stir in the vanilla and cooled red beans.

3. Transfer the mixture to a large mixing bowl and stir in the remaining cream. Set over a larger bowl of ice and water and stir occasionally until cool to the touch, about 40°F. Alternatively, cover and refrigerate until cold.

4. Transfer the mixture to your ice cream maker and freeze following the manufacturer's instructions. Enjoy immediately, or freeze for a firmer ice cream. The ice cream is best enjoyed fresh, but it will keep in an airtight container in the freezer for up to 3 days.

■

MANGOSTEEN SHERBET

Makes 1 quart

Mangosteen is the queen of Thai fruits, with a unique floral and fruity juiciness unlike anything else. In Asia, fresh mangosteens are available in the summer, but, sadly, we have only the mushy fresh frozen ones, so I recommend, especially for this purpose, the canned variety that is readily available. While their flavor is subtle, it is ambrosial enough—even in canned form—to stand on its own without any adornments or accompaniments.

CHEF'S TIP: Fresh mangosteens may be available in the United States in the near future. In the meantime, canned mangosteens are available at most Asian markets.

⅔ cup (4½ ounces/126 grams) sugar

¼ teaspoon salt

1 teaspoon fresh lemon juice

Two 20-ounce cans mangosteens, drained, rinsed well, and drained again

1. Put the sugar, salt, lemon juice, and 1¼ cups water in a medium saucepan and bring to a boil over high heat, stirring occasionally, to dissolve the sugar.

2. Transfer the sugar syrup to a blender and add the mangosteens. Blend until they are pureed, with a few small fruit chunks remaining. Transfer the mixture to a large mixing bowl, set over a larger bowl of ice and water, and stir occasionally until cool to the touch, about 40°F. Alternatively, cover and refrigerate until cold.

3. Transfer the mixture to your ice cream maker and freeze following the manufacturer's instructions. Enjoy immediately, or freeze for a firmer sherbet. The sherbet is best enjoyed fresh, but it will keep in an airtight container in the freezer for up to 3 days.

■

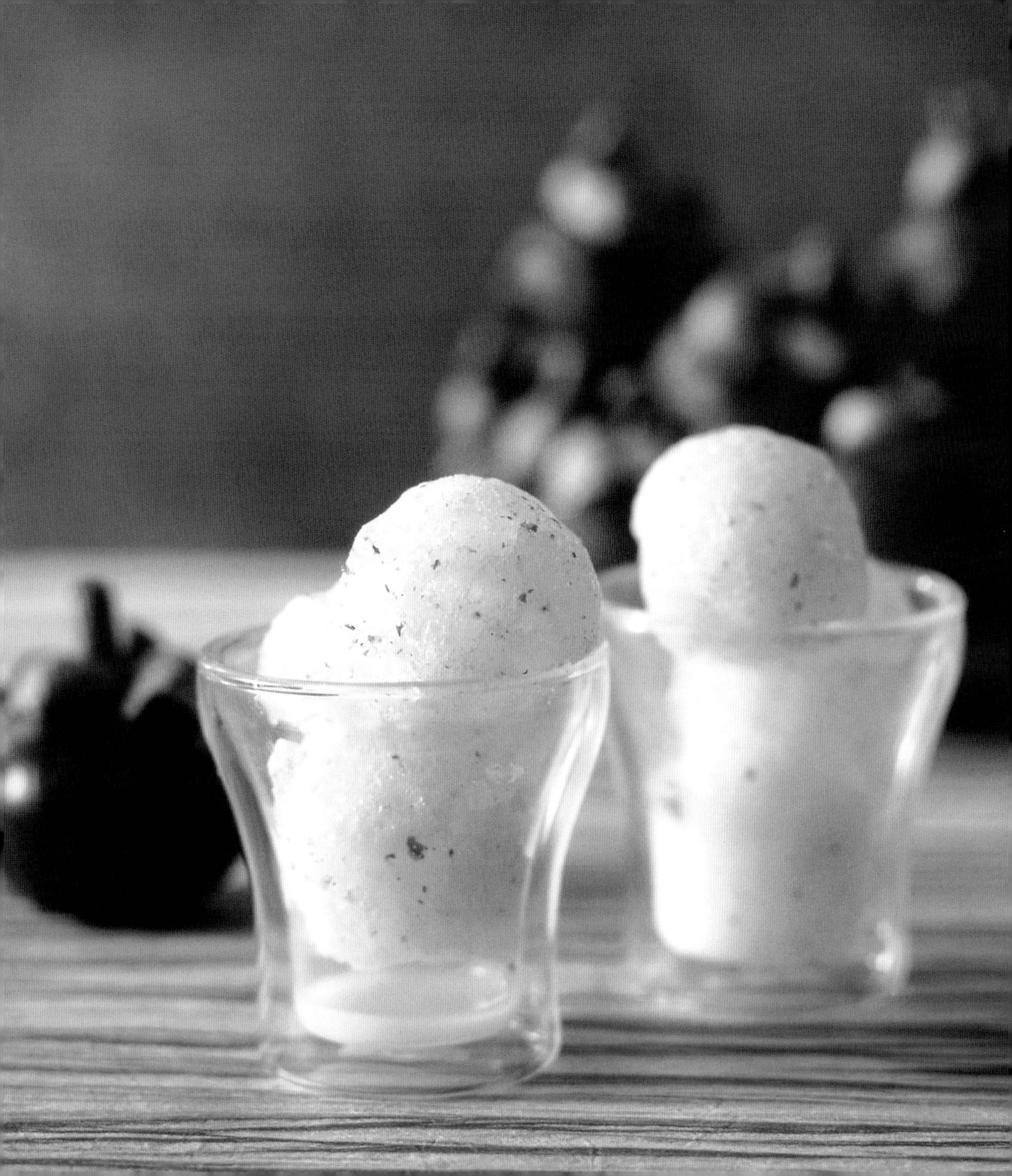

VIETNAMESE COFFEE ICE CREAM

Coffee ice creams fall into two camps: those that just taste sweet with a faint mocha aroma and those that are so intensely strong that one may as well bite into a coffee bean. The two camps meet in Vietnamese coffee, which is essentially strong, dark coffee mixed with sweetened condensed milk. When churned into an ice cream, the results are heavenly.

6 large egg yolks

1½ cups (12 ounces/339 grams) whole milk

½ cup (4 ounces/113 grams) heavy whipping cream

½ cup (1⅛ ounces/32 grams) Vietnamese, chicory, or French Roast coffee powder

½ teaspoon salt

1¼ cups (14 ounces/396 grams) sweetened condensed milk

1. Whisk the egg yolks in a medium mixing bowl until broken; set aside. Put the milk, cream, coffee powder, and salt into a medium saucepan and warm over medium heat, stirring occasionally, until bubbles begin to form around the edges. Remove from the heat and pour ½ cup of the warm milk mixture onto the yolks in a slow, steady stream, whisking constantly. Transfer the yolk mixture back to the saucepan, set over low heat, and cook, stirring constantly, until the mixture is thick enough to coat the back of a wooden spoon and registers 165°F, about 5 minutes.

2. Strain the mixture through a fine-mesh sieve into a large mixing bowl. Stir in the sweetened condensed milk. Set the mixture over a larger bowl of ice and water and stir occasionally until cool to the touch, about 40°F. Alternatively, cover and refrigerate until cold.

3. Transfer the mixture to your ice cream maker and freeze following the manufacturer's instructions. Enjoy immediately, or freeze for a firmer ice cream. The ice cream is best enjoyed fresh, but it will keep in an airtight container in the freezer for up to 3 days.

■

FROZEN ORANGE WEDGES

> At 66 restaurant, Jean-Georges Vongerichten asked me to make a fun version of the orange slices served at the end of every Chinese meal. We came up with these frozen wedges of light refreshing orange sherbet encased in candied orange peel. Pine nuts were folded into the sherbet to resemble orange seeds. These orange slices sent many very happy customers and food critics out the door.

4 large oranges

3 cups (20½ ounces/583 grams) sugar

⅛ tablespoon salt

1 tablespoon fresh lemon juice

¼ cup pine nuts

1. Cut the oranges crosswise in half and juice them; strain out the seeds but add the pulp to the juice. Keep the rinds intact and reserve them. You should end up with about 2 cups juice.

2. Put the juice in a small saucepan with ¼ cup of the sugar and the salt warm over medium heat, stirring occasionally, until the sugar dissolves. Remove from the heat, stir in the lemon juice, and pour into a bowl. Chill in the refrigerator.

3. Bring a large pot of water to a boil and add the orange rinds. Let the water return to a boil, then drain the rinds, rinse under cold water, and drain again. Repeat the process two more times.

4. Put the orange rinds, cut edges up, in the pot and cover with the remaining 2 ¾ cups sugar. Add 2 cups water and bring to a steady simmer over medium heat, then turn the heat to low and simmer for 30 minutes.

5. Flip the oranges over and simmer for another 10 minutes; the rinds should be soft. Let cool to room temperature in the saucepan, then transfer the rinds and syrup to a container that will hold the rinds snugly. Let the rinds stand in the syrup for at least 2 hours, or as long as overnight in the refrigerator.

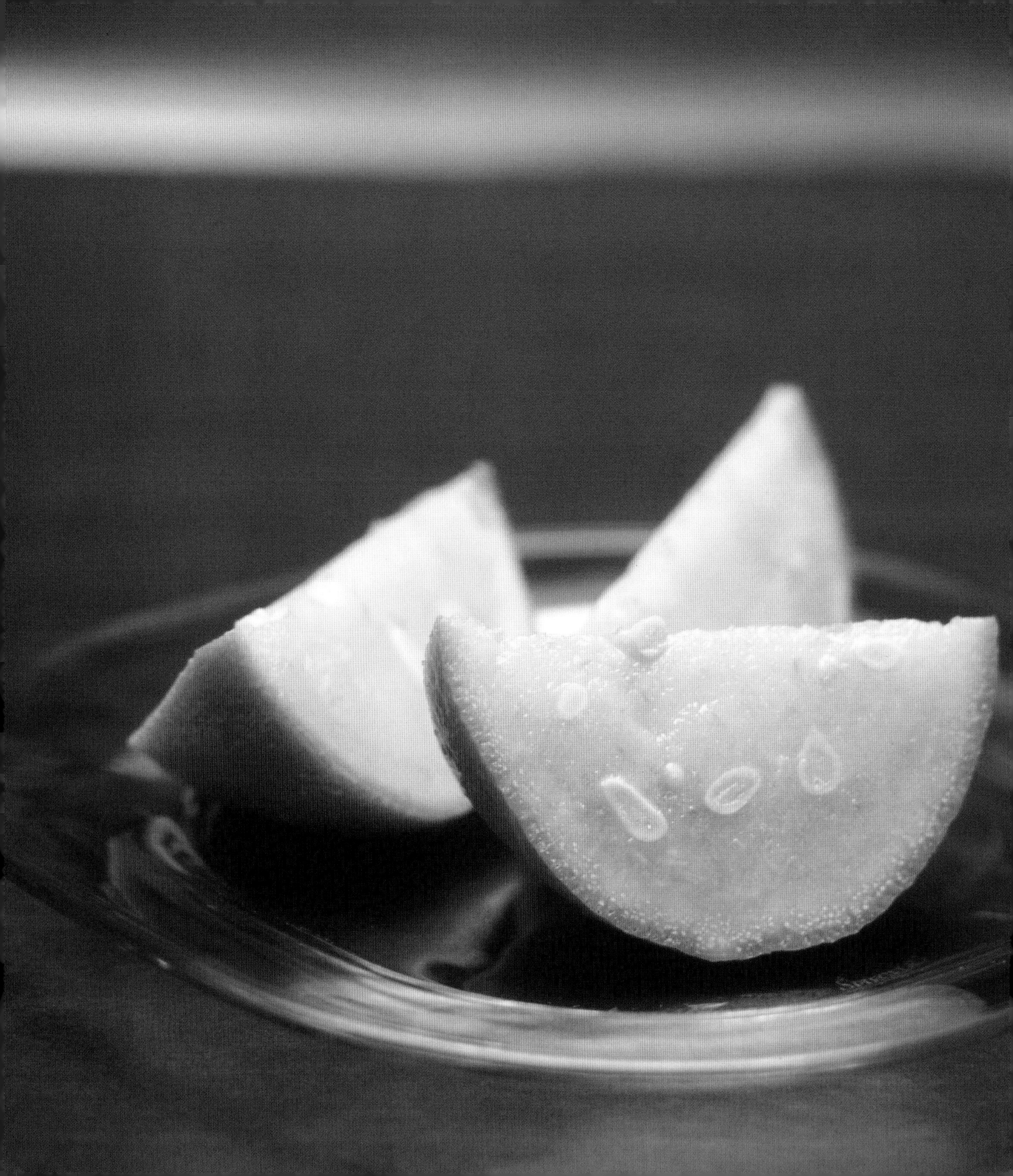

6. To assemble the dessert, remove the rinds from the syrup. Use a spoon to scoop out the remaining pulp from each one, then use the edge of the spoon to scrape out enough of the white pith to leave a shell about ⅛ inch thick. Put the rinds in individual cups or in a muffin tin that will hold them snugly.

7. Freeze the chilled orange juice mixture in an ice cream machine according to the manufacturer's instructions. When the sherbet is ready, fold in the pine nuts.

8. Fill the orange cups with the sherbet, packing it in and smoothing out the tops with the back of a knife. Cover and freeze until frozen hard.

9. To serve, cut the orange halves into wedges and arrange on serving plates.

■

BANANA–PASSION FRUIT SHERBET

Makes 1 quart

Unlike the painfully sweet rainbow sherbet in the supermarket, this version is pleasantly tart, with just enough bananas to round out the tang. I pair this with rich desserts like Jasmine Rice Pudding (page 167). It's also great on its own as a light ending to a heavy meal.

CHEF'S TIP: Passion fruit puree can be found at specialty stores and online, but be sure to get the puree and not the beverage. I use Perfect Puree of Napa Valley for this recipe. Taste the puree and adjust the sugar content to your liking.

2 cups (16 ounces/454 grams) passion fruit puree

¼ cup (2 ounces/57 grams) fresh orange juice

3 ripe bananas, peeled and roughly chopped

1½ cups (10 ounces/283 grams) sugar

1 teaspoon salt

1. Put all of the ingredients and 1¾ cups water in a large saucepan and bring to a steady simmer over medium-low heat. Cook, stirring occasionally, for 5 minutes.

2. Transfer the mixture to a blender and blend until smooth, then transfer to a large mixing bowl. Set over a larger bowl of ice and water and stir occasionally until cool to the touch, about 40°F. Alternatively, cover and refrigerate until cold.

3. Transfer the mixture to your ice cream maker and freeze following the manufacturer's instructions. Enjoy immediately, or freeze for a firmer sherbet. The sherbet is best enjoyed fresh, but it will keep in an airtight container in the freezer for up to 3 days.

■

POMEGRANATE SHERBET

Pomegranates are known as *tup thim* in Thailand, which translates as "rubies." The brilliant red seeds are as beautiful as jewels and their color only intensifies in the context of this silky sherbet. This dessert also accentuates the distinct, complex flavor of pomegranates, at once sharp and rich. Plus, they are chock-full of antioxidants and vitamin C. What more could you want?

CHEF'S TIP: To make fresh pomegranate juice, liquefy pomegranate seeds in a blender with a little bit of water. Strain through a fine-mesh sieve.

3 cups (24 ounces/680 grams) pomegranate juice

½ cup (3¾ ounces/106 grams) sugar

2 tablespoons pomegranate molasses or honey

2 teaspoons fresh lemon juice

1. Put all the ingredients into a large saucepan, set over medium heat, and warm, stirring, just until the sugar is completely dissolved.

2. Transfer the mixture to a large mixing bowl. Set over a larger bowl of ice and water and stir occasionally until cool to the touch, about 40°F. Alternatively, cover and refrigerate until cold.

3. Transfer the mixture to your ice cream maker and freeze following the manufacturer's instructions. Enjoy immediately, or freeze for a firmer sherbet. The sherbet is best enjoyed fresh, but it will keep in an airtight container in the freezer for up to 3 days.

■

LEMONGRASS FROZEN YOGURT

Makes 1 quart

Lemongrass is exactly what it sounds like—a refreshing combination of bright citrus and grassy herb. Although it's more often used in savory dishes than in sweet, I enjoy playing with this Southeast Asian staple in my desserts. When combined with yogurt, the lemongrass takes on a more pronounced tang, ideal for hot summer days. This yogurt is so good I eat it straight out of the ice cream machine, but I also like adding a scoop to creamy desserts like Lemongrass Tapioca and Tropical Fruit (page 275).

CHEF'S TIP: Choose fresh lemongrass stalks that are firm and fragrant.

2 stalks lemongrass, trimmed, smashed, and chopped

2½ cups (20 ounces/568 grams) whole milk

1 cup (7 ounces/200 grams) sugar

¼ teaspoon salt

4 large egg yolks

1¾ cups (14⅛ ounces/400 grams) plain whole-milk yogurt

2 teaspoons fresh lemon juice

1. Put the lemongrass and milk in a blender and blend until the lemongrass is finely chopped. Transfer the mixture to a medium saucepan, add the sugar and salt, and warm over medium heat, stirring occasionally, until bubbles begin to form around the edge. Remove from the heat and let sit for 10 minutes.

2. Whisk the egg yolks in a medium mixing bowl until broken; set aside. Pour ½ cup of the warm milk mixture onto the yolks in a slow, steady stream, whisking constantly. Transfer the yolk mixture back to the saucepan, set over low heat, and cook, stirring constantly, until the mixture is thick enough to coat the back of a wooden spoon and registers 165°F, about 5 minutes.

3. Strain the mixture through a fine-mesh sieve into a large bowl, pressing all of the liquid out of the lemongrass. Cool the mixture until it is lukewarm, about 20 minutes.

4. Stir the yogurt and lemon juice into the milk mixture. Set the bowl over a larger bowl of ice and water and stir occasionally until cool to the touch, about 40°F. Alternatively, cover and refrigerate until cold.

5. Transfer the mixture to your ice cream maker and freeze following the manufacturer's instructions. Enjoy immediately, or freeze for a firmer frozen yogurt. This is best enjoyed fresh, but it will keep in an airtight container in the freezer for up to 3 days.

Lemongrass-Vodka Frozen Yogurt: Substitute 2½ teaspoons lemon or citrus vodka for the lemon juice.

Light Lemongrass Frozen Yogurt: Omit the egg yolks. After the milk steeps with the lemongrass and cools until it is lukewarm, stir in the yogurt and lemon juice and proceed as above.

■

COCONUT ICE CREAM SANDWICHES WITH TROPICAL FRUIT SALAD

Makes 8 to10 servings

Ice cream is always a welcome dessert at parties, but it's even better when transformed into a finger food you can prepare completely ahead of time. If you want to make this a pretty plated dessert, serve it with the fresh fruit salad. The kaffir lime leaves add a perfumey citrus flavor with just a hint of tartness to the fruit. Either component can be eaten alone and thoroughly enjoyed. Taking everything together in one bite? Even better.

CHEF'S TIPS: You can find fresh kaffir lime leaves in Asian and some specialty markets. To make this even simpler, cut the whole cookie sheet in half, spread the ice cream evenly onto one half, and top with the other. Freeze until firm, then cut into squares or triangles and freeze again until ready to serve. Or you can break the cookie into free form shapes as in the photograph.

Coconut Ice Cream

¾ cup (6 ounces/170 grams) whole milk

⅔ cup (6 ounces/170 grams) unsweetened coconut milk

1½ cups (4⅝ ounces/130 grams) finely shredded unsweetened dried coconut

¾ cup (5¼ ounces/150 grams) sugar

¼ teaspoon salt

8 large egg yolks

1½ cups (12 ounces/340 grams) heavy whipping cream

3 tablespoons coconut-flavored rum, preferably Malibu, optional

Toasted Coconut Cookies

Nonstick cooking spray

2 large eggs, at room temperature

1 teaspoon grated lime zest

½ cup (3½ ounces/100 grams) sugar

⅛ teaspoon salt

½ teaspoon vanilla extract

1⅓ cups (4 ounces/115 grams) finely shredded unsweetened dried coconut

Tropical Fruit Salad

¼ cup diced papaya

¼ cup diced strawberries

¼ cup diced mango

1 tablespoon sugar

1 tablespoon fresh lime juice

1 teaspoon minced kaffir lime leaves (about 3 leaves)

1. To make the coconut ice cream: Put the milk, coconut milk, dried coconut, sugar, and salt in a medium saucepan and set over medium heat. Bring to a steady simmer and cook, stirring occasionally, for 10 minutes. Remove from the heat.

2. Whisk the egg yolks in a medium mixing bowl until broken. Pour ½ cup of the warm milk mixture onto the yolks in a slow, steady stream, whisking constantly. Transfer the yolk mixture back to the saucepan, set over low heat, and cook, stirring constantly, until the mixture is thick enough to coat the back of a wooden spoon and registers 165°F, about 5 minutes.

3. Strain the mixture through a fine-mesh sieve into a large mixing bowl, then pour the cream through the sieve, pressing on the coconut flakes to extract as much liquid as possible. Stir in the rum, if desired. Set the mixture over a larger bowl of ice and water and stir occasionally until cool to the touch, about 40°F. Alternatively, cover and refrigerate until cold.

4. Transfer the mixture to your ice cream maker and freeze following the manufacturer's instructions. Transfer to an airtight container and freeze.

5. Meanwhile, make the coconut cookies: Preheat the oven to 300°F. Lightly spray a 13 × 9-inch rimmed baking sheet or baking pan with nonstick cooking spray, line with parchment paper, and spray the paper; set aside.

6. Put the eggs, lime zest, sugar, and salt into the bowl of an electric mixer fitted with the whisk attachment. Whisk on medium speed until thick, pale yellow, and doubled in volume, about 8 minutes. Stir in the vanilla extract, and gently fold in the coconut.

7. Spread the batter evenly onto the prepared baking sheet. Bake until golden brown, about 20 minutes. Remove from the oven and cool in the pan for 5 minutes.

8. Invert the cookie onto a cutting board. While warm, use a 2¼-inch round biscuit cutter to cut out 16 circles. Cool the circles completely.

9. To make the fruit salad: Toss the fruit with the sugar and lime juice. Cover and refrigerate until ready to serve. Immediately before serving, stir in the kaffir lime leaves.

10. To assemble the ice cream sandwiches: Put a scoop of ice cream on top of 8 of the coconut cookies. Top with the remaining 8 cookies and press down gently to form sandwiches. Cover and freeze until frozen hard.

11. Serve the ice cream sandwiches with the fruit salad on the side.

■

THE ORIGINAL ICE DESSERT: SHAVED ICE

Ice seems like an unlikely inspiration for any great dish. But its humble status as, well, frozen water is exactly why it is the perfect foundation for fabulous desserts. Sadly, snow cones and Italian ices are the only well-known ice desserts in America. But there's so much more out there.

In Asia, ice has long been among the most popular foundations for summer treats. Despite the region's increased consumption of Western ice cream treats in recent decades, shaved ice desserts remain popular, and nothing is more refreshing on a hot and humid summer day.

Few places have hotter or more humid summers than Singapore, and I grew up eating the Singaporean national summer dessert, *ice kachang,* made in the street food stalls. Condensed and evaporated milks are drizzled over shaved ice to make a bracingly fresh and cold "ice cream." Mali syrup, flavored by jasmine flowers, adds a sweet floral aroma. This glorious concoction is then topped with a mixture of tropical fruits—like jackfruit and palm seeds—and sweet red and white beans. Perfect.

Taiwan is known for shaved ice creations with esoteric toppings such as grass jelly, taro, and pearl barley, although the standard accompaniments—like sweet beans and lychee—are also common. The "toppings" go on the bottom, and the mountain of shaved ice that tops them is then drizzled with sweetened condensed milk for a creamy finish.

The Korean version of this treat, called *paht bing-su,* has a decidedly Western flair. Fresh fruit like strawberries, bananas, kiwis, and cantaloupe often supply the flavor, while ice cream lends depth and richness to the dish. While it may seem like overkill to combine ice and ice cream—trust me, it's not. The combination of creamy cold and crunchy cold is fabulous. The occasional dash of chocolate syrup, whipped cream, and Fruity Pebbles cereal doesn't hurt either.

Perhaps the most Westernized version of Asian shaved ice desserts is the Filipino dish *halo-halo,* or "mix-mix," in which shaved ice tops a layer of flan—yes, flan. Native Filipino fruits like coconut and pineapple complete this fusion frozen treat.

I have tasted just about every shaved ice dessert that Asia has to offer. Now I've combined my favorite parts of each to create my own version—Thai Jewels and Fruits on Crushed Coconut Ice. These shaved ice treats are meant to be enjoyed any time of day. Light and refreshing after a meal, delightful in the middle of the afternoon, or palate-cleansing between spicy bites at an Asian feast.

SHAVED ICE WITH SUMMER CORN, AVOCADO, AND RED BEANS

Makes 8 servings

I grew up eating *ice kachang* on the streets of Singapore on hot summer days. Each vendor had his own special toppings—the ones below are mine. Crisp summer corn is offset by creamy avocado, tender sweet beans, and crunchy peanuts. The coconut milk sauce binds all those flavors together. This refreshing treat tastes best after a barbecue or spicy meal.

CHEF'S TIP: If you have an ice-shaving machine, either electric or hand-crank, use it here. Otherwise, my technique below is the closest you can get to delicate, snowflake-like shaved ice.

½ cup (2⅞ ounces/80 grams) crushed palm sugar

1½ cups (14 ounces/400 grams) unsweetened coconut milk

¼ teaspoon salt

3 tablespoons granulated sugar

2 ears corn, shucked

1 avocado, peeled, pitted, and cut into ¼-inch cubes

1½ cups (16⅓ ounces/463 grams) cooked sweet red beans (see page 240) or canned sweet red beans, drained, rinsed, and drained again

¾ cup (4 ounces/115 grams) unsalted peanuts, toasted

½ cup (4 ounces/113 grams) evaporated milk

1. Put the palm sugar and 1 cup water in a small saucepan, set over medium-high heat, and cook, stirring occasionally to dissolve the sugar, until the syrup becomes a dark caramel brown, about 10 minutes. Stir in the coconut milk, bring to a boil, and add the salt. Transfer to a bowl and refrigerate until cold.

2. Put 6 cups water in a large baking pan or tray and transfer to the freezer. As soon as it solidifies, scrape the surface with a fork to make tiny, fluffy ice crystals. If the ice begins to melt as you're scraping, freeze for 5 minutes, and resume. To expedite the process, you can freeze multiple pans of water simultaneously, as thinner layers of ice will freeze faster. You can also scrape the ice ahead of time and freeze until ready to use.

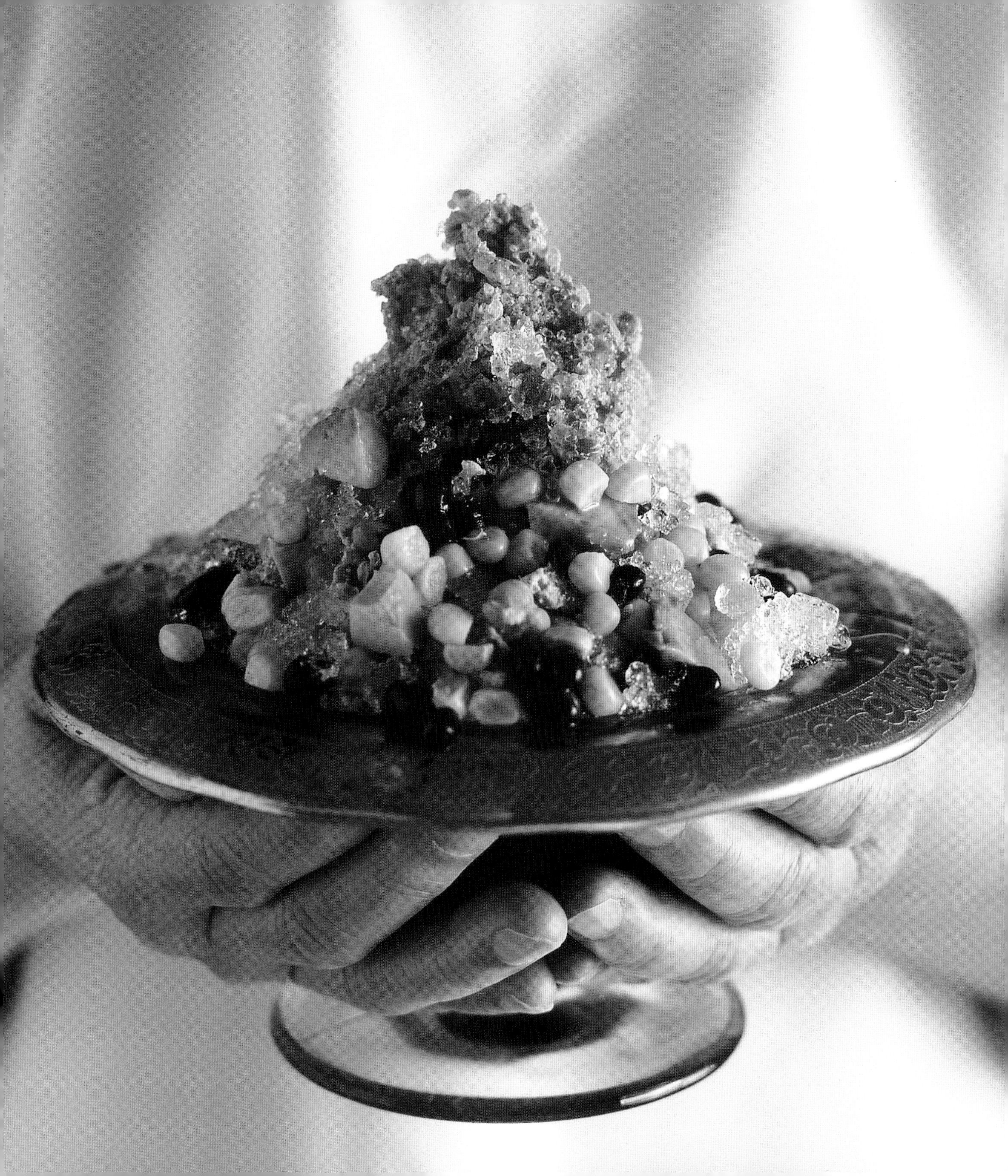

3. While the ice is freezing, bring a large pot of water to a boil. Add the sugar and corn, return to a boil, and cook just until the corn is warmed through but still crisp, about 3 minutes. Drain and cool completely.

4. Cut off the corn kernels and set aside.

5. Fluff the shaved ice with a fork and divide among eight serving bowls, forming the ice into little peaked mountains. Divide the avocado, beans, peanuts, and corn among the bowls, drizzle the tops with the chilled coconut sauce and the evaporated milk, and serve immediately.

■

THAI JEWELS AND FRUITS ON CRUSHED COCONUT ICE

Makes 8 servings

The inspiration for this incredibly popular dessert was the endless variations on shaved ice snacks enjoyed in street markets throughout Asia. At its core, the dish is just a heap of tapioca dumplings, crushed young coconut juice, and chilled coconut sauce. I found that fragrant jasmine flowers, in the form of mali syrup, pair perfectly with earthy, aromatic vanilla beans. Adding vibrant tropical fruits turns this dessert into a veritable greenhouse of goodness.

CHEF'S TIP: If you can't find red sala syrup, substitute grenadine.

Coconut Sauce

1 cup (7½ ounces/212 grams) sugar

1 teaspoon salt

3½ cups (30⅞ ounces/875 grams unsweetened coconut milk

2 vanilla beans, split lengthwise in half, seeds scraped out, and seeds and pods reserved

1 cup (8 ounces/227 grams) whole milk

Mali Syrup

⅔ cup (4 ounces/112 grams) crushed palm sugar

1 vanilla bean, split lengthwise in half, seeds scraped out, and seeds and pod reserved

1¾ teaspoons salt

1 tablespoon mali syrup

Thai Jewels

9 ounces (255 grams) fresh water chestnuts, peeled and cut into ¼-inch dice

½ cup (4 ounces/113 grams) red sala syrup

2½ teaspoons green pandan paste

3 cups (12½ ounces/354 grams) tapioca flour

2⅔ cups (21 ounces/597 grams) frozen unsweetened coconut juice, thawed, coconut pieces removed and sliced, and juice refrozen

1 cup (4 ounces/114 grams) palm seeds, rinsed and quartered

1 cup (5 ounces/142 grams) thinly sliced jackfruit

1 cup (5 ounces/142 grams) diced papaya, preferably red

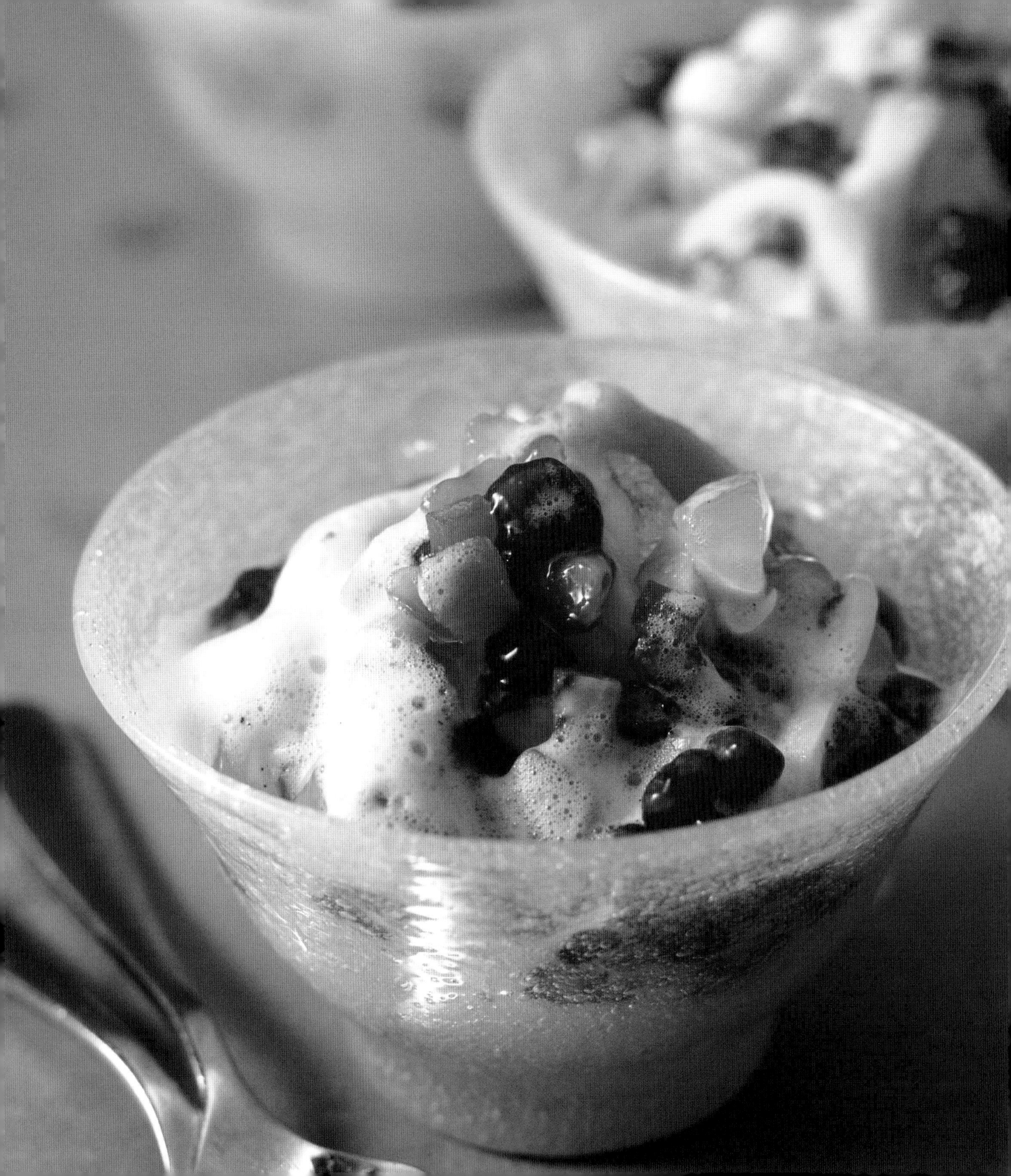

1. To make the coconut sauce: Put the sugar, salt, coconut milk, and vanilla seeds and pods in a medium saucepan, set over medium heat, and bring to a simmer, stirring occasionally, until the sugar dissolves. Remove from the heat and stir in the milk and the remaining palm sugar syrup. Transfer to a container with a tight lid, cover, and refrigerate until completely chilled.

2. To make the syrup: Put the palm sugar, vanilla seeds and pod, 1¼ teaspoons of the salt, and 1 cup water in a medium saucepan, set over medium heat, and cook, stirring occasionally, until the sugar is dissolved. Remove from the heat, stir in the mali syrup, and let cool to room temperature.

3. Meanwhile, make the Thai jewels: Divide the water chestnuts between two small mixing bowls. Add the red sala syrup to one bowl and the green pandan paste to the other and mix well to coat and color the water chestnuts. Let sit for at least 10 minutes, or cover and refrigerate overnight.

4. Drain the water chestnuts, reserving the soaking liquid in two large bowls and keeping the red and green chestnuts separate. Add ⅓ cup of the palm sugar syrup to each of the two bowls.

5. Bring a large pot of water to a boil over high heat and add the remaining ½ teaspoon salt. Toss the red water chestnuts with half of the tapioca flour in a mixing bowl—shake vigorously to coat well. Transfer the water chestnuts to a sieve and tap the sides to remove any excess starch, which could cause clumping. Add the chestnuts to the boiling water and cook, stirring constantly, until they float to the surface, about 5 minutes. Drain, transfer to a large bowl of ice and water, and cool completely. Drain again and add to the bowl of red syrup. Repeat with the green water chestnuts, putting them in the green syrup after cooling them. Refrigerate both until ready to serve.

6. To assemble: Transfer the frozen coconut juice to a large sturdy plastic bag and pound it with a heavy skillet until it becomes finely crushed ice. Drain the water chestnuts and toss with the coconut pieces, palm seeds, jackfruit, and papaya. Divide the coconut ice among eight serving bowls and top with the red and green jewels and mixed fruit. Shake the coconut sauce until foamy, divide among the serving bowls, and serve immediately.

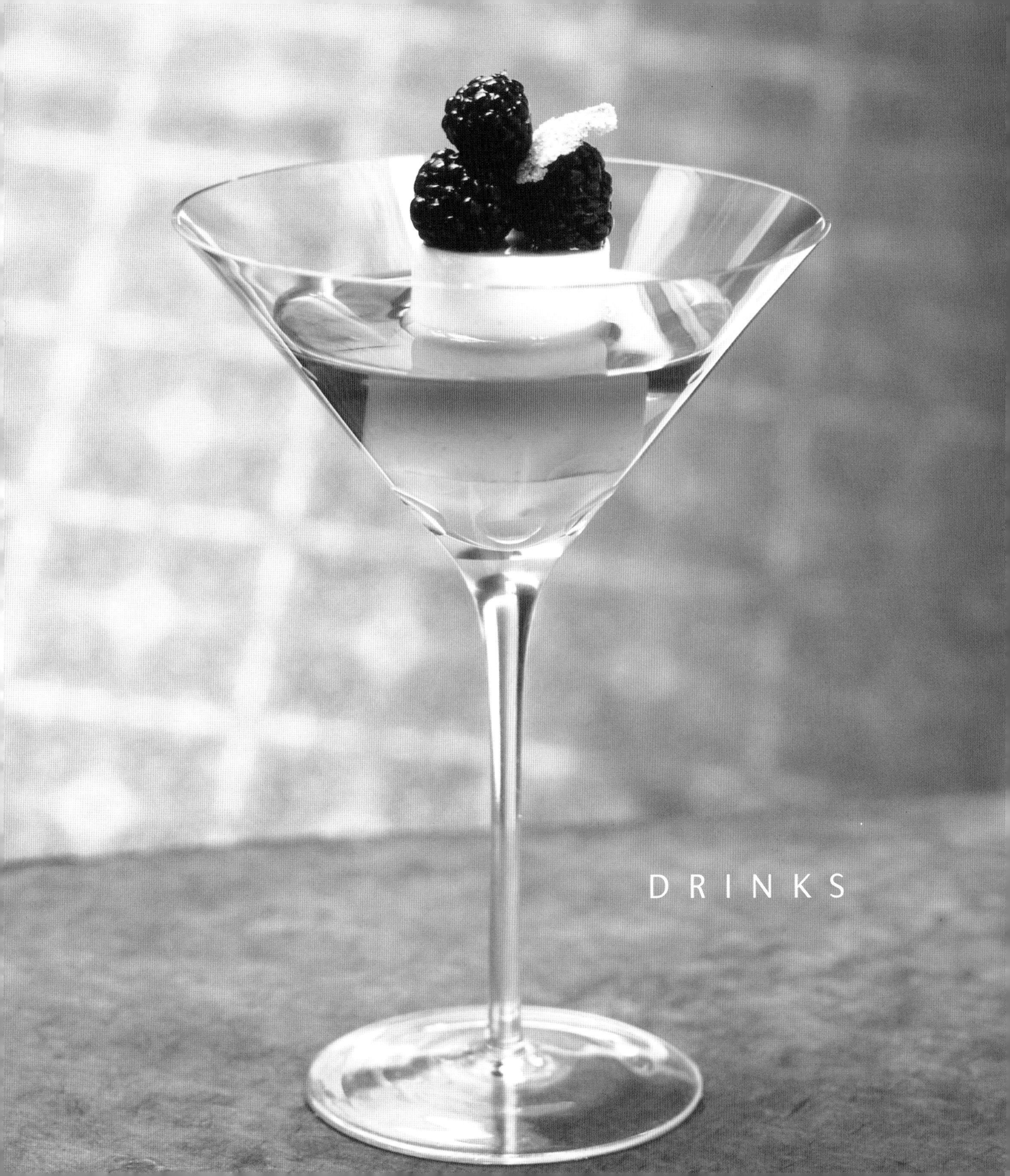

DRINKS

To say that tea is an important part of Asian life is an understatement. In Asia, tea *is* life. As soon as you enter someone's home, they offer you hot tea. Your teapot is constantly refreshed throughout your meal at an Asian restaurant. Tea is used to make deals, to tie families together at weddings, to celebrate births, and to mourn deaths. More than a beverage, tea has influenced the economics, politics, culture, and cuisine of the entire region.

As important as tea is in Asia, however, there is a universe of drinks beyond it. And given the hot and humid climate that predominates throughout much of Asia, many of these drinks take the form of icy, refreshing treats to be enjoyed before, during, or after a meal. These concoctions often take advantage of the tropical fruits native to the region, but they also employ two other ingredients—sweetened condensed milk and tapioca.

Sweetened condensed milk, which is evaporated milk mixed with sugar, was originally introduced to dairy-poor Southeast Asia as a nutritional supplement. These days, although condensed milk is still used to fortify diets, its rich sweetness and luscious creaminess have found a more extravagant use in various desserts and drinks, particularly tea and coffee, where it is used as a sugar substitute. The interaction of flavors between coffee and sweetened condensed milk is especially compelling and utterly unique—it's

one of my favorite pairings and a trustworthy foundation for many of my desserts.

Tapioca pearls are small round balls processed from the starchy root of the cassava plant. Cassava is indigenous to South America, but its hardiness led to widespread growth in Asia and Africa, where its other qualities helped it become a staple, particularly in war-torn regions in the early and mid-twentieth century. Like sweetened condensed milk, tapioca pearls have been adapted for use in desserts, where their chewiness and relatively neutral flavor match well with a variety of sweet and crunchy ingredients.

TAPIOCA TEA

In New York, it started with the neighborhood kids in Chinatown. After school, they would pop into little bakeries and tea shops and emerge with plastic cups filled with colorful liquid and an insidious-looking black mass at the bottom of the cup. Their wide smiles signaled it was something good. Adventurous foodies started to follow them into those shops, emerging grinning like kids. Soon, chic restaurants started presenting cocktails in tall slender glasses filled with those same tiny black balls. Almost at the same time, tiny tumblers of those same little balls were being passed around at parties, weddings, and every other hot social event.

Tapioca tea, also known as bubble tea, boba tea, or pearl tea, exploded on the drink scene in the 1990s. Unlike many other pan-Pacific food trends, which start on one side of the ocean and travel to the other, the bubble tea phenomenon unfolded nearly simultaneously in America and Asia. The story starts in the early 1980s, in Taiwan, although no one knows exactly where or with whom. In any case, some culinary genius figured out that you could add cooked tapioca pearls to sweetened flavored tea, supply a fat straw for slurping, and watch the customers come in droves. The drink soon spread to Hong Kong and other parts of Asia, while Taiwanese transplants in America began re-creating the drink here.

For generations of Americans, the word "tapioca" conjures up memories of dreadful cafeteria lunches or disappointing lunch bag "treats." In Asia, however, tapioca has long been a valued dessert component, and that tradition has led to sophisticated and delicious preparations of the ingredient. In fact, tapioca pearls—like those in tapioca tea—form the basis of many Asian desserts. Although these desserts often feature "black" tapioca pearls—so colored because of the brown sugar added during the manufacturing process—I prefer the more traditional small white pearls. Flavorless, they are ideal for enhancing the texture of any dessert and make for a much prettier presentation.

VIETNAMESE COFFEE TAPIOCA "AFFOGATO"

Makes 8 servings

In New York City, Chinatown and Little Italy are next-door neighbors. Since I love both Taiwanese tapioca milk teas from Chinatown storefronts and affogatos from the sidewalk cafés in Little Italy, I decided to see what would happen if I combined the two. The results are spectacular. If you don't have Vietnamese coffee and don't want to make condensed milk ice cream, you can revert to the traditional espresso and vanilla ice cream pairing, but the tapioca is a must.

CHEF'S TIP: You can prepare each component—the tapioca, coffee, and ice cream—ahead of time. (Room-temperature coffee works fine.) Transfer the drained tapioca pearls to a large container and add enough cold water to cover the tapioca by 1 inch. Stir well and then drain before using.

Condensed Milk Ice Cream

5 large egg yolks

2 cups (16 ounces/454 grams) whole milk

1¼ cups (14 ounces/396 grams) sweetened condensed milk

1 vanilla bean, split lengthwise in half, seeds scraped out, and seeds and pod reserved, or ½ teaspoon vanilla extract

½ teaspoon salt

Vietnamese Coffee Affogato

½ cup (3¾ ounces/106 grams) sugar

½ teaspoon salt

½ cup (2⅞ ounces/80 grams) small tapioca pearls (⅛-inch diameter)

¼ cup (½ ounce/14 grams) Vietnamese, chicory, or French-roast coffee powder

8 Walnut Cookies (page 104), crushed to small crumbs, optional

1. To make the ice cream: Whisk the egg yolks in a medium mixing bowl until broken; set aside. Put the milk, condensed milk, vanilla seeds and pod, if using, and salt in a medium saucepan and set over medium heat. When bubbles start to form around the edges, remove from the heat. Pour ½ cup of the warm milk mixture onto the yolks in a slow, steady stream, whisking constantly. Transfer the yolk mixture back to the saucepan, set over low

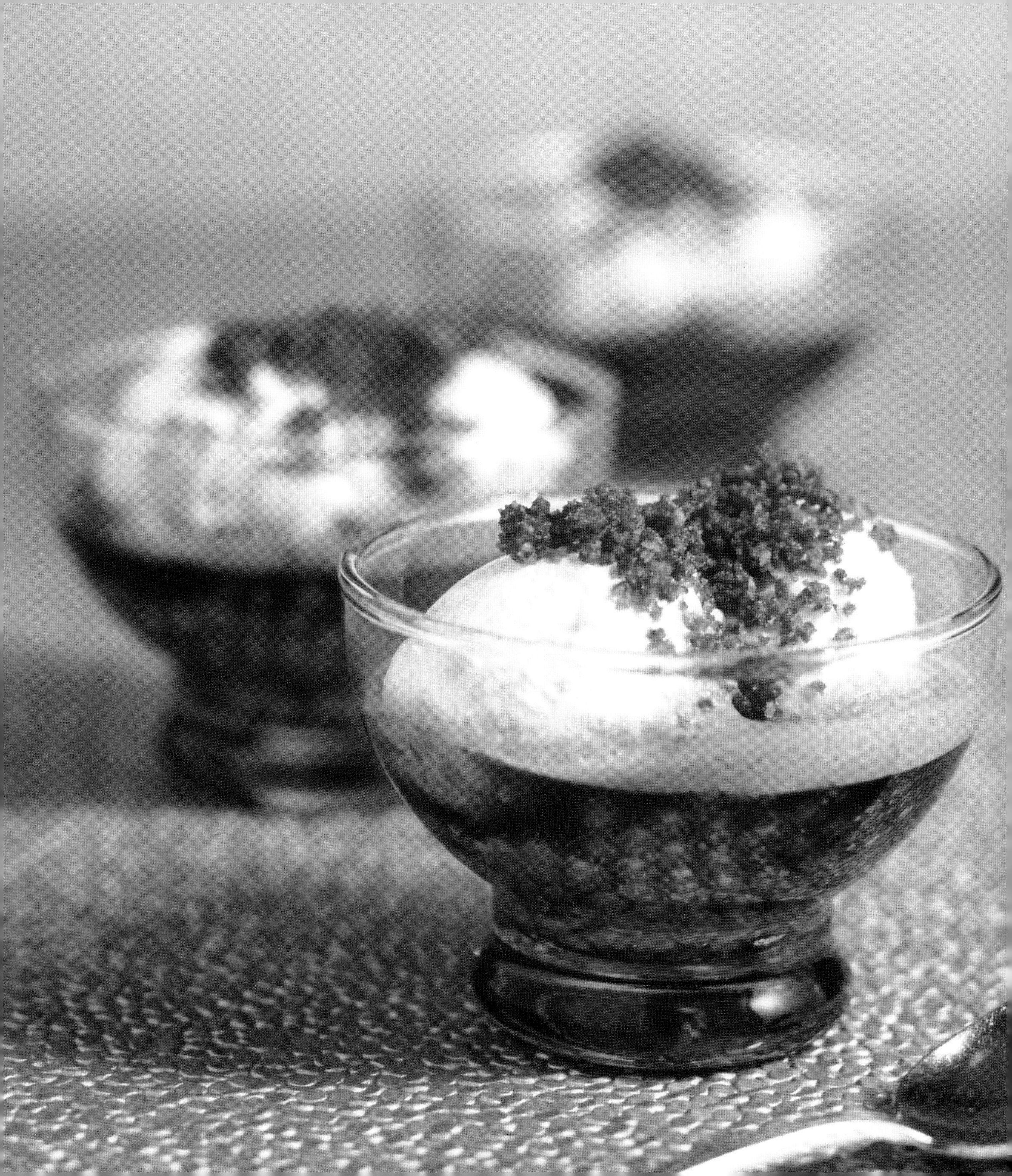

heat, and cook, stirring constantly, until the mixture is thick enough to coat the back of a wooden spoon and registers 165°F, about 5 minutes.

2. Strain the mixture into a large mixing bowl. Stir in the vanilla extract, if using. Set the mixture over a larger bowl of ice and water and stir occasionally until cool to the touch, about 40°F. Alternatively, cover and refrigerate until cold.

3. Transfer the mixture to your ice cream maker and freeze following the manufacturer's instructions. Transfer to a freezer container and place in the freezer. The ice cream is best fresh, but it will keep in an airtight container in the freezer for up to 3 days.

4. To make the affogato: Put the sugar, salt, and 6 cups water in a large saucepan and bring to a boil over high heat. Add the tapioca and cook, stirring, until the water returns to a rapid boil. Turn the heat to medium and continue stirring occasionally until the tapioca is cooked through, about 15 minutes. It's done when it's almost translucent, with a pinpoint of white in the center; the balls should be tender but still chewy. Drain, rinse under cold water, drain again, and immediately divide among eight serving bowls or glasses.

5. Brew the coffee: If you have a traditional Vietnamese drip coffee canister, use it; otherwise, use a coffee machine. Line the filter with two paper filters and pack in the coffee tightly. Add 3 cups water to the machine, and use the slow drip option if available. You should end up with about 2 cups of very strong coffee.

6. Divide the hot coffee among the bowls and put 2 scoops of ice cream on top. Garnish with cookie crumbs, if desired. Serve immediately with fat straws or spoons.

■

FRESH MELON AND TAPIOCA

This is both a classic haute Chinese dessert and a humble home-style treat whipped up in minutes by mothers across Asia. It's the ideal use for ripe, musky melons. This preparation heightens their juicy sweetness while simultaneously mellowing it with chewy tapioca pearls and creamy coconut milk.

CHEF'S TIP: Give the dessert a shake or stir before eating to combine the tapioca with the creamy, fragrant liquid.

4 cups (22½ ounces/636 grams) chopped ripe cantaloupe, honeydew, or other melon

3 tablespoons sugar, plus more to taste

⅛ teaspoon salt

1 cup (5⅔ ounces/160 grams) small tapioca pearls (⅛-inch diameter)

1 cup (9 ounces/255 grams) unsweetened coconut milk

1. Put the melon and 2 tablespoons of the sugar and salt in a blender and blend until completely smooth. Taste and add more sugar, if desired. Transfer to a medium mixing bowl, cover, and refrigerate until ready to use.

2. Bring 8 cups water to a rolling boil in a large pot over high heat. Add the tapioca and cook, stirring, until the water returns to a rapid boil. Turn the heat to medium and continue stirring occasionally until the tapioca is cooked through, about 25 minutes. It's done when it's almost translucent, with a pinpoint of white in the center; the balls should be tender but still chewy.

3. Drain the tapioca, rinse under cold water, and drain again. Put in a medium mixing bowl and stir in the coconut milk and the remaining 1 tablespoon sugar.

4. Divide the pureed melon among eight serving glasses or bowls and top with the tapioca mixture. Serve immediately with fat straws or spoons, instructing your guests to stir the dessert to combine.

■

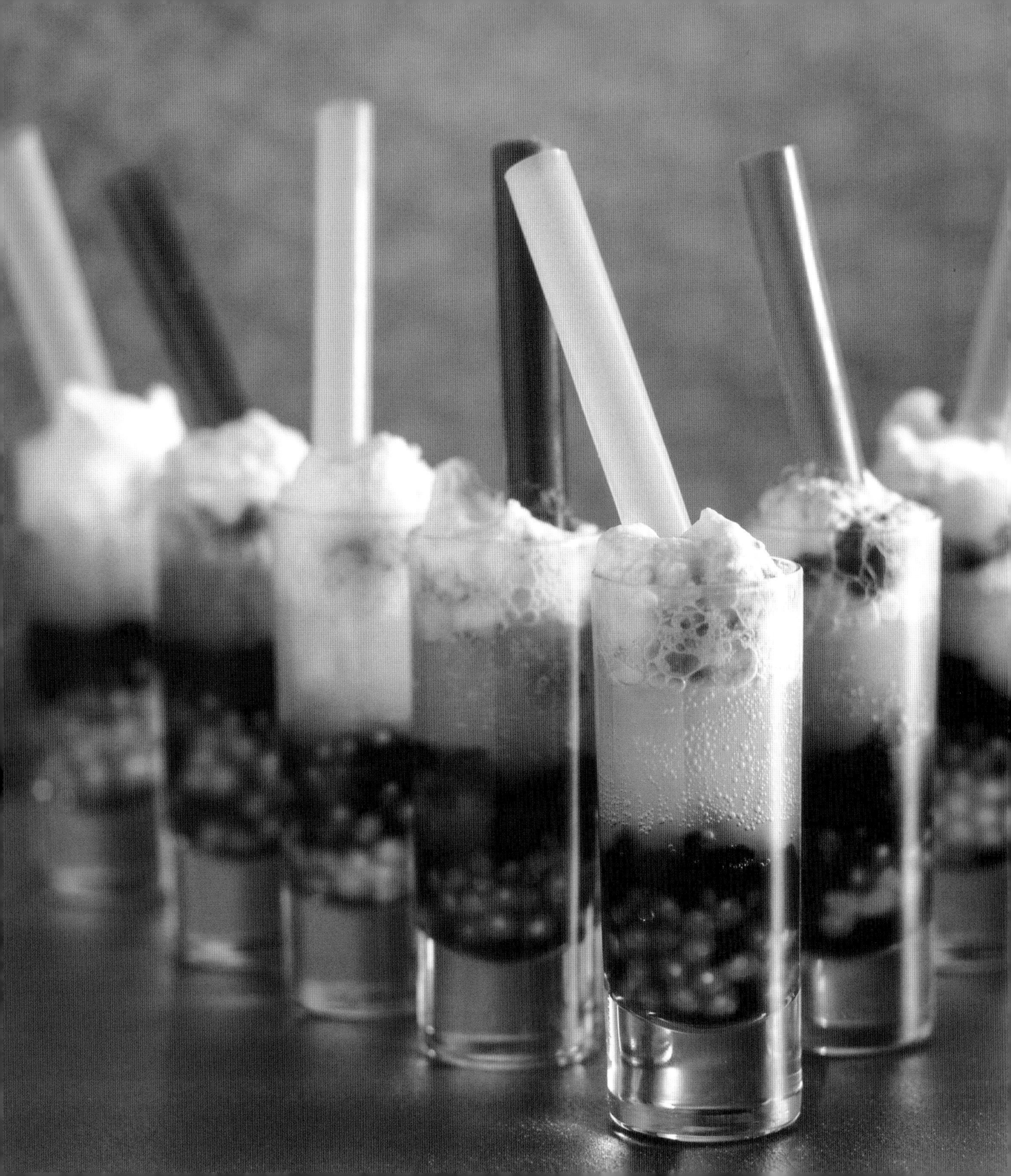

CONCORD GRAPE TAPIOCA FLOAT WITH GINGER SOUR CREAM SHERBET

Makes 8 servings

Concord grapes are a deep purple-black variety indigenous to North America. Their gorgeous color, robust flavor, sweet aroma, and unique juicy texture make them my favorite grape. Because the harvesting season is short, I like to make Concord grape preserves, which will last the entire year. Plus, when the grapes are cooked, the flavor and color become even more intense. At once warming and refreshing, this drink is an exotic finish to any meal.

CHEF'S TIP: Fresh Concord grapes are usually available for only a brief period in the fall, generally around late September and early October. If you miss the chance to make your own preserves, you can buy Concord grape jam year-round at nearly any supermarket.

Concord Grape Preserves

2 pounds (908 grams) Concord grapes, stemmed, rinsed, and drained

¼ teaspoon salt

2¼ cups (15 ounces/424 grams) sugar

2 lemons

Ginger Sour Cream Sherbet

1 cup plus 2 tablespoons (7½ ounces/212 grams) sugar

One 4-inch piece fresh ginger, chopped

½ teaspoon salt

2 cups (16 ounces/454 grams) buttermilk

¾ cup (6⅜ ounces/180 grams) sour cream

½ cup (2⅞ ounces/80 grams) small tapioca pearls (⅛-inch diameter)

¼ teaspoon salt

4 cups (32 ounces/908 grams) club soda, chilled and preferably from unopened bottles

1. To make the grape preserves: Bring a large heavy saucepan of water to a boil. Add the grapes and salt and bring back to a boil. Immediately remove from the heat and drain the grapes in a large fine-mesh sieve. Set the sieve over the empty saucepan and press on the grapes with a wooden spoon to extract all the juices, straining out the seeds and skin.

2. Add the sugar to the grape juice. Zest the lemons directly into the saucepan. Cut the lemons in half and juice them into the saucepan, straining out the seeds. Set over medium-low heat and cook, stirring occasionally, until the mixture is thick enough to coat the back of a wooden spoon, about 40 minutes. Remove from the heat and cool completely. The preserves can be refrigerated in an airtight container for up to 2 weeks.

3. To make the sherbet: Put the sugar, ginger, salt, and 1 cup water in a medium saucepan, set over high heat, and bring to a boil, stirring occasionally. Turn the heat to medium and simmer until the ginger syrup is reduced by one-third and thick, about 20 minutes.

4. Strain the ginger syrup through a fine-mesh sieve into a large mixing bowl. Pour the buttermilk through the sieve and press hard on the ginger pieces to extract as much liquid as possible. Add the sour cream to the bowl and whisk until it melts. Set the bowl over a larger bowl filled with ice and water and cool until cold, stirring occasionally.

5. Transfer the sour cream mixture to an ice cream machine and freeze according to the manufacturer's instructions.

6. Meanwhile, bring 5 cups water to a boil in a large saucepan over medium-high heat. Add the tapioca and cook, stirring, until the water returns to a rapid boil. Turn the heat to medium and continue stirring until the tapioca is cooked through, about 15 minutes. It's done when it's almost translucent, with a pinpoint of white in the center; the balls should be tender but still chewy. Drain, rinse under cold water, and drain again. Divide the tapioca among eight tall glasses.

7. Put 2 tablespoons of the grape preserves in each glass and top with a scoop of the sherbet. Pour ½ cup club soda in a slow, steady stream into each glass; there should be a lot of foam at the top of the glass. Serve immediately with fat straws or spoons.

■

YIN AND YANG—THE CHINESE PHILOSOPHY OF A BALANCED DIET: WARM SOUPS AND ICY DRINKS

Many Americans know that the fundamental dynamic of Chinese philosophy is the interaction between two countervailing forces, yin and yang. Derived from the *Book of Changes,* which is one of the Five Classics in Confucian social thought and philosophy, yin and yang are opposing yet complementary forces that must be balanced to achieve harmony. This same philosophy animates Chinese cuisine as well. Chinese chefs believe that each dish should have some yin and some yang elements and that the human body needs a diet that balances yin and yang foods. Not only does this philosophy result in good health and well-being, it also makes for aesthetically pleasing and delicious meals.

In the Chinese approach to food and health, yin generally represents cool (or cooling) elements and yang generally represents hot (or heating) ones. However, the philosophy of yin and yang is quite fluid. There is no food pyramid to dictate how much yin and yang should be consumed. For that matter, there is no food item that is purely yin or yang. Some have more of one than the other, while others are effectively neutral.

There are other considerations as well, including the way the food is prepared—steaming, for example, is yin, while deep-frying is yang. And your body's own balance must be taken into account. If you're a yin person, you need more yang, and vice versa.

Even the categorization of yin and yang foods is a source of debate. Some are obvious—a spicy meat dish is yang. Others are not—a glass of ice water is yang, too. (The ice is thought to be so bracing that the body becomes yang in its consumption.) Although there are plenty of Chinese gurus out there, I have found that yin and yang food philosophies most often come from mothers. Every mother knows what her child should eat to maintain balance.

The philosophy of yin and yang also influences Asian desserts. After all, dessert is the best way to remedy any imbalance at the end of a meal. For that reason, fruit and tea, which are slightly yin, are frequently served at the end of a meal, since meat and seafood main courses tend to be yang. And when special desserts are in order, they tend to be warm soups. Now, the fact that the soup is warm does not make it yang. Warm soups are thought to have mild cooling properties, since they are easy for the body to handle and do not shock the system by being either too cold or too hot. In fact, many soups are made with "neutral" ingredients, like red bean or walnuts, but my favorites are made with a coconut milk base, which is both yin and delicious.

If desserts are meant to be yin, why are icy-cold drinks among the most popular Asian sweets? (Remember that icy is actually yang.) The answer is that these drinks usually aren't consumed after a meal, but instead are midday pick-me-ups. Plus, the yang of the ice in the drink is usually counterbalanced by a sweet yin ingredient, such as fruit or cream. The pairing of these elements leads to wonderfully refreshing drinks.

You can try to adhere to a diet that balances yin and yang for better health, but try these desserts just because they taste so good.

LEMONGRASS TAPIOCA AND TROPICAL FRUIT

Makes 6 servings

If Hong Kong had a national (or "territorial") dessert, it would be tapioca in coconut milk soup. It's the fancy ending to restaurant banquets, the quick fix for weeknight dinners, and the dish everyone brings to potlucks. Though it's nice and warming, this dessert also works well served cold. Bits of tropical fruit and mint make it immensely refreshing during those unbearable Hong Kong summers. It is traditionally served in rice bowls and eaten with a spoon, but putting it in parfait glasses and swapping fat straws for spoons makes it an ideal dessert party starter.

CHEF'S TIP: You can prepare the whole dessert a few hours ahead of time and mix all the fruit together into a thick beverage. Right before serving, give it a stir, and ladle out the fun. If it's too thick, just add a splash more milk.

2½ cups (22 ounces/625 grams) un-sweetened coconut milk

1½ cups (7⅞ ounces/224 grams) crushed palm sugar

One 5-inch-long lemongrass stalk, lightly smashed

1 vanilla bean, split lengthwise in half, seeds scraped out, and seeds and pod reserved

¾ teaspoon salt

2 cups (6⅞ ounces/196 grams) large tapioca pearls (¼-inch diameter)

1 cup (8 ounces/227 grams) whole milk

¾ cup (5½ ounces/157 grams) ¼-inch dice pineapple

¾ cup (6 ounces/170 grams) ¼-inch dice mango

¾ cup (5 ounces/140 grams) ¼-inch dice kiwi

Lemongrass Frozen Yogurt (page 250), optional

1 teaspoon grated lime zest, optional

1. Put the coconut milk, sugar, lemongrass, vanilla seeds and pod, and ¼ teaspoon of the salt in a large saucepan. Stir well, set over medium heat, and bring to a boil. Turn the heat to low and simmer, stirring occasionally, until the sugar dissolves, about 5 minutes. Transfer to a large bowl and set aside.

2. Bring 4 quarts water to a boil in a large pot and add the remaining ½ teaspoon salt. Add the tapioca and cook, stirring constantly, until the water returns to a rapid boil. Turn the

heat to medium and continue stirring occasionally until the tapioca is cooked through, about 25 minutes. It's done when it's almost translucent, with a pinpoint of white in the center; the balls should be tender but still chewy.

3. Drain the tapioca, rinse under cold water, and drain again, then immediately transfer to the coconut milk mixture. Stir in the whole milk, then refrigerate until cold before serving.

4. Remove the lemongrass and vanilla pod from the tapioca mixture. Divide the mixture among six serving bowls and arrange 2 tablespoons of each diced fruit on top of each portion. If desired, top with a scoop of frozen yogurt and a sprinkle of lime zest. Serve immediately with spoons.

KABOCHA AND BANANA IN GINGERED COCONUT MILK

Makes 8 servings

This yin and delicious warm soup is one of the most popular home-style desserts in Southeast Asia. You can use any sweet vegetable, like sweet potato, taro, or even corn, but I love buttery Kabocha squash best. The bananas are a must, as they give the soup body and a sweet, hearty aroma.

CHEF'S TIPS: If using other vegetables, be sure to add them in stages, according to their texture. Start cooking the firmest ones first and add the softer ones later. Ultimately, you want all the ingredients to have the same tenderness.

You can find pandan leaves in the frozen section of Asian markets.

2 ripe baby bananas, peeled and cut into ½-inch-thick slices

1 teaspoon fresh lemon juice

1 cup (9 ounces/255 grams) unsweetened coconut milk

¼ cup (1⅜ ounces/40 grams) crushed palm sugar

One 1-inch piece fresh ginger, cut into ¼-inch slices

4 frozen pandan leaves, thawed

1 vanilla bean, split lengthwise in half, seeds scraped out, and seeds and pod reserved

½ teaspoon salt

One 6-ounce (170-gram) wedge Kabocha squash, seeded and cut into ¼-inch-thick slices

2 teaspoons white sesame seeds, toasted

1. Toss the bananas with the lemon juice and set aside.

2. Put the coconut milk, sugar, ginger, pandan leaves, vanilla seeds and pod, salt, and ¼ cup water into a medium saucepan and bring to a steady simmer over medium-high heat, stirring occasionally. Add the squash, turn the heat to low, and simmer until the squash is softened, about 5 minutes. Remove from the heat, add the banana slices, cover the saucepan, and let the mixture stand for 5 minutes.

3. Remove the ginger slices, pandan leaves, and vanilla pod from the mixture. Divide among eight serving bowls, garnish with the sesame seeds, and serve warm.

ICED "DRAGON EYES" TEA

Longan, which translates to "dragon eyes," is a refreshing musky fruit. It's similar to lychee, but smaller and less juicy, with a smooth mustard-yellow skin and a more subtle sweetness. The fruit is only in season from mid-July through August, but the dried version used here is available throughout the year. The succulent juiciness and purported health benefits of this drink make it one of the most popular in China and Southeast Asia. It's usually drunk warm in the winter and cold in the summer, but I prefer it iced year-round. Reconstituting dried fruits in a light syrup to make sweet "teas" is a popular Asian dessert technique. Dried persimmons, jujubes, and orange peel are also commonly used. You can substitute any of these dried fruits and adjust the sugar to taste.

CHEF'S TIP: Dried longan and rock sugar can be found in most Asian markets. In late summer, when fresh longan are available, you can add fresh, peeled fruits to the drink.

2 cups (16 ounces/454 grams) rock
sugar, broken into small pieces

½ cup (2 ounces/54 grams) dried longan

1. Put the sugar in a small saucepan, cover with 2 cups water, and bring to a boil over medium-high heat, stirring until the sugar dissolves. Remove from the heat and add the longan. Let the longan sit in the syrup until they plump up and the mixture cools to room temperature.

2. Fill eight cups halfway with crushed ice, then divide the longan mixture among them. Serve immediately.

■

AVOCADO MILK SHAKE

Makes 8 servings

In the West, avocados are almost exclusively used in savory dishes, such as guacamole, salads, and sandwiches. But avocados (which are, after all, fruits) can be delicious in desserts as well. In fact, this avocado milk shake is one of the most popular drinks in Southeast Asia. Creamy and smooth with a subtle but complex sweetness, this shake makes for a healthy and filling snack. In Vietnam, where it's called *sinh to,* the shake mixture is sometimes blended with other fruits, made into ice cream, or shaken with iced coffee.

2 ripe avocados, preferably Hass, pitted and peeled

¾ cup (6 ounces/170 grams) cold whole milk

1 tablespoon fresh lime juice

¼ cup plus 2 tablespoons (4¼ ounces/119 grams) sweetened condensed milk

⅛ teaspoon salt

Put all of the ingredients in a blender, add 4 cups ice, and blend until the ice is completely crushed. Divide among eight glasses and serve immediately.

■

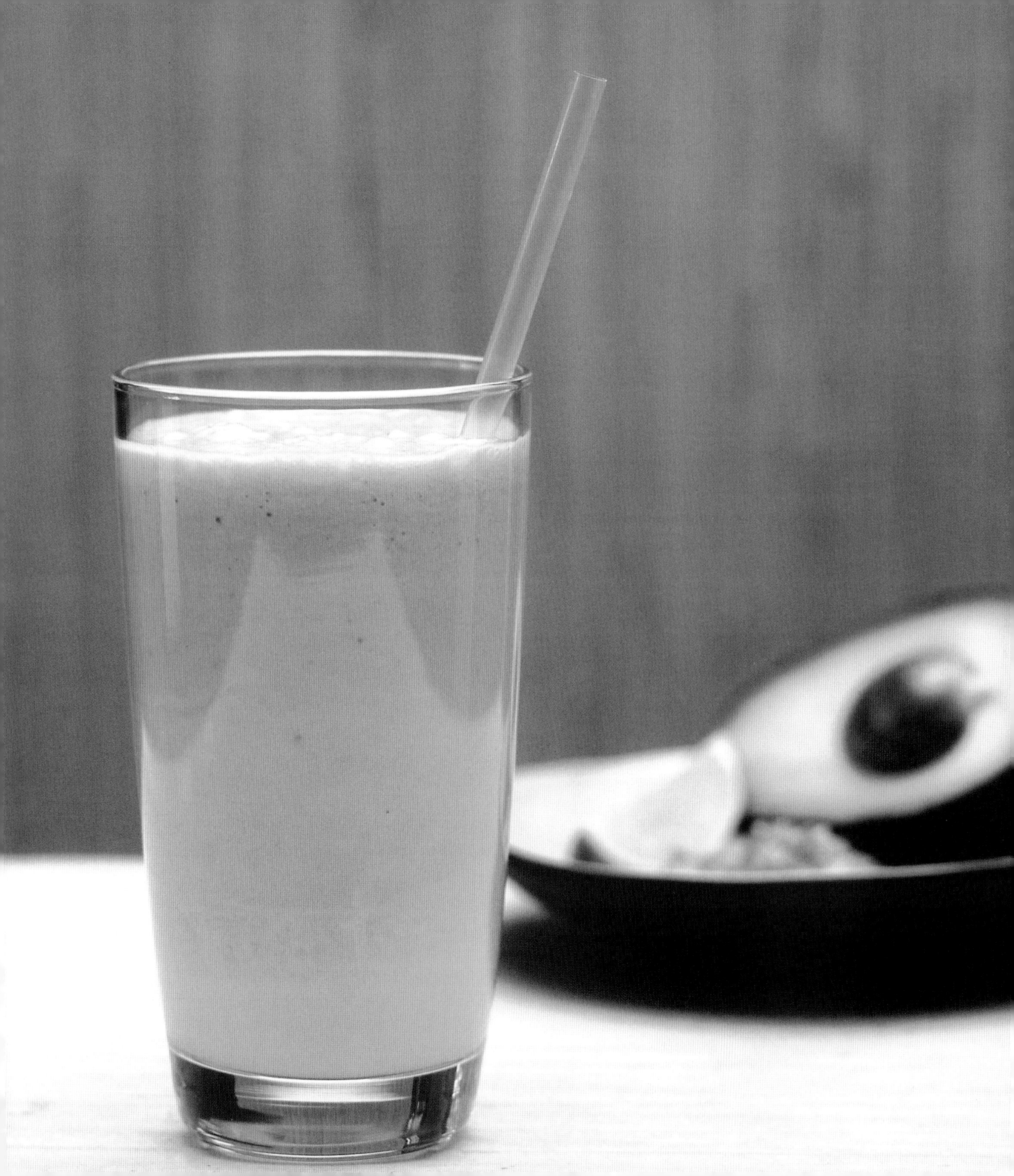

S O U R C E S

Many of the ingredients in this book can be found in your supermarket. Your best bet for a lot of the Asian ingredients is your local Asian market. If you live in a major metropolitan area, you can probably even choose a market by country. Otherwise, try a general Asian market that carries a range of regional items. Well-stocked supermarkets, specialty or gourmet shops, and natural food markets will also carry many of the Asian ingredients.

Mail-Order and Internet Sources

Amazon.com
www.amazon.com
A great one-stop shop for the specialty dry ingredients needed in this book. The "Gourmet Food" category offers items from many different sources, all of which you can order from your Amazon account.

The Chef's Warehouse
www.thechefswarehouse.com
The name says it all—this is a great source for fine chocolates, fruit purees, nuts, and hard-to-find pastry items.

Dean & Deluca
560 Broadway
New York, NY 10012
www.deandeluca.com
A good source for specialty items, including teas, spices, and chocolates.

Foods of India
121 Lexington Avenue
New York, NY 10016
(212) 683-4419
This is my favorite place for Indian spices, ingredients, and cookware, such as kulfi molds. They take phone orders and ship to all fifty states.

In Pursuit of Tea, Inc.
866-TRUE TEA
www.inpursuitoftea.com
The finest teas from all over the world, with a big selection of Asian teas, such as oolong, white peony, pu-erh, and Lapsang Souchong, as well as matcha powder. The website is like a tea encyclopedia!

J. B. Prince
36 East 31st Street
New York, NY 10016
(800) 473-0577
www.jbprince.com
An incredible source for big and small kitchen tools, cookbooks, and high-end kitchen equipment.

Kalustyan's
123 Lexington Avenue
New York, NY 10016
(212) 685-3451
www.kalustyans.com
Carries spices, coffees, teas, beans, nuts, flours, and many other specialty items; a good source for South Asian spices, rose products, and dried produce.

Korin Japanese Trading Corp.
57 Warren Street
New York, NY 10007
(212) 587-7021
www.korin.com
Great source for high-quality Japanese knives and kitchen tools, as well as beautiful
tableware.

Melissa's World Variety Produce, Inc.
P.O. Box 21127
Los Angeles, CA 90021
(800) 588-0151
www.melissas.com
Ships fresh, exotic, and hard-to-find organic produce.

Mr. Recipe
(646) 261-4460
Email: mrrecipe@gmail.com
Great specialized bulk-order business that carries vanilla products, including powder and oil,
and rare spices, including beautiful Sri Lankan (Ceylon, or True) cinnamon.

Oriental Pantry
423 Great Road
Acton, MA 01720
(800) 828-0368
www.orientalpantry.com
Carries Asian beans, nuts, flours, spices, and sauces.

Le Sanctuaire
2710 Main Street
Santa Monica, CA 90405
(310) 581-8999
www.le-sanctuaire.com
Fabulous store with top quality spices, oils, and extracts, next to unique small tools, high-tech
equipment, and imported books.

Penzeys Spices
P.O. Box 933
Muskego, WI 53150
(414) 679-7207
www.penzeys.com
High-quality spices, whole and ground, from around the world.

Sur La Table
www.surlatable.com
Professional kitchenware and gourmet ingredients for home cooks are available at retail stores nationwide.

Uwajimaya
519 Sixth Avenue South
Seattle, WA 98104
(800) 889-1928
www.uwajimaya.com
A good place for Japanese food products from dried beans to spices and seasonings.

Williams-Sonoma
www.williams-sonoma.com
A wonderful gourmet food and cookware store with retail outlets across the country.

I N D E X

lemongrass, 20
 frozen yogurt, 250–51
 frozen yogurt, light, 251
 tapioca and tropical fruit, 275–76
 -vodka frozen yogurt, 251
lime:
 –cream cheese frosting, 70–72
 key, dahn taht, 148
 tart pastry, 136
longans, 17
 iced "dragon eyes" tea, 279
lychee, pineapple, and kiwi carpaccio with jalapeño
  cream, 203–4
lychees, about, 17

mali syrup, 20
malted chocolate layer cake, 73–76
maltose (malt sugar), 20
mango(es), 17
 -chocolate cheesecake parfait with chocolate
  macadamia cookie crumbs, 85–86
 pudding, 155
 sticky rice, 218–19
mangosteens, about, 17–18
mangosteen sherbet, 242
matcha, 20
 green tea cream and fresh fruit cake, 66–69
 green tea cream filling, 66–67
 green tea cream puffs, 118
 green tea pops, 237–38
 green tea pudding, 157–58
 truffle centers, chocolate cakes with, 59–61
melon, 18
 fresh, and tapioca, 269
 watermelon shaved ice with salt and pepper,
  208–9
milk, 20
 almond, fresh, 20
 evaporated, about, 15–16
 shake, avocado, 280
 soy, fresh, 20
 see also sweetened condensed milk

mochi:
 cakes, about, 194
 rice flour, about, 16
 yuzu, 195
mukwa, 21

nut(s):
 buying and storing, 21
 caramel tart, 141–42
 pistachio kulfi with pomegranate soup, 231–33
 pistachio rose thumbprint cookies, 99–100
 rasmalai with rose water and pistachios,
  177–78
 salt and pepper cashew dragées, 186
 toasting, 21
 see also almond(s); peanut(s); walnut(s)

oatmeal ginger raisin cookies, 91–92
oils, in desserts, 21
olive oil and yogurt cake, 35–36
orange blossom water, 21
 chenna, drunken cherries with, 174
 sabayon, 205–7
oranges with orange blossom sabayon, 205–7
orange wedges, frozen, 245–47
Ovaltine, about, 21–22
Ovaltine and milk chocolate kulfi with caramelized
  banana, 229–30

palm seeds, 18
palm sugar, 22
pandan (leaves), 22
 cake, steamed, 44
 layer cake, steamed, 40–42
passion fruit, 18
 –banana sherbet, 248
 dahn taht, 148
pastry cream, ginger, 132–33
peanut butter cookies, 93–94
peanut(s):
 and milk chocolate bars, 181–83
 peanut butter cookies, 93–94